Belongings

Belongings
Property, Family, and Identity in Colonial South Africa (An Exploration of Frontiers, 1725–c. 1830)

Laura J. Mitchell

www.gutenberg-e.org

COLUMBIA UNIVERSITY PRESS
NEW YORK

Columbia University Press
Publishers Since 1893
New York   Chichester, West Sussex
Copyright © 2009 Columbia University Press

Library of Congress Cataloging-in-Publication Data

Mitchell, Laura Jane, 1963–
Belongings : property, family, and identity in colonial South Africa : an exploration
of frontiers, 1725–c. 1830 / Laura J. Mitchell.
p. cm. — (Gutenberg-e)
Print edition to accompany multimedia work of the same title published in the
Gutenberg-e online history series by Columbia University Press.
Includes bibliographical references.
ISBN 978-0-231-14252-6 (cloth : alk. paper) — ISBN 978-0-231-51229-9 (ebook)
1. Frontier and pioneer life—South Africa—Cedar Mountains.   2. Land settlement—
South Africa—Cedar Mountains—History.   3. Land tenure—South Africa—Cedar
Mountains—History.   4. Real property—Social aspects—South Africa—Cedar
Mountains—History.   5. Social conflict—South Africa—Cedar Mountains—
History.   6. Family—South Africa—Cedar Mountains—History.   7. Group identity—
South Africa—Cedar Mountains—History.   8. Nederlandsche Oost-Indische
Compagnie.   9. Cedar Mountains (South Africa—Colonization.   10. Cedar
Mountains (South Africa) —Ethnic relations.   I. Title.   II. Series.

DT2400.C43M57 2009
968.73′4—dc22
2009003836
www.gutenberg-e.org

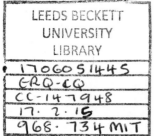
Columbia University Press books are printed on permanent
and durable acid-free paper. This book is printed on paper
with recycled content. Printed in the United States of America.

c 10 9 8 7 6 5 4 3 2 1

References to Internet Web sites (URLs) were accurate at the time
of writing. Neither the author nor Columbia University
Press is responsible for URLs that may have expired
or changed since the manuscript was prepared.

CONTENTS

ACKNOWLEDGMENTS

I've been living with the eighteenth-century residents of the Cedarberg for over a decade. They are not all likable people, but they have made for interesting neighbors in my mental landscape. Their book sprang to life as a research proposal about slaves, then morphed into a dissertation about land tenure. Now it is an analysis of community, with implications for rethinking South Africa's national history.

The "New South Africa" was really new when I began this endeavor; many individuals and institutions have helped me along the way. My journey to this book included excursions through the Cedarberg, but I did most of the work in classrooms, libraries, archives, and at my own desk, often in the company of extraordinary people. It is an honor to acknowledge my guides and traveling companions.

I dedicate *Belongings* to Claudia Wright, the first teacher who helped me see the possibilities of history. At Berkeley, Eugene Irschik introduced me to social history and Helen Ettlinger expanded my notion of what research could be. I doubt they would remember a shy undergraduate in a long procession of students, but lessons from their classrooms have stayed with me for more than twenty years. Markus Rediker pushed me to think about theory and methods that can account for the lived experiences of working people who left too few records of their own. At UCLA I benefited tremendously from the knowledge, generosity, and scholarly examples of Bill Worger, Ned Alpers, and Chris Ehret, who encouraged me to sustain my interest in early-modern history while pursuing specialist training as an Africanist. I am also grateful for Bob Kirsner's patience as I learned both Dutch and Afrikaans. Bill, Ned, and Bob, along with Jan de Vries at Berkeley, formed a supportive dissertation committee that encouraged me to pursue wide-ranging, shifting questions, even when that pursuit kept me in South Africa for four years.

While far from home, I received invaluable council from Nigel Worden, Antonia Malan, Susie Newton-King, Rob Shell, John Parkington, and Tony Manhire in Cape Town, Robert Ross in Leiden, and Jim Armstrong from various points around the globe. I owe each of them particular intellectual debts, acknowledged in the notes to this book. Their guidance and company, along with that of Gerald Groenewald, Candy Malherbe, Lalou Meltzer, Sandy Rouwalt, and Christopher Saunders make it a joy to work in the "Tavern of Two Seas." I owe special thanks to Gerald as my virtual eyes, finding documents in the Cape Archives when I wasn't in Cape Town. I am particularly indebted to Nigel Penn, who introduced me to the Cedarberg; to Robert Ross, whose role as critic, interlocutor, and careful reader has contributed greatly to my work; and to Roger Beck, whose generous, meticulous reading of the entire manuscript left me humbled—and the book much improved.

The staff at the Cape Archives is always friendly and helpful. I appreciate receiving permission to reproduce material from the collections and am grateful to Erika Le Roux for helping me to navigate that bureaucracy, as well as for cheerful assistance in the reading room. Thanks especially to Jaco van der Merwe for his ongoing advice in the reading room, and to Peter Jafta for his assistance with reproduction and microfilming. At the Deeds Office, the help of Mike Schoeman and Mr. Wicomb was invaluable. At the Surveyor General's Office, I would like to thank Ken Lester in Mowbray and Eddie Sparrow in Cape Town for the time they took explaining the practice and history of surveying in South Africa.

While I was a graduate student, my "desk" was really an expanding box of research notes. We moved a lot, that box and me; without friends I could not have managed to pursue research on three continents. I am particularly grateful for the hospitality of the Vet family in Leiderdorp, the Foresters in Somerset West, the Ross family in Gordon's Bay, and Susan Bendel and Daryl Collins in Cape Town, all of whom helped me keep hearth, heart, and box together.

From archives in the Hague and Cape Town, then back to North America, Kerry Ward and Martha Chaiklin have been stalwart friends and colleagues, sharing translations, carefully reading drafts, offering sage advice and welcome moral support. Kairn Klieman, a model and mentor since graduate school, has been an example of sanity and accomplishment, as well as a trusted sounding board. Stephanie Magid, a constant friend for enough decades to warrant a history of its own, continues not only to tolerate my arcane interest in people long-dead, but to provide unflagging encouragement.

At the University of Texas in San Antonio, several colleagues read and commented on early versions of various chapters. Thanks to Kirsten Gardner, Anne Hardgrove, Ben Johnson, and Gregg Michel. I also appreciate the unwavering support of Antonio Calabria, the good counsel of Wing Chung Ng, and the valuable research assistance of Cyndi McCowen.

Irvine has been a stimulating, dynamic, productive, and generous place to live and work. Marc Baer, Sharon Block, Carolyn Boyd, Dave Bruce, Helen Chenut, Alice Fahs, Rebeca Helfer, Julia Lupton, Michelle Molina, Rachel O'Toole, Ken Pomeranz, Kathy Ragsdale, Vicki Ruiz, Uli Strasser, Tim Tackett, and Anne Walthall have all read and commented on at least one stage of this project. Graduate students April Anderson, Lindsay Holowach, Dan Rood, and Laura Sextro provided crucial research assistance; Glen Watt generously shared her careful reader's eye. Four years of conversations with Dan Rood have sharpened my own thinking and expanded my reading, for which I am grateful. Many thanks to Tony Soeller for introducing me to GIS, to Nina MacDonald, Melinda Choudhary, and Bonnie Shea of Pixel Loom for getting me started with the kinship charts, and to Susan Reese for preparing the maps.

I greatly appreciate the conversations, convergences, and questions that consistently emerge in the meetings of the UC Multi-campus Research Group in World History. I've received many helpful suggestions there; especially from Terry Burke, Ray Kea, Randy Head, and Benjamin Lawrence.

Thanks to my *Past-Tense* coconspirators—Thomas Andrews, Kathleen Donnegan, Michelle Nickerson, and Jenny Price—along with all the seminar participants, I am a better writer. Finding a community of like-minded writers in Irvine greatly enhanced my ability to enjoy the process of transforming a dissertation and additional research notes into newly-envisioned book. Lisa Alvarez, Roger Gloss, Bhasha Leonard, and Michelle Mitchell-Foust sustained my faith that this book might have readers outside the academy, while Jonathan Cohen proofread the entire manuscript and provided valuable editorial advice, too.

Since this book builds on years of work, some of its ideas and evidence had previous appearances in print. Three chapters are adapted from published articles. Chapter Three draws on "Traces in the Landscape: Hunters, Herders and Farmers on the Cedarberg Frontier, South Africa 1725–1795," *Journal of African History* 43:3 (2002) 431–450. Chapter Six draws on "'This is the Mark of the Widow': Domesticity, and Frontier Conquest in Colonial South Africa," *Frontiers: A Journal of Women's Studies*, 28: 1 & 2 (Spring 2007) 47–76. Chapter Five had two previous incarnations, first as "Belonging: Kinship and Identity at the Cape of Good Hope, 1652–1795," in *Contingent Lives: Social Identity and Material Culture in the VOC World*, edited by Nigel Worden (University of Cape Town Press, 2007, 247–265), and then in a revised form as "Belonging: Family Formation and Settler Identity in the VOC Cape," *South African Historical Journal* 59 (December 2007) 103–126.

The editorial staff at Columbia University Digital Knowledge Ventures helped realize my goals for a digital book. Without the hard work of Kate Wittenberg, Nathaniel Herz, Merran Swartwood, Risa Karaviotis, and Emily Molanphy, my ideas would still be just words on a page, instead of text and images to guide readers through the Cedarberg in the eighteenth century.

All the friendship, intellectual engagement, and moral support in the world cannot, however, produce a book without concomitant material support. I undertook the initial research for this book as a graduate student, serially funded by a number of institutions whose faith in my work is redeemed finally with the production of this long–promised book. A fellowship from the UCLA Department of History, a UCLA Chancellor's Dissertation Fellowship, a FLAS grant from UCLA's Ralph Bunche Center for African Studies, travel support from UCLA's International and Area Studies Center, a Fulbright-Hayes Dissertation Research Abroad Fellowship, and the Mary Louise Remy Endowed Scholarship from P.E.O. all contributed directly to my ability to work in the Netherlands and South Africa. I enjoyed the extraordinary opportunity of four years abroad devoted to this project. Those experiences enriched my scholarship and my life in ways that year-end reports will never capture. My gratitude for these foundational years will be lifelong.

More recently, the UCI Humanities Center funded two trips to South Africa for additional research for this book, and the UCI School of Humanities provided assistance for travel to conferences where I was able to get valuable feedback on chapter revisions and new work. The Gutenberg-e Prize from the American Historical Association and the Mellon Foundation provided financial support for travel, research assistance, and technical help preparing the manuscript. The generous funding of an ACLS/SSRC/NEH International and Area Studies Fellowship for the 2005–6 academic year and a 2005–6 UC President's Humanities Research Fellowship gave me the luxury of a year without teaching responsibilities so that I could devote myself full-time to writing this book.

I am overwhelmed by the time, advice, and material support I've received for this project. Despite all this help, some errors will undoubtedly persist; the responsibility for them is all mine.

My final words of appreciation are for those who are first in my heart, and who certainly had a right to feel taken for granted in the final months of this book's preparation. My parents, Les and Cosette Mitchell, have stood by me for as long as I have memories. My brother Roger is always ready with searing, witty observations to celebrate life and put the tribulations of work in perspective. Virginia Mitchell and the Elders—Craig, Carolyn, Christian, Colin, and Corrina—have kept my family feeling grounded and at home in Southern California. The Proctors—David and Judy, John, Richard, Treintje, Jade, Steve, Jeanine, Stuart, and Vaughn—enliven our too infrequent visits to South Africa, and have opened their hearts to give me a family there. Most important of all, Graham and Ian fill my days with joy, not letting me think for a minute that family is just a research topic or an intellectual construct. They have shared me with this book, which was too much for me to ask, and yet what I needed. That they could give it is the treasure of a lifetime.

ABBREVIATIONS

AHR	*American Historical Review*
ARA	Algemeene Rijksarchief, The Hague
AYB	*Archives Yearbook of South African History*
CA	South African National Archives, Cape Depot, Cape Town
DO	Deeds Office, Cape Town
dV&P	C.C. de Villiers, *Geslagsregisters van die Ou Kaapse Families* (*Genealogies of Old South African Families*), Completely revised, augmented and rewritten by C. Pama. 1st ed. Cape Town and Rotterdam: A.A. Balkema, 1966; 2nd ed., 1981
H&L	J.A. Heese and R.T.J. Lombard. *Suid-Afrikaanse Geslagregisters*, 5 vols. Pretoria: Protea Book House, 1999
IJAHS	*International Journal of African Historical Studies*
JAH	*Journal of African History*
JCCH	*Journal of Colonialism and Colonial History*
JSAS	*Journal of Southern African Studies*
Kronos	*Kronos: Journal of Cape History*
Leibbrandt, *Précis*	H. C. V. Leibbrandt, *Précis of the Archives of the Cape of Good Hope Requesten (Memorials) 1715–1806*, 5 vols. Cape Town and London: Cape Times Limited, Government Printers (Vols. 1–2), 1905. Cape Town: South African Library (Vols. 3–5), 1989

LFL	Loan Farm Ledgers in the Stellenbosch Magistrate's archives (CA: 1/STB)
MOOC	Master of the Supreme Court, documents of the Orphan Chamber
NGK	Nederlands Gereformeerde Kerk
OBP	*Overgekomen brieven en papieren uit Kaap van Goede Hoop en Mauritius*
OSF	Old Stellenbosch Freeholds
RCC	George McCall Theal, *The Records of the Cape Colony.* London: for the Government of the Cape Colony, 1905
RLR	Receiver of Land Revenue, *Oud Wildschutte Boeke*
RxD	Rixdollars
SAHJ	*South African Historical Journal*
VOC	*Verenigde Oostindische Compagnie/Dutch East India Company*

A NOTE ON ORTHOGRAPHY

Spelling, especially of proper names, was not consistent in seventeenth- and eighteenth-century records. In the text, I have chosen one form and used it consistently. For place names, I used current South African spellings so that readers might connect locations in this book with modern maps and road signs. In citations and quotations from specific documents, however, I left the spelling as it appears in the original, hence Piketberg in text and Piquetberg in the notes, or Maria Fick and Maria Tik in reference to the same person.

I

Beginnings

It starts small, a spring of clear water in the Witsenberg Valley, trickling past boulders and seeping across sandy washes, flooding small marshes that nourish seasonal lilies. It takes the easy way down over steep and rocky terrain, not quite precipitous or spectacular enough for a waterfall. The Olifants is an unassuming river, not long, not navigable, not particularly scenic. But it is liquid and cool and perennial—remarkable features in an otherwise arid landscape.

The river is an unassailable starting point for a discussion of colonial intersections in South Africa. The source of the Olifants River is certain, its route is defined, its place in the landscape—geographical, social, and economic—is understood. Compared to events on a human timescale the Olifants River is constant, knowable, controllable. The river is a solid anchor in a history of uncertainty in the Western Cape.

For a century, the Olifants River ran at the heart of a colonial frontier. Piecemeal expansion of the harbor-side victualing station at Table Bay slowly transformed a small but crucial outpost of the Dutch East India Company into a settler colony. Within a decade of establishing a permanent presence at the Cape of Good Hope, European explorers had traveled north of the river's mouth and into Namaqualand, but it was nearly 75 years before colonial hunters and farmers began regularly to exploit the resources near the Olifants. Even that initial usage began tentatively. Few of the first land claimants actually lived in the area; instead they used their loan farms as grazing posts, sending livestock and herdsmen while they remained closer to Cabo, as nascent Cape Town was then known.

Demographic pressure in the growing colony eventually propelled families ever further into land already used regularly by Khoikhoi herders and San foragers,[1] so colonial land claims along the Olifants River and in the surrounding Cedarberg mountains increasingly became sites of permanent settler households—and the region became a place of contention.

This book explores the contours of conflict among Company officials, settlers, Khoisan, and slaves. It details the ways in which settlers themselves—rather than Company policy or an imperial army—brought a distant region first into a colonial orbit, then gradually under colonial control. This process was contested violently; Khoisan resisted displacement, the appropriation of their livestock and hunting grounds, involuntary servitude in settler households, and subordination in colonial society. Settlers, for their part, resisted the Company's efforts to control territorial expansion, limit their interaction with independent Khoisan groups, and regulate bonded labor. Individuals across a variegated colonial social spectrum struggled, too. Illicit trade, illegitimate children, and repeated desertions bear witness to ongoing social tensions. At the same time, the increasing presence of European material culture in frontier areas provides concrete evidence of people affirming their relationship to the source of colonial power.

Against a backdrop of resistance on many fronts—often violent, always present—settlers claimed land one farm at a time. Family by family, household by household, the inhabitants of the Cedarberg were bound to each other and to a colonial society based near the Cape's harbor.[2] Conquest was ultimately quotidian and domestic, rather than martial.[3] Flocks of sheep grazing on steep hillsides, a kitchen garden growing near the river, small houses made of rock and dried earth—eventually expanded and rebuilt in bricks and plaster—signaled colonial conquest. Farmers protected these newly claimed assets at gunpoint, supported by the commando system and occasionally by soldiers stationed at the Company's outpost at the Warm Baths.[4] Their ultimate success depended less on the militia than on their families' persistence, though. A shared sense of community, tightly entwined relationships and reciprocal obligations, enabled the continued survival of livestock, crops, and frontier households. Settlers achieved hegemony on an apron string.[5]

Telling a story of that frontier from a starting point in the metropole—either Amsterdam or Cape Town—then expanding outward, benefits too much from hindsight; the ending is preordained, a familiar conclusion from the age of European expansion. While it would be counterintuitive (and counterfactual) to locate colonial settlement near the Olifants outside of the global and globalizing processes of modern imperialism, individuals such as Barend Lubbe, Maria Vosloo, Engela Koopman, and Cupido van Bengal certainly did not see themselves as players in a historical metanarrative. Their daily challenge of surviving inhospitable surroundings was local, material, and specific. As a farmer and colonial official, a mixed-race illegitimate daughter who married three prominent settlers in succession, a mixed-race woman who owned her own land, and a runaway slave, these four people experienced frontier life differently. Each, undoubtedly, would start the story of frontier interactions in a different place: perhaps in Westphalia, in the Cape's Cedarberg Mountains, or in India. I am choosing to start this story with the waters of the river upon which they all, at one time or another, depended.[6]

Beginning with the river situates the story of a colonial frontier firmly in place. The origins of the river are a geographical rather than a temporal issue, since the Olifants' genesis introduces a time span much older than the history of human interactions at the heart of this book.

Beginning with the river introduces a crucial actor as well as the setting for this story. Without the Olifants, the Cedarberg would not have been an attractive place for human settlement. The hunters, herders, and farmers who lived in this region would have found it uninhabitable and undesirable without water.

Beginning with the river also postpones the question of whose version of the frontier should take priority. Instead of indigenes, or second-comers, or those involuntarily transported, we focus on the primacy of location and resources. Ironically, such a deft sidestepping of contentious human issues only emphasizes the problematic nature of periodizing colonial history. Even environmental history is bracketed according to man-made changes. The final section of this book is a mediation on the significance of periodization and its implications for understanding the concept of frontier. I defer that discussion because it depends on the first three parts of the book.

The four parts of the book together constitute a narrative—though the nature of historical sources means there are holes as well as connections that bind people, places, and stories in the Cedarberg. I have ordered the chapters in the service of this book's arguments, but I do not presume this order is the only way to read it. Consequently, most chapters have several points of cross-reference that indicate more information is available in another part of the book. Readers who click on the cross references will be redirected to the relevant chart, map, or section of text. You may use your browser's "back button" to return to the cross reference point.

In Part I, "Establishing the Cedarberg" details the setting; "Establishing Frontiers" lays out the parameters of debate. Part II, "Terms of Contest," populates the region and elaborates the points of conflict in colonial society. Part III, "Mechanics of Conquest," uses four extended families to illustrate the extent to which land tenure and the control of labor were rooted in family networks. Successful claims to land and labor were the key to the eventual ascendancy of a hegemonic settler identity. Although the state authorized the legitimacy of these claims, the actual assertion and subsequent maintenance of property rights and the control of bonded and family labor depended on individual households. Settler success thus rested firmly within domestic relationships. So deferring to the river at the outset is only a temporary solution, the first stop on a journey through the Cedarberg frontier.

NOTES

1. Note on terminology: Early European travelers and settlers referred to the indigenous herders of the southwestern Cape as Hottentots. This term acquired a derogatory connotation through its historical use. The term Khoikhoi is now the accepted convention. The hunter-gatherers of the region were known collectively as Bushmen. The modern appellation of San recently has been disputed, since it derives from a derogatory Khoikhoi term. In most cases, reference to specific groups of Khoikhoi and Bushmen are preferred, but this convention is not practical for general discussion. I use Khoikhoi when referring specifically to pastoral peoples, San when referring to hunters, and the admittedly awkward Khoisan when referring to indigenous people when it is not possible to differentiate them.

2. Mary S. Hartman powerfully articulates the premise that households were instruments of change, not simply reacting to the wider world in *The Household and the Making of History: A Subversive View of the Western Past* (Cambridge: Cambridge University Press, 2004).

3. On the intimate or domestic as a site of colonial rule, see Antoinette Burton, *Dwelling in the Archive: Women Writing House, Home and History in Late Colonial India* (Oxford: Oxford University Press, 2003), 5–7; and Ann Laura Stoler, *Carnal Knowledge and Imperial Power: Race and the Intimate in Colonial Rule* (Berkeley: University of California Press, 2002), 9, 12–14.

4. D. Sleigh, *Die Buiteposte: VOC-buiteposte onder Kaapse bestuur, 1652–1795* (Pretoria: Haum, 1993), 534–538.

5. Sara Berry, "Hegemony on a Shoestring: Indirect Rule and Access to Agricultural Land," *Africa: Journal of the International African Institute* 62:3 (1992), 327–55.

6. For an example of how effective it can be to geographically recenter a historical narrative, see Norman Etherington, *Great Treks: The Transformation of Southern Africa, 1815–1854* (London: Longman, 2001).

1. ESTABLISHING THE CEDARBERG

The Olifants River originates in the craggy heights of the Cape Fold Belt Mountains. It gathers momentum as it runs towards the coastal plain, accumulating water from the seasonal springs and streams that sparkle amid dusty brush. Now regulated by a dam near Clanwilliam, the river's flow played an important part in shaping plant and animal life in its vicinity. There is, understandably, evidence of concentrated human activity along the river in both precolonial and colonial eras. A perennial source of water and a remarkable feature in the landscape, the Olifants River was a reference point among Europeans from the earliest days of their penetration in the region. Consequently, the river valley and surrounding area were an important zone of interaction between settlers and indigenous hunting and herding populations in the eighteenth century.

The upper Olifants River valley and the surrounding Cedarberg Mountains were a crucible of frontier life. From the headwaters above present-day Tulbagh to the place where the river meets the sandy coastal plain near Heeren Logement, steep mountains with few natural passes separate the river from the Swartland and Sandveld to the west and the Bokkeveld to the east.[1] Despite the rugged terrain, people moved regularly through the mountains, so any discussion of human settlement near the river must necessarily follow the links that people maintained to the coast and to the interior valleys.

SITUATING THE CEDARBERG

The Cedarberg region lies 250 kilometers north of Cape Town—about nine days' travel in an ox wagon during the mid-eighteenth century. The mountainous terrain of the Cape Fold Belt consists largely of shale and nutrient-poor soil. Rainfall is less than 40 millimeters per year; surface water is limited and scattered. Despite the aridity, the vegetation is diverse. Areas of Renosterveld, Nama Karoo, and Succulent Karoo biomes are interspersed among the predominant Fynbos, providing different densities and ranges of plants within a relatively contained space.[2] People and animals need only climb partway up a mountainside to find a change of foliage. Cresting a pass can be enough to change not just vegetation but water availability as well.

Fynbos is mostly low, scrubby brush without grasses or trees. The biome has three major elements: Cape reeds replace the grasses typical in other ecosystems, local heaths known as erica compose the second major element, and Proteas round out the trio.[3] Renosterveld, though less diverse than Fynbos, has abundant geophytes—plants that store their nutrients underground as bulbs, tubers, or corms.[4] The irises, lilies, and orchids of the Renosterveld were an important seasonal food source for hunters in the region prior to colonial settlement.[5] Renosterveld also supports grasses, though it is overgrazed easily. The Nama Karoo and Succulent Karoo biomes occur in the driest zones. Daisies, a major component of the Succulent Karoo, produce the spectacular spring wildflower displays that now draw significant numbers of tourists each year.[6]

In general, the land has a relatively low carrying capacity. There are no large herds of ungulates and it is unlikely that they existed in the region in earlier eras because the existing resources would not support them, at least not year-round. The highly variable and seasonal availability of water restricts the range of larger herbivores and carnivores in the Cedarberg. Many plants flower and reproduce after the winter rains, so forage is abundant in spring.[7]

The rocky terrain, steep mountain slopes, and characteristic shrubland impede but do not prohibit the movement of animals and humans. The passage of the Olifants River and other watercourses provide passes through the landscape. The many rocky outcroppings that hamper the construction of paths or wagon roads instead offer natural shelter.

The hunting and herding populations that inhabited the region prior to the arrival of European explorers and settlers were mobile; Khoikhoi and San did not establish permanent settlements. The first colonial farmers to claim land in the Olifants River valley also built impermanent dwellings. Moreover, their homesteads were scattered and it was not until the beginning of the nineteenth century that the first signs of a concentrated settlement began to appear at the place then known as Jan Dissels Vlei.[8] Although the landscape does not conform to Victorian notions of romantic beauty,[9] the nascent village inspired this description by a nineteenth-century English visitor:

> "Set in surroundings of somewhat stark grandeur, the village was sited on a low rise in the tongue of land . . . Immediate to the east it is flanked by the Karooberg Mountain, 1,015', part of the Cedarberg range which rise majestically to form a mighty eastern bulwark and the source of many streams."[10]

Regardless of the era or the reason for their interest in the Cedarberg, visitors and inhabitants of the region focused on water—in a semiarid place they had to. So the perennial Olifants River and the relative fecundity of its valley provided both habitat and battleground for the groups of people that resided there.

POPULATING THE CEDARBERG

Although not a lush environment, the Cedarberg has accommodated human settlement for at least 10,000 years.[11] The region's numerous rock art sites and Paleolithic remains have attracted intense archaeological investigation for over twenty years, shedding new light on the relationship between hunter-gatherers and pastoralists and on centuries of migrations.[12]

San hunters and gatherers predated Khoikhoi herders at the Cape.[13] People who subsisted predominantly by foraging used land and resources differently from pastoralists. Although archaeological, documentary, and ethnographic data is not conclusive, it strongly suggests that the indigenous populations of the Cape had a clear sense of territoriality and regular ranges through which different groups moved systematically. Communities gathered and dispersed in response to climatic and economic stimuli.[14] Such movement among people engendered both cooperation and conflict. Open hostility and struggle for specific territory seems likely before the seventeenth century, but it appears as though the notions of individual land claims and land ownership arrived in the region with colonial settlers.

Europeans first arrived in the Olifants River valley in 1660. On that visit, Jan Danckaert saw herds of elephants, and so named the river for them. Europeans subsequently returned to the river valley on hunting expeditions, further exploratory treks in search of the Copper Mountains, or journeys to barter for cattle with Namaquas.[15] The colony's expansion began to affect the region full-time in 1725, when the Company issued the first grazing permit along the river.[16] Stock farmers began regularly using the area from that point onward; by the late 1730s settlers began arable farming.

Colonial land claims under Dutch East India Company (referred to by its Dutch initials, VOC) rule rested on a two-tiered system of permanent grants (freehold property) and temporary permits (loan farms). Homesteads in out-lying areas such as the Cedarberg were almost exclusively loan farms—annual permits granted by the VOC to free burghers. A loan farm gave a settler exclu-sive right to a fixed tract of land in exchange for annual rent. The permit was renewable indefinitely. *Burghers*, or free citizens, could build, farm, hunt, and graze on their loan farms without restrictions. Although they technically could not sell the land, settlers could transfer the improvements, so in prac-tice the grants conferred permanent, alienable property rights on the permit holders.[17]

For the existing hunting and herding populations of the Cedarberg, the in-troduction of loan farms meant intensified competition for access to land and resources such as water, grazing, and game. More importantly, loan farms rep-resented the advent of a new land tenure regime based on notions of private ownership that was intrinsically inimical to Khoisan seasonal migration.

The establishment of colonial farming also introduced a demand for agri-cultural labor to the region. Settlers brought with them both chattel slaves and the habit of indenturing captive Khoisan. Settler encroachment in the Cedarberg thus imported a two-tiered system of bonded labor in which the distinction between chattel slave and indentured Khoisan was not fixed. This permeable boundary meant that a porous conception of race and ethnicity prevailed in frontier regions during the eighteenth century.[18]

Although social distinctions of race may have been flexible and unevenly ap-plied on the frontier, the elaborate nomenclature developed in colonial soci-ety also pertained in the Cedarberg. From the settler perspective, there were distinctions among various classifications of people, free and bonded, Europe-ans and "others." The Company officials were at the top of the colonial hierar-chy. Next were burghers. The VOC soldiers and sailors had few rights and limited opportunities, but the Company gave some men permission to work for wages among the burgher population. The occupations of these *knechts* spanned a wide range, from overseer to teacher.[19] The term *free black* applied to individuals who were not of European origin, not indigenous, and not enslaved. Colonists referred to the indigenous population as *Hottentots* (Khoikhoi) and Bushmen. They further differentiated between classifications of mixed-race individuals, labeling the descendants of European-Khoisan unions as *Bastaards* and the children of Khoisan and slaves or free blacks as *Bastaard-Hottentots*. Finally, slaves imported mostly from the Indian Ocean rounded out the population at the Cape in the eighteenth century.[20] In spite of this elaborate social classifica-tion, on the frontier individuals had a greater choice in adopting social identity, as long as they wanted to live within colonial norms.

Khoisan response to this intrusion was uneven, consisting of various de-grees of engagement, resistance, and flight. Toward the end of the late 1730s, violent resistance predominated, culminating in the fierce frontier war of

1739. Its conclusion effectively ended the possibility of independent existence for local hunters and herders living near colonial settlements in the Land van Waveren (present-day Tulbagh) and regions to the north. Colonial commandos crushed concerted, armed Khoisan resistance and opened the frontier to more intensive settler use.[21]

The end of orchestrated warfare was not, however, the end of violence, nor was it the beginning of uncontested colonial settlement in the Cedarberg. In fact, frontier inhabitants disputed the terms of labor relations, land tenure, and social control until well into the nineteenth century. Although the balance of power began to shift in favor of land-owning settlers in the 1740s, the terms of living in the Cedarberg—and in particular the terms of exercising authority—remained contested for nearly a century afterward.

THE COLONIAL CONTEXT

In the seventeenth and eighteenth centuries, the shifting frontier regions in South Africa differed from most other colonial frontiers in the world in an important aspect of administration. Europeans established a foothold at the southern tip of Africa not in the name of king and country, not for the glory of God, but rather in the direct pursuit of profit. The first European settlement at Table Bay was a commercial enterprise, established in 1652 by the Dutch East India Company to support its lucrative operations in the Indian Ocean.[22] The VOC explicitly and self-consciously did not want to colonize the Cape, but rather sought to establish the barest infrastructure necessary to resupply the passing East Indiamen with fresh food, water, and sailors to replace hands who took ill or died on the perilous Atlantic and Indian Ocean passages that linked the Cape to the economically more important ports of Amsterdam and Batavia.[23]

The officials making decisions for the VOC did not intend for the settlement at Table Bay to be an independent economic or political entity, although they did hope that the resupply efforts would become self-financing. Initially, the affairs of the Cape had no direct claim on the attention of the *Heren XVII*, the seventeen gentlemen who ruled the VOC. At first, the commander of the Cape reported both to the VOC governor in Batavia and to the Heren XVII in Amsterdam. In 1732 the unwieldy system was streamlined so that the Cape's administrator, by then promoted to governor, reported directly to Amsterdam. Even so, the Cape's pleas for more soldiers, more labor, and more funds often went unanswered, because in the commercial structure of the VOC, the needs of Java and the Spice Islands were always more important.[24]

The Dutch East India Company was a private venture. Although it held a charter from the States-General that authorized monopoly trade and the exercise of sovereign rights—raising an army, negotiating treaties, and administering justice—the Company's primary interests lay with its shareholders, not with the complicated politics of the Republic of the United Netherlands.[25]

The Company's structure represented its diverse commercial origins and mirrored the decentralized structure of the Dutch Republic. Created in 1602 as the world's first joint-stock company, the VOC was comprised of six member chambers, known as *kamers*, which were the legacy of the various smaller commercial organizations folded into the VOC. The six kamers—Amsterdam, Rotterdam, Zeeland, Delft, Hoorn, and Enkuizen—each had representatives among the Heren XVII. The individuals appointed to serve among the 17 lords all came from the ruling classes of the member cities; the conservative decisions made by the Heren XVII reflect the patrician origins and commercial priorities of its members.[26]

The first Europeans at the Cape were all in the direct service of the VOC, employed as soldiers, sailors, or administrators. Soon after their arrival, the Company decided it would be more efficient (and less costly) to grant some of the VOC servants the status of free citizens (burghers) and offer them tracts of land. The farmers would then produce agricultural goods at their own cost and sell the product to the VOC—the only buyer in the market.[27]

The growing settlement at Table Bay consisted of Company officials, contracted VOC soldiers and sailors, Company slaves, burghers, the burghers' slaves, and a small number of free blacks.[28] A Company-appointed governor administered the Cape, advised by the Council of Policy, which consisted entirely of Company officials. The burghers had three seats on the Council of Justice, which decided criminal matters.[29] The Company and the Council of Policy controlled appointments to the Council of the official Dutch Reformed Church, often filling the Church Council with Company administrators. The Church ministers themselves were employed by the VOC, which meant that the Company either controlled or strongly influenced most civic and social life at the Cape.[30]

As the free burghers began to seek land further and further from the settlement at Table Bay, the Company created a second tier of administration for the interior. The first *landdrost*, or magistrate, was appointed to serve in Stellenbosch in 1679. Members of the *heemraad*, or citizens' advisory council, assisted the landdrost, a Company official. The heemraden were local residents, as were the *veldkornets*, burghers assigned responsibility for local districts.[31] Thus, free farmers in outlying areas had more influence on government administration than did burghers living in or near the settlement at Table Bay.

Frontier residents, regardless of their status, were therefore distant bureaucratically as well as geographically from the colonial government that claimed to rule them. From the perspective of a slave, the exercise of state authority began with his or her master, who was legally permitted to mete out corporal punishment.[32] The master was in turn subject to the authority of the veldkornet, the landdrost, and the heemraden. The landdrost reported to the *fiscaal*, the Company's prosecutor, and the governor. [33]

This strict bureaucratic structure had consequences for frontier districts of the growing Cape colony. In some instances, the great distance from the seat of administrative power offered relative freedom for frontier residents seeking escape from rigid colonial social structures.[34] In other cases, colonial justice penetrated to the outer reaches of colonial settlement. In still other circumstances, the rigid application of hierarchical and elitist Company policies led directly to settler rebellions.[35]

The development of a sizeable settler community was anomalous in the VOC world, though not in the wider Dutch imperial experience.[36] The sprawling East India Company linked three continents, two oceans, and identities beyond enumeration. In the context of a trading company run by elite married men, staffed primarily by bachelor soldiers and sailors, dependent on the labor of slaves, and striving for control of both indigenous populations and colonial settlements, it might seem surprising to locate a conversation about colonial identity with settler marriage and family networks at the Cape. It is, however, precisely in the relationships established and entrenched through matrimony that we can see evolving—but not rigid—class distinctions, changing attitudes about race, and the creation of a settler identity distinct from indigenous African communities (Khoikhoi, San, and Xhosa) as well as from other emerging colonial groups including free blacks and mixed-race communities such as Griqua and Bastaards.

Within and against the corporate structure and commercial goals of the VOC, settlers, Khoikhoi, and slaves used conflict, collaboration, and sex to work their way toward an uneasy equilibrium dominated by colonists. The components of this contest were laid bare on the frontier, where ultimately no one—no matter how physically distant—could avoid the ascendancy of social, political and economic structures conceived in Europe, shaped in Cape Town, and applied in the Cedarberg.[37]

NOTES

1. See P.S. Scholtz, "Die historiese ontwikkeling van die Onder-Olifantsrivier, 1660–1902: 'n Geskiedenis van die Distrik Vanryhsdorp," *AYB* (1966) for the history of the lower Olifants River area. My thanks to Robert Ross for sharing his copy of Scholtz with me.

2. Gretel van Rooyen and Hester Steyn, *South African Wild Flower Guide 10: Cedarberg, Clanwilliam and Biedouw Valley* (Cape Town: Botanical Society of South

Africa, 1999), 17. Thanks to Fiona Ballantyne of the Botany Department at the University of Cape Town for a plant-oriented expedition in the Cedarberg, Dec. 2006.

3. The scientific family names of the plants are Restionaceae, Ericaceae, and Proteaceae.

4. Renosterveld geophytes include Iridaceae, Asphodelaceae, Colchicaceae, Hyacinthaceae, Eriospermaceae, and Orchidaceae; van Rooyen and Steyn, 19.

5. John Parkington, personal communication, July 1997.

6. The daisies belong to the Asteraceae family.

7. Present-day wildflower season tourism in August and September makes an important contribution to the local economy.

8. The village at Jan Dissels Vlei was renamed Clanwilliam in 1814.

9. J.M. Coetzee, "The Picturesque, the Sublime, and the South African Landscape," in *White Writing: On the Culture of Letters in South Africa* (New Haven: Yale University Press, 1988), especially 37–39 and 41.

10. Graham Brian Dickason, *Irish Settlers to The Cape: History of the Clanwilliam 1820 Settlers from Cork Harbour* (Cape Town: A.A. Balkema, 1973), 18.

11. Tony Manhire, *Later Stone Age Settlement Patterns in the Sandveld of the South-Western Cape Province, South Africa* (Oxford: BAR, 1987). John Parkington, "Time and Place: Some Observations on Spatial and Temporal patterning in the Later Stone Age Sequence in Southern Africa," *South African Archaeological Bulletin* 35 (1980), 73–83.

12. John Parkington, "Changing Views of Prehistoric Settlement in the Western Cape," in Parkington and Hall, eds., *Papers in the Prehistory of the Western Cape*, vol. I, 4–23. Tony Manhire, *Later Stone Age Settlement Patterns in the Sandveld of the South-Western Cape Province, South Africa* (Cambridge Monographs in African Archaeology, 21. Oxford: BAR, 1987). Richard Klein, "The Prehistory of Stone Age Herders in the Cape Province of South Africa," *Prehistoric Pastoralism in South Africa* (South African Archaeological Society Goodwin Series 5 [June 1986]), 5–11.

13. Andrew B. Smith, "Competition, Conflict and Clientship: Khoi and San Relationships in the Western Cape," *Prehistoric Pastoralism in South Africa* (South African Archaeological Society Goodwin Series 5 [June 1986]), 37.

14. R.B. Lee, *The !Kung San: Men, Women and Work in a Foraging Society* (Cambridge: Cambridge University Press, 1979); Klein, "The Prehistory of Stone Age Herders," 5.

15. Scholtz, "Die historiese ontwikkeling van die Onder-Olifantsrivier," 7–27.

16. CA: RLR 6:58, Permit issued to Johannes Ras at Lange Valleij, 18 Oct. 1725.

17. C. Graham Botha, *Early Cape Land Tenure* (Cape Town: Cape Times Limited, 1919. Reprinted from the *South African Law Journal*, May and August 1919); Leonard Guelke. "Early European Settlement of South Africa" (PhD diss., University of Toronto, 1974). Both Botha and Guelke disagree with the British assumption that the loan farm system created insecurity, L.C. Duly, *British Land Policy at the Cape 1795–1844: A Study of Administrative Procedures in the Empire* (Durham: Duke University Press, 1968).

18. This argument was first championed by Martin Legassick, whose articulation was framed as a challenge to the then-prevailing orthodoxy among South African historians that racial biases were solidified on the frontier; "The Frontier Tradition in South African Historiography," in Shula Marks and Anthony Atmore, eds., *Society and Economy in Pre-Industrial South Africa* (London: Longman, 1980), 44–79. This

position was subsequently supported and eloquently elaborated by Robert Ross, whose work in this regard is cataloged by Susan Newton-King, *Masters and Servants on the Eastern Cape Frontier* (Cambridge: Cambridge University Press, 1999), 41n35. I engage more fully in frontier historiography in Chapter 2.

19. Robert C.-H. Shell, *Children of Bondage: A Social History of the Slave Society at the Cape of Good Hope, 1652–1838* (Hannover and London: University Press of New England, 1994), 11n30. Newton-King, *Masters and Servants*, 16–17.

20. Richard Elphick and Robert Shell, "Intergroup Relations: Khoikhoi, Settlers, Slaves, and Free Blacks, 1652–1795," in *The Shaping of South African Society, 1652–1840,* 2nd edition, eds. Richard Elphick and Hermann Giliomee (Johannesburg: Maskew Miller Longman, 1989), 194–204.

21. Nigel Penn, "The Frontier in the Western Cape, 1700–1740," *Papers in the Prehistory of the Western Cape, South Africa.* (Oxford: BAR, 1987), 492–93. Penn restates this argument in *The Forgotten Frontier: Colonist and Khoisan on the Cape's Northern Frontier in the Eighteenth Century* (Athens: Ohio University Press and Cape Town: Double Storey Books, 2005).

22. See C.R. Boxer, *The Dutch Seaborne Empire 1600–1800* (Middlesex: Penguin 1965) for a general discussion of VOC activities in the Indian Ocean and the relative position of the Cape in the VOC structure.

23. Slightly fewer than 1 million men (and a few women) set sail from Europe on board VOC ships between 1602 and 1705. Only about one-third returned to Europe. For more details about the high mortality rate, see J.R. Bruijn, F.S. Gaastra, and I. Schoeffer, assisted by E.D. van Eyck van Histinga, *Dutch Asiatic Shipping in the Seventeenth and Eighteenth Centuries* (The Hague: Nijhoff: 1979), a detailed account of the VOC as an enterprise and its commercial activities in the Indian Ocean. For a relevant overview of European commercial activities, see P.H. Boulle, Leonard Blussé and Femma S. Gaastra, eds., *Companies and Trade: Essays on Overseas Trading Companies in the Ancien Régime* (Leiden: Leiden University Press, 1981).

24. For a general history of the VOC, see Femma S. Gaastra, *De Geschiedenis van de VOC,* 2nd ed. (Zutphen: Walberg Pers, 1991). For a pithy survey of the VOC literature as it relates to the Cape, see Robert Ross, "The First Imperial Masters of Colonial South Africa," *SAHJ* 25 (1995), 177–83.

25. For a political history of the United Provinces, see Jonathan I. Israel, *The Dutch Republic: Its Rise, Greatness, and Fall, 1477–1806* (Oxford: Oxford University Press, 1995). For social history, see J.H. Huizinga, *Dutch Civilization in the Eighteenth Century and Other Essays,* translated by Arnold J. Pomerans (New York: Frederick Ungar Publishers, 1968). For cultural history, see Simon Schama, *The Embarrassment of Riches: An Interpretation of Dutch Culture in the Golden Age* (London: Fontana Press, 1991). For economic history, see Jan de Vries and Ad van der Woude, *The First Modern Economy: Success, Failure and Perseverance of the Dutch Economy, 1500–1815* (Cambridge: Cambridge University Press, 1997).

26. Femma S. Gaastra, *Bewind en Beleid bij de VOC, 1672–1702* (Zutphen: Walberg Pers, 1989), points out the particular business and political acumen exercised by VOC leadership.

27. For an excellent description of the VOC at the Cape, see Gerrit Schutte, "Company and Colonists at the Cape, 1652–1795" in Elphick and Giliomee, *Shaping*, 283–323.

28. For a demographic analysis of the Cape, see Leonard Guelke, "Anatomy of a Colonial Settler Population, Cape Colony 1657–1780," *IJAHS* 21:3 (1988), 453–73.

29. The burghers' frequent complaints about lack of representation were answered in 1785 when three more of the Council's 12 seats were set aside for burghers, giving them equal representation with Company officials in matters of justice.

30. For a recent analysis of the Dutch Reformed Church at the Cape, see Gerrit Schutte, "Between Amsterdam and Batavia: Cape Society and the Calvinist Church Under the Dutch East India Company," *Kronos* 25 (1998–1999), 17–49. For the Church in Stellenbosch prior to 1730, see Ad Biewinga, "Kerk," Chap. 4 and "Gemeente," Chap. 5 in *De Kaap de Goede Hoop: Een Nederlandse vestigingskolonie, 1680–1730* (Amsterdam: Uitgeverij Prometheus and Bert Bakker, 1999).

31. Floris Albertus van Jaarsveld, "Die Veldkornet en sy aandeel in die opbou van die Suid-Afrikaans Republiek tot 1870," *AYB* 13:2 (1950), 187–354. My thanks to Rob Shell for this reference.

32. Hans Heese, *Reg en Onreg: Kaapse Regspraak in die Agtiende Eeu* (Bellville: Instituut vir Historiese Navorsing, 1994), 19–28. Robert Ross, "The Rule of Law in the Cape Colony in the Eighteenth Century," in *Beyond the Pale: Essays on the History of Colonial South Africa* (Johannesburg: Witwatersrand University Press, 1994), 155–65.

33. The Cape reported to Batavia only until 1732.

34. This interpretation coincides with Guelke's dual frontier thesis articulated in "The Making of Two Frontier Communities." Nigel Penn, "Fugitives on the Cape Frontier, c.1680–1770," in *Rogues, Rebels and Runaways: Eighteenth Century Cape Characters* (Cape Town: David Philip 1999), 73–100.

35. For example, consider the rebellion against Governor Simon van der Stell led by Adam Tas, see Margaret W. Spillhaus, *The First South Africans and the Laws Which Governed Them, to Which is Appended the Diary of Adam Tas* (Cape Town: Juta, 1949). Also consider the case of the fugitive Estienne Barbier; see Nigel Penn, "Estienne Barbier: An Eighteenth-Century Cape Social Bandit," in *Rogues, Rebels and Runaways*, 101–46. Finally, there is the classic example of the Cape Patriots' movement; see Coenraad Beyers, *Die Kaapse Patriotte gedurende die laaste kwart van die agtiende eeuw in die voortlewing van hul denkbeelde* (Pretoria: J.L, 1967).

36. Linda M. Rupert, "Contraband Trade and the Shaping of Colonial Societies," *Itinerario* 30:3 (2006), 35–54; Jaap Jacobs, *New Netherland: A Dutch Colony in Seventeenth-Century America* (Leiden: Brill, 2005); Wim Klooster, *Dutch in the Americas, 1600–1800* (New Castle, DE: Oak Knoll Press, 1997).

37. To compare the vastly different application of European customs by the VOC in Asia, see Jean Gelman Taylor, *The Social World of Batavia: Europeans and Eurasians in Dutch Asia* (Madison: University of Wisconsin Press, 1983). Also see Leonard Blussé, *Strange Company: Chinese Settlers, Mestizo Women and the Dutch in VOC Batavia* (Dordrecht: Foris Publications, 1986).

2. ESTABLISHING FRONTIERS

The frontier in history is a powerful image; the notion of a zone of engagement has captured scholarly imaginations for generations.[1] The idea of the
frontier looms particularly large in South African history and historiography,
frequently inviting comparisons with the westward movement of settlers in
North America and encompassing attendant explorations of conquest and resistance, cross-cultural contact, colonial dialectics, environmental resource allocation, European hegemony, and debates about race and national identity.[2]
The frontier as both geographic place and as method of inquiry continues to
have salience—in South Africa and elsewhere—despite a long and contested
historiography. Notwithstanding all the ink spilled in efforts to define, demarcate, and deconstruct frontiers, the idea still has intellectual rigor.[3]

One reason for the persistence of frontier as an analytical category is its
flexibility. The notion of a boundary both fixed and porous, a region simultaneously claimed and fought over, a moment that is both fixable in time and
yet open-ended is particularly alluring. The frontier can be poked and prod-
ded and stretched without being convoluted beyond recognition. Its plasticity
gives the frontier the ability to bridge temporal, spatial, and theoretical gaps,
making it well suited to a variety of critical circumstances, but also in need of
careful scrutiny every time it is invoked.

My own understanding of frontier is rooted specifically in South African
debates, inflected by Africanist and comparative colonial contributions. The

frontier was a hinterland, at the margins of effective governmental control but not completely beyond the Company's reach. I am indebted here to Leonard Guelke's formulation of "outlaw" and "orthodox" frontiers for suggesting a way to go beyond simply "opening" and "closing" fluid "contact zones," thereby progressively bringing more territory into the colonial orbit.[4] A conception of frontiers as serially opened then closed assumes rather than explains the terms of conquest. The idea of outlaw and orthodox social formations, by contrast, offers a more nuanced understanding of frontiers by probing the ways which individuals and groups interacted among themselves and with colonial authority.[5]

Building on Guelke's formulation, I assert a conceptualization of the frontier as both a region and period of time in which orthodox and heterodox ideas, practices and social relationships were in tension. Broadening the description of outlaw to the more inclusive term heterodox creates a more capacious intellectual category. Heterodox encompasses a range of resistance from outright lawlessness to the creation of alternative households and the staking of marginal or unofficial claims to land. This heterodox/orthodox formulation lets us think about a space and time in which some people exploited the space beyond dominant conventions. Others—typically those with access to land and livestock—increasingly saw their lot as invested in conformity with the established colony rather than tied to the opportunities and risks of life beyond it. Thus I am using Guelke's perspective to portray colonial engagements not only in terms of "settler" and "native," but significantly also to characterize frontiers as space where both colonizing and colonized peoples contested metropolitan expectations. Orthodoxy, then, was an affinity with colonial authority.[6]

The explanatory power of the frontier is strong, as Penn and others have noted, but it is not unassailable.[7] Robert C.-H. Shell, for example, makes an argument that the dynamics of slavery and slave holding, not the frontier, framed the character of subsequent historical developments, particularly race relations.[8] I walk not a middle ground but a different path to explaining South Africa's past.

The agrarian nature of the colonial enterprise at the Cape—the struggle to coax a living from the land—offers the most appropriate context in which to comprehend early South African history.[9] Within that context, family structure and household organization are fundamental. Neither the independence of the frontier nor a brutal system of forced labor premised on violence completely encompasses the socioeconomic dynamics at play in the eighteenth century. But where these two strands intersect—on the loan farms of the frontier—we can see clearly the contested efforts to claim land, control territory, and assert preeminence that were made first by colonial settlers and then exerted by the state.

To describe the region surrounding the upper Olifants River Valley as a frontier is more than a geographical marker indicating the outer limits of colonial settlement. From 1725 until about 1750, farms claimed along the Olifants River and in the surrounding Cedarberg did, in fact, represent the furthest reaches of colonial land claims in a northwesterly direction from Cape Town.[10] The Cedarberg, however, remained a frontier long after an advancing perimeter of loan farms had extended to the north and the west.[11] As Guelke notes, "The frontier was not a simple geographical phenomenon but a complex region which offered opportunities to many different kinds of people."[12]

Some of those people homesteaded in the Cedarberg for nearly a century before the colonial government established a local administrative presence in Clanwilliam. Consequently, the region was long-lived as a contested zone—but one with a paper trail that shows successive generations of settlers transforming violently-contested land claims into widespread, year-round ranching properties anchored by well-stocked houses and multiply-intersecting family relationships.

TEXTURES OF FRONTIER LIFE

Social diversity characterized the Cedarberg from the time of the first land claims until well into the nineteenth century. The composition and density of frontier society changed over the course of one hundred years, adding a temporal element to Guelke's depiction while emphasizing the variety he describes. For Khoisan, frontier regions afforded continued, though restricted, access to land—not so much an opportunity as a mitigated misfortune. Among Khoisan who could no longer sustain an independent community, some individuals in frontier regions made limited land claims, some women married or established permanent relationships with settler men, and many found employment in colonial households, though in admittedly subordinate positions.

For settlers, frontier opportunities were both material and social. The prospect of land plus the availability of game and other resources meant the elements of subsistence for some and the chance of enrichment for others. Outlaws and scofflaws lived in community with state-appointed veldkornets. Soldiers and slaves fled to the frontier.[13] Even European travelers visited the colony's remote outposts and reported on the differences there in comparison to Cape Town and its closer hinterlands at Stellenbosch and Drakenstein.[14]

The frontier offered socioeconomic mobility, porous racial distinctions, and refuge from the law; however, it was not beyond the reach of either legal or social mechanisms of conformity. Frontier residents may have challenged prevailing social norms, the availability of frontier land may have been a safety valve diverting demographic pressure and thus deflecting dramatic social change, but the frontier experience did not fundamentally reshape the contours of society that began forming at the Cape with the arrival of the first VOC garrison in 1652. After all, our knowledge of outlaws and runaways in frontier regions comes from landdrosts' reports and criminal trial proceedings, evidence that distance and a heterogeneous, heterodox population was not refuge enough from the state's justice. Eventually, the norms established in Cape Town prevailed throughout the colony.

This conquest came slowly to the Cedarberg. The century-long process was a daily struggle for countless Khoisan, four generations of settler families, and their slaves. They did not live "on the frontier," but rather at Kridouw Krans, or on the farm Halve Dorschvloer, or at other recognized places in the landscape. They may have moved, some individuals quite often, but their families and communities were connected firmly to the region, networks of watering and resting places supplanted by a network of farms occupying the same places. This book tells the story of how one society both displaced and absorbed another, a particular, specific version of colonial dynamics that unfolded around the world in the eighteenth century.

SPECIFICS OF FRONTIER SCHOLARSHIP

Characterizing the Cedarberg as a frontier zone evokes direct comparisons with other areas of colonial settlement in seventeenth- and eighteenth-century South Africa. The Cape saw two broad strands of colonial expansion into the interior: easterly and northerly migrations. The eastern frontier moved away from Stellenbosch, over the Hottentots Holland Mountains, and across the Overberg to Swellendam. In 1785 the creation of the Graaff-Reinet district extended the eastern colonial boundary to the Great Fish River.[15]

The northern frontier, more arid than the east, historically attracted fewer colonial settlers. The climate supported pastoralism, but not widespread cultivation. Consequently, the settler frontier economy was based on stock farming, in contrast to the lucrative wine and wheat farms of the better-watered regions.[16] Poorer and more sparsely populated, the northern frontier attracted less Anglophone scholarly attention than Swellendam and Graaff-Reinet. P.J. van der Merwe's trilogy in Afrikaans remained the major contribution until Martin Legassick's pathbreaking dissertation renewed historians' interest in the region.[17] Subsequent work by Robert Ross, Fred Morton, Barry Morton, Jean and John Comaroff, and Nancy Jacobs greatly enhances our understandings of nineteenth-century dynamics in regions north of the Orange River.[18]

Most recently, Nigel Penn's work forces a reconsideration of the northern frontier areas below the Orange River and before the nineteenth century.[19] Penn's painstaking archival work opens up a new range of possibilities for historical inquiry in areas from the Cedarberg north to Namaqualand, and east-southeast to the Bokkeveld and Roggeveld. His work focuses much-needed attention on frontier areas not directly affected by Bantu-speaking peoples or by missionaries during the eighteenth and early nineteenth centuries.

A closer examination of the Cedarberg frontier is a case in point. Both in temperament and geography, the Clanwilliam district and Cedarberg region fall within the classification of the northern frontier as pioneered by Penn. The broader conceptualization of the northern frontier as used by authors such as Legassick and the Comaroffs leaves the Cedarberg well behind the front lines of colonial expansion. The northern frontier writ large began moving beyond the Cedarberg to Namaqualand and northeast to Griqualand and Trans-Orangia by the 1760s and 1770s, long before frontier struggles in the Cedarberg were settled. There, the crucial terms of labor relations and land tenure were not firmly in control of orthodox settlers and the colonial administration until well into the nineteenth century.

BOUNDARIES, METHODS, AND SOURCES

This process of asserting orthodoxy was entwined with the creation of colonial identities. Struggles over land and labor produced relationships of dominance, subordination, and resistance, the details of which lie bound in the volumes of the VOC archives, embedded in genealogies, painted on rock walls, and buried in the earth of the Cedarberg.

The Dutch East India Company kept copious records, meaning that the Cape has an abundance of written source materials, unlike most regions of Africa in the eighteenth century. However, the ledgers, accounts, and administrative reports of a merchant company do not record the whole story of colonial interactions. To understand the social implications of land tenure, family structures, and the basis of identity, we need to delve into carefully preserved archival documents, stretching them as far as they can go, a method with significant precedent.

Social history was founded on the practice of prodding documents to reveal stories they were not originally intended to tell.[20] Then postmodern criticism exploded the definition of text and readability, which expanded the notion of what constitutes an archive.[21] By necessity, African history has been at the leading edge of such methodological innovations. Since the 1960s, Africanists working with limited written sources have been reimagining ways of reconstructing and narrating the past.[22]

In that tradition, this book interrogates the relationship between narrative history and its constituent source materials. Each chapter in Part III reconstructs a family history from different kinds of written documents. None of these sources stands alone—all of the chapters rely on a wide range of materials for context. But emphasizing different sources in sequence demonstrates a range of possibilities for historical research.

Part II offers a way to rethink connections between archaeology and history.[23] I foreground archaeology because of its fundamental relationship with African history[24] and because it provides evidence crucial to understanding changing land use and land tenure in the Cedarberg, detailed in Chapter 3. The traces in the landscape left by brushes dipped in ochre, by beads, and by bits of stone tools also hint at subordinated colonial identities—contested social formations that were lost during a period of extreme transformation, discussed in Chapter 4.

Equally important, this juxtaposition of archaeological and documentary evidence challenges traditional notions of periodization. The colonial and precolonial collided in the Cedarberg. Individuals from vastly different traditions cooperated, collaborated, cohabited, procreated, and married. They fought violently and transmitted virulent diseases. They transferred technology conceptually across millennia and spatially across the subcontinent. In these interactions, the historic and the prehistoric cohabit, populating the same narrative and destabilizing categories of knowledge. In a world where historic and prehistoric bleed into each other, it is possible to adjust our vision of the past and to project this refracted periodization back across the Atlantic. Imagine a "precolonial Europe": France before sugar, England before tobacco, Spain before a tremendous influx of silver.

The term precolonial, applied to regions that would become colonies of European states, implicitly suggests a time or a place of waiting, peoples somehow living in anticipation of their subordination to an external power. This description resonates with Dipesh Chakrabarty's characterization of postcolonial states existing in a condition of a global "not yet."[25] Could we not equally envision Europeans waiting for commodities, luxuries, and the mass availability of cheap labor to fuel unprecedented economic change?[26] Admittedly, "precolonial" imperfectly describes Europe, but it is equally uncomfortable for Africa. Global inequalities of power—then and now—are embedded in the terminology we use to discuss the past. We are unlikely to discard the category of precolonial, but we should at least be aware that a wide range of attributes rooted in, or relegated to, a murky, unwritten past did, in fact, persist well into the time of colonization, as both documentary and archaeological evidence from the Cedarberg attests.[27]

NOTES

1. Particularly interesting reconceptualizations of frontiers in historical analysis include James F. Brooks, *Captives and Cousins: Slavery, Kinship, and Community in*

the Southwest Borderlands (Chapel Hill: The University of North Carolina Press, 2001); Richard White, The Middle Ground: Indians, Empires, and Republics in the Great Lakes Region, 1650–1815 (Cambridge: Cambridge University Press, 1991); Peter Sahlins, Boundaries: The Making of France and Spain in the Pyrenees (Berkeley: University of California Press, 1989); and Igor Kopytoff, ed., The African Frontier: The Reproduction of Traditional African Societies (Bloomington: Indiana University Press, 1987).

2. For an elegant historiography of the frontier in South African history, see Nigel Penn, The Forgotten Frontier: Colonist and Khoisan on the Cape's Northern Frontier in the Eighteenth Century (Cape Town: Double Storey Books and Athens: Ohio University Press, 2005), 9–13. On comparisons between North America and South Africa, see Howard Lamar and Leonard Thompson, eds. The Frontier in History: North American and South Africa Compared (New Haven: Yale University Press, 1981).

3. Susan Newton-King's Masters and Servants on the Eastern Cape Frontier, 1760–1803. (Cambridge: Cambridge University Press, 1999) and Penn's The Forgotten Frontier are both excellent recent narrative accounts of frontier tensions, and testament to the continued salience of frontier studies in South African history.

4. Leonard Guelke, "The Making of Two Frontier Communities: Cape Colony in the Eighteenth Century." Historical Reflections/Reflexions Historiques 12:3 (1985), 419–48. The idea of open and closed frontiers is Giliomee's, articulated in "Processes in Development of the Southern African Frontier," in Lamar and Thompson, 76–119. "Contact zone" comes from Mary Louise Pratt, Imperial Eyes: Travel Writing and Transculturation, (London: Routledge, 1992).

5. Guelke's theoretical contribution has been underrepresented in South African frontier historiography.

6. My use of the term "orthodox" is not the same as Bourdieu's, embedded in habitus—the social reproduction of structures in a stable society. Pierre Bourdieu, "Structures, Habitus, Power: Basis for a Theory of Symbolic Power," in Culture/Power/History, N. B. Dirks, G. Eley and S. B. Ortner , eds., 155–99 (Princeton, NJ: Princeton University Press, 1983). In following Guelke's use of the term in a frontier context, I instead use "orthodox" to describe the visible markers linking individuals and communities with the settler identity that dominated colonial society. This orthodoxy in a frontier zone represented a choice to identify with the dominant culture—thereby extending its dominance.

7. Martin Legassick, "The Frontier Tradition in South African Historiography," in Shula Marks and Anthony Atmore, eds., Society and Economy in Pre-Industrial South Africa (London: Longman, 1980), 45–47; Saunders, The Making of the South African Past, 70–71; Ken Smith, The Changing Past: Trends in South African Historical Writing (Johannesburg: Southern Book Publishers, 1988), 96.

8. Robert C.-H. Shell, Children of Bondage, xxxi.

9. My thinking on agrarian societies stems from Ester Boserup, The Conditions of Agricultural Growth: The Economics of Agrarian Change Under Population Pressure (New York: Aldine Publishing Company, 1965). The importance of agrarian history is by no means overlooked in South African historiography. Notable examples include Marks and Atmore's collection, Economy and Society in Pre-Industrial South Africa; William Beinart, Colin Bundy and Stanley Trapido, eds., Putting a Plough to the Ground: Accumulation and Dispossession in Rural South Africa, 1850–1930 (Johannesburg: Ravan

Press, 1986); and Charles van Onselen, *The Seed is Mine: The Life of Kas Maine, a South African Sharecropper, 1894–1985* (New York: Hill and Wang, 1996). For work confined to the Western Cape, see Wayne Dooling, "Agrarian Transformation in the Western Districts of the Cape Colony, 1838–c.1900" (PhD diss., Cambridge University, 1996); Mary Rayner, "Wine and Slaves: The Failure of an Export Economy and the Ending of Slavery in the Cape Colony, South Africa, 1806–1834" (PhD diss., Duke University, 1986); and Robert Ross, "The First Two Centuries of Colonial Agriculture in the Cape Colony: A Historiographical Review," *Social Dynamics* 9:1 (June 1983), 30–49.

10. Bergh and Visagie, *The Eastern Cape Frontier Zone, 1660–1980: A Cartographic Guide for Historical Research* (Durban: Butterworths, 1985), 4.

11. Among the earliest record of farms north of the Olifants River Valley include CA: RLR 16:107, 8 Jan. 1761, permit for Willem Koopman on the farm Klip Rugh, described as "over de Olifants en Doorn riviers in die Hantam."

12. Leonard Guelke, "The Making of Two Frontier Communities," 446.

13. Penn, in *Rogues, Rebels and Runaways*, 73.

14. O.F. Mentzel, *A Geographical and Topographical Description of the Cape of Good Hope (1787)*, trans. G. V. Marais and J. Hoge, ed. H. J. Mandelbrote (Cape Town: Van Riebeeck Society, 1925); Anders Sparrman, *A Voyage to the Cape of Good Hope Towards the Antarctic Polar Circle Round the World and to the Country of the Hottentots and the Caffres from the Year 1772–1776*, trans J. &. I. Rudner, ed. V. S. Forbes (Cape Town: Van Riebeeck Society, 1975); Carl Peter Thunberg, *Travels at the Cape of Good Hope 1772–1775*. ed V. S. Forbes (Cape Town: Van Riebeeck Society, 1986).

15. J.S. Bergh and J.C. Visagie beautifully illustrate the expanding eastern frontier in *The Eastern Cape Frontier Zone*. A good early study of easterly colonial migration is Edmund H. Burrows, *Overberg Outspan: A Chronicle of People and Places in the Southwestern Districts of the Cape* (Cape Town: Maskew Miller Limited, 1952; reprint, Swellendam: Swellendam Trust, 1988). For a more contemporary reassessment of the eastern frontier, see Clifton Crais, *The Making of the Colonial Order: White Supremacy and Black Resistance in the Eastern Cape, 1770–1865* (Johannesburg: Witwatersrand University Press, 1992). Susan Newton-King's outstanding *Masters and Servants on the Cape Eastern Frontier* is set in the eighteenth century and focuses on the tensions between Khoisan and colonists. Thus it is both a model and a foil for my exploration of colonial labor relations in the Cedarberg.

16. P.J. van der Merwe, *The Migrant Farmer in the History of the Cape Colony, 1658–1842*, trans. Roger B. Beck (Athens: Ohio University Press, 1995); Leonard Guelke, "Freehold Farmers and Frontier Settlers, 1657–1780," in *The Shaping of South African Society, 1652–1840*, eds. Richard Elphick and Hermann Giliomee, 66–108. 2nd ed. (Johannesburg: Maskew Miller Longman, 1989).

17. P.J. van der Merwe, *Die Noordwaarste Beweging van die Boere voor die Groot Trek (1770–1842)* (The Hague: W.P. van Stockum & Zoon, 1937; reprint, Pretoria: Die Staatsbiblioteek, 1988); *Die Trekboer in die Geskiedenis van die Kaapkolonie, 1657–1842* (Cape Town: Nasionale Pers Beperk, 1938); *Trek: Studies oor die Mobilitiet van die Pioniersbevolking aan die Kaap* (Cape Town: Nasionale Pers Beperk, 1945). Roger B. Beck's meticulous English translation of *Die Trekboer* appeared in 1995 as *The Migrant Farmer in the History of the Cape Colony, 1658–1842* (Athens: Ohio University Press).

Martin Legassick, "The Griqua, the Sotho-Tswana and the Missionaries." A shorter formulation of his principal arguments appears as "The Northern Frontier to 1840: The Rise and Decline of the Griqua People," in Elphick and Giliomee, *Shaping*, 358–420.

18. Robert Ross, *Adam Kok's Griquas: A Study in the Development of Stratification in South Africa* (Cambridge; Cambridge University Press, 1976); Fred Morton and Elizabeth Eldredge, editors, *Slavery in South Africa: Captive Labor on the Dutch Frontier* (Boulder: Westview Press, 1994); Barry Morton, "Servitude, Slave Trading and Slavery in the Kalahari," in Morton and Eldredge, 215–50. John and Jean Comaroff, *Of Revelation and Revolution: Christianity, Colonialism and Consciousness in South Africa*, Vol. 1 (Chicago: University of Chicago Press, 1991) and *Of Revelation and Revolution: The Dialectics of Modernity on a South African Frontier*, Vol. 2 (Chicago: University of Chicago Press, 1997) Nancy Jacobs, "The Flowing Eye: Water Management in the Upper Kuruman Valley, South Africa, c. 1800–1962," *Journal of African History* 37:2 (1996), 237–260. Julian Cobbing's seminal contribution sparked an ongoing reconsideration of frontier dynamics that include areas of the northern frontier "The Mfecane as Alibi: Thoughts on Dithakong and Mbolompo," *JAH* 29 (1988), 487–519. Also see Carolyn Hamilton, ed., *Mfecane Aftermath: Reconstructive Debates in Southern African History* (Johannesburg: Witwatersrand University Press, 1995).

19. Nigel Penn, *The Forgotten Frontier*. My own research owes a great debt to Penn's dissertation, which demonstrates the breadth and richness of material available in the Cape Archives for understudied regions of the northern frontier: "The Northern Cape Frontier Zone, 1700–c.1815" (PhD diss., University of Cape Town, 1995). Penn and Newton-King both adeptly demonstrate the possibilities of reconstructing histories of Khoisan and Khoisan – settler relationships from documents not always intended to reveal the complexities of frontier encounters.

20. Natalie Zemon Davis, *Fiction in the Archives: Pardon Tales and Their Tellers in Sixteenth-Century France* (Stanford: Stanford University Press, 1987); Ranajit Guha, ed., *A Subaltern Studies Reader 1986–1995* (Minneapolis: University of Minnesota Press, 1997).

21. Carolyn Hamilton, et al, *Refiguring the Archive* (Cape Town: David Phillip, 2002); Antoinette Burton, ed. *Archive Stories: Facts, Fictions and the Writing of History* (Durham: Duke University Press, 2005).

22. John Edward Philips, ed. *Writing African History* (Rochester: University of Rochester Press, 2005). For a discussion of how Africanist scholarship changed historical method, see Steven Feierman, "African Histories and the Dissolution of World Histories," in Robert H. Bates, V.Y Mudimbe, and Jean O'Barr, eds., *Africa and the Disciplines: The Contributions of Research in Africa to the Social Sciences and Humanities* (Chicago: University of Chicago Press, 1993), 167–212; Heidi Gengenbach, *Where Women Make History: Gendered Tellings of Community and Change in Magude, Mozambique* (New York: Columbia University Press, 2005), http://www.gutenberg-e.org/geho1/guide.html.

23. My approach is detailed in Laura J. Mitchell, "Material Culture and Cadastral Data: Documenting the Cedarberg Frontier, South Africa 1725–1795" in *Sources and Methods in African History: Spoken, Written, Unearthed*, Toyin Falola and Christian Jennings, eds. (Rochester: University of Rochester Press, 2003), 16–32.

24. Kairn Klieman, *"The Pygmies Were Our Compass": Bantu and Batwa in the History of West Central Africa, Early Times to c. 1900 C.E.* (Portsmouth , NH : Heinemann, 2003); Flordeliz T. Bugarin, "Trade and Interaction on the Eastern Cape Frontier: An Historical Archaeological Study of the Xhosa and the British during the Early 19th Century," (PhD diss., University of Florida 2002).

25. Dipesh Chakrabarty, *Provincializing Europe: Postcolonial Thought and Historical Difference* (Chicago: University of Chicago Press, 2000), 7–9.

26. For a discussion of social and cultural changes in Europe after Britain's contact with the Americas, see William Brandon, *New Worlds For Old: Reports From the New World and Their Effect on the Development Of Social Thought in Europe, 1500–1800* (Athens: Ohio University Press, 1986). On Europe's economic transformation as a result of colonial territories, see Kenneth L. Pomeranz, *The Great Divergence* (Princeton: Princeton University Press, 2000).

27. For a clear articulation of "precolonial" persistence into later periods, see Gareth Austin, " 'Developmental' Divergences and Continuities Between Colonial and Pre-Colonial Regimes: The Case of Asante, Ghana, 1701–1957," paper presented at the African Studies Association Annual Meeting, New Orleans, LA, 11–14 Nov., 2004.

II

Terms of Contest

The cool, clear streams of the Cedarberg nourish hardy plants that have sustained life in this region for longer than human memory. The arrival of European colonists in this landscape in the eighteenth century brought violently contested changes and particular forms of record keeping, so we know more about shifting land use and the social transformations in this period than we do for past ones. As a colonial frontier, the Cedarberg was the site of two major struggles, one for the control of land and another over the contours of identity.

These battles intertwined; land was crucial not only as a means of subsistence, but also as a component of identity for Khoisan and settler communities. Over the course of the eighteenth century, two parallel processes played out in the Cedarberg. Colonial land tenure practice was increasingly regularized and intensified, while fluid social categories became gradually reified.

Even as communities solidified, the social taxonomy created at the Cape was hardly monolithic. Slaves, indentured servants, land owners, and independent Khoisan formed variously permuted relationships with each other and with the natural environment. Identities proliferated, defying static categorization; people across the social spectrum challenged conventions, and many subordinated people worked their way through colonial structures.

The VOC's mania for lists flattened some of this variety. Property claims and *opgaaf* rolls, or census and taxation returns, must be coaxed to give up their stories. More texture emerges in narrative documents such as landdrost's correspondence and criminal records, but the Company's regular accounting of loan farms, settler agricultural production, and slave ownership do, in fact, reveal more than statistics. The chapters in Part II demonstrate the possibilities of social history reconstructed from ledgers. Loan farm claims preserved in the *Oud Wildschutte Boeke*, ongoing loan farm rent payments noted in the Stellenbosch landdrost's account books, and the annual opgaaf which recorded the settler population, their slaves, and their taxable agricultural production all document individual lives. The title to a farm and large flock of sheep cannot stand for an entire life; the tally mark next to a master's name is even less representative of a slave's existence. Nevertheless, read in conjunction with each other and in light of other sources, these lists produce remarkable stories about the terms of struggle in the Cedarberg.

Chapter 3 examines specific land-use patterns and links sites in the landscape to indigenous Khoisan identity, using lists compiled by twentieth-century archaeologists to contextualize colonial land claims. Chapter 4 explores colonial identities forged through interactions among various communities, and documents the basis of belonging to the dominant settler society.

3. TRACES IN THE LANDSCAPE

Although inhospitable, the Cedarberg is far from uninhabitable or innavigable. For at least the last 10,000 years, people lived from foraging and hunting. They responded to environmental change and either adapted to the arrival of pastoralists or selectively adopted herding practices.[1] Specific histories of these communities remain irretrievable, but the general contours of settlement are clear.

Hunters and herders used the Olifants River area extensively, and in some places intensively, long before the arrival of colonial explorers and settlers.[2] The relative paucity of references to Khoikhoi and San in contemporary colonial documents may well reveal more about European reporting priorities than about actual indigenous land and resource use.[3] Although the colonial records are imperfect, read critically and in conjunction with archaeological evidence they provide a basis for understanding the tendentious and uneven encounters between settlers and Khoisan.[4]

Early colonial relations ranged from awkward coexistence to armed conflict. From the beginning of permanent VOC settlement in 1652, interaction between the groups was ambivalent; both Khoisan and colonists had reason to be wary of the other. Thus European exploration was cautious and the settler frontier advanced in fits and starts during the eighteenth century. Whether it was the result of selective viewing, edited reporting, or the cyclical, seasonal use of territory by the Khoisan, the first things Jan Danckaert saw when he arrived in the Olifants River Valley were elephants. The earliest official, documented European expedition to breach the Piekeniers Kloof Pass and travel in the river valley was Danckaert's party in 1660.[5] Other expeditions followed Danckaert's trail at irregular intervals until sustained colonial occupation began in 1725.[6]

KHOISAN LAND USE

Colonization, however, was not the first catalyst for shifting human settlement patterns in the region. Environmental changes influenced population distribution over the preceding 15,000 years. In general terms, people altered the size of the groups they lived in, moved their territorial range, and shifted to plant-oriented food strategies from game-oriented organization in response to changing climatic conditions.[7] Between 8000 and 4000 BP, lower rainfall and higher sea levels caused people to move into the mountains, adapting to available plant and animal life.[8] Then, as the climate approached present conditions, people were able to establish links between the mountains and the coast.

Around 2000 BP, the advent of pastoralism in the Western Cape caused a new series of changes. "The very large number of sites dated to the last two millennia at the coast and in the more isolated parts of the mountains may reflect a reorganization of hunter-gatherer subsistence in the face of this incursion."[9] Under this most recent pattern, it is likely that groups gathered in the mountains on either side of the Olifants River during the late summer months, the driest part of the year.[10] From early winter through the spring, winter rainfall would make the Karoo and the Sandveld more attractive, causing people to spread out from the mountains. Seasonal population dispersal in these areas is consistent with archaeological data and early travelers' accounts.[11]

In much of the Southwestern Cape, herders and hunters shared the environment, but not without struggle. In mountainous areas and dry reaches of the interior, however, hunters were not challenged for the use of land until the arrival of European settlers in the eighteenth century. In areas where hunters were confronted by herders, the two groups were not always easy to distinguish, either to contemporary observers or in their archaeological signature. ". . . [B]road continuities in stone artifact traditions and in hunting-gathering patterns before and after the introduction of stock and pottery to the Cape suggest that acculturation (diffusion) was at least as important as population movement in promoting the spread of pastoralism."[12]

When herders began arriving at the Cape 2000 years ago, they displaced hunters and put pressure on San society.[13] The archaeological evidence is suggestive of conflict during the process. For example, an increase in the creation of rock art and a change in the art itself indicates a society under stress.[14] On the coastal plain and in the better-watered areas of the interior, hunters and herders would have been in direct competition for occupancy of land and access to water. Domestic herds gradually displaced wild game, so hunters who did not merge with pastoralists either entered into the client relationships reported in colonial records or they retreated higher into the mountains and resorted to smaller prey.[15] "The idea of hunting peoples being forced into less productive areas is . . . implied in both the historical and archaeological data."[16]

The Khoikhoi's main domestic animals were cattle and sheep, the ratio of which varied in space and time. Goats were extremely rare. They kept dogs for both hunting and herding. Khoikhoi used cattle for dairy products as well as transportation of goods and people, but rarely for meat. Like San, Khoikhoi also hunted, trapped small game, and fished. Groups near the coast exploited marine resources, eating shellfish, seals, and whatever else they could catch or gather.

Although Khoikhoi could not smelt metal, they did incorporate metal pieces into tools and weapons when it was available. For the most part, however, their technology was limited to the bone, stone, and wooden implements associated with Late Stone Age assemblages. Khoikhoi made distinctive pottery, which San did not, though they appear to have used Khoikhoi pots and shards when they were available. Khoikhoi lived in small, nomadic groups, housed in huts of woven mats that were easy to take apart, move, and rebuild.[17]

Both Khoikhoi and San groups were mobile and probably aggregated at certain times of the year. For most of the time, however, indigenous groups were small, dispersed, and—with the exception of San rock painting—left little permanent trace on the landscape. Thus it is possible that land either looked or was empty of human habitation when first encountered by Europeans.

The illusion of an empty interior was not sustainable, however. An expanding colonial frontier brought pastoralist-pastoralist competition.[18] *Trekboere* (migrant farmers) moving just ahead of the colonial frontier with their herds, flocks, and households brought with them unprecedented competition for limited grazing land and access to water. Their arrival increased the pressure on game and was the harbinger of permanent settlement with permanent structures in the landscape. They brought with them new ideas and technology, most importantly the notions of exclusive access to land and the concept of fixed boundaries, as well as ironmongery and guns.

Both within and beyond colonial territories, the imposition of European notions of land tenure brought colonists into direct conflict with indigenous hunting and herding populations.[19] Colonial expansion produced competition for territory and resources that was unprecedented in Khoisan experience.[20] There may well have been tension between hunting and herding groups that resulted in hunters inhabiting the rockier mountain regions while herders stuck to the coastal plains, but this debate among archaeologists is not resolved.[21] There is rock art in the Cedarberg suggestive of combat, but it is impossible to situate in specific temporal or geographical context.[22] There is also evidence that trade goods such as ostrich eggshell beads—and probably people as well—circulated with regularity between the coast and the mountains.[23]

LOAN FARMS AND THE COLONIAL FRONTIER

The earliest settler land claims in the Olifants River region were hunting and grazing permits granted by the Dutch East India Company to free burghers who requested them.[24] This land tenure system was an outgrowth of the early mineral exploration and hunting permits that the VOC used to regulate travel to the interior from the 1650s. By the eighteenth century, most of the permits were for grazing land, rather than hunting or mineral extraction. As outlying areas were settled, land first used for seasonal grazing gradually became used more intensively. Crops, buildings, wells, dams, and other permanent improvements were introduced and loan farms became an integral part of the Cape's agricultural economy.

The annual rent for a loan farm of 24 *rixdollars* was standard throughout the colony for most of the VOC period, though the consistency with which it was paid and the level of arrears tolerated by the Company varied greatly according to region and to the individual farmers. A loan farm permit had to be renewed each year, but this practice was followed rather loosely, with an extension being taken for granted unless transfer or termination was requested specifically. Rent, which could be paid in specie or livestock, was payable either at the landdrost or the Castle at the Cape.[25] Farmers in outlying areas often paid several years at once, presumably due in part to the long journey from their farms to the seats of colonial authority. Even when combined payments of up to ten years at once did not completely eliminate arrears on a loan farm's rent, in most cases occupancy continued unchallenged. Despite directives from the Heren XVII that local authorities should be diligent in collecting payments to make the administration of the Cape less of a drain on the Company's coffers, cases of farmers in the Olifants River region being unable to renew their loan permits for nonpayment of arrears were rare.[26]

A loan farm agreement did not grant title to the land—only permission to use the land—so loan farms could not actually be sold or bequeathed. However, a remnant of Dutch feudal land tenure practice stipulated that a tenant be compensated for physical improvements made to the land.[27] Thus the value of buildings, crops, and any other nonmovable assets belonged to the tenant, not the landlord. At the Cape, this practice meant that although a loan farm holder could not transfer the land directly, he could dispose of the *opstal* (farm house and outbuildings). Since it was not possible to separate buildings and other improvements from the land they stood on, the value of the land—accessibility, fertility, and water sources—was embedded in the price of the opstal. Settlers and the Company understood any transfer to include the loan farm permit with its annual 24 rixdollars obligation, although technically the land itself was not sold and did not appreciate in monetary terms beyond the value of the rent to the Company.

A loan farm was legally a limited land claim, but in practice it was de facto land ownership. This notion of ownership was conceived of in specific terms with roots in European practice. Settlers brought with them the idea of land as a partible, bounded commodity, owned by an individual (or self-selected partnership), transferable, and exclusive in perpetuity. This view of land ownership transcended the formal boundaries of the colonial frontier as the trekboere staked out territory for themselves beyond the claimed and administered districts of the VOC colony.[28]

SITES OF STRUGGLE IN THE LANDSCAPE

Settler expansion into the Olifants River Valley pushed indigenous populations onto increasingly marginal land. San who had been able to accommodate the pressure of encroaching pastoralists for nearly two millennia were virtually eliminated from the Southwestern Cape in less than two centuries of interaction with European colonists. The pastoralist Khoikhoi whose migration to the Cape changed the distribution of both human and animal populations were unable to retain an independent means of subsistence in the face of challenges from another pastoralist society, particularly once that society claimed land for permanent settlement. Khoisan reaction to colonial expansion included peaceful interaction, violent resistance, and complete withdrawal. The irrefutable material evidence of widespread and long-standing Khoisan presence in the Cedarberg adds resonance to the colonial documentary accounts of brutal and desperate battles for that land.

It is possible that this and other eighteenth-century confrontations were more than generalized struggles over water sources and hunting or grazing terrain.[29] Given the extent to which settlers established loan farms on land that harbors evidence of intensive Khoisan activity,[30] they may have incited particular ire—knowingly or not—by exercising exclusive claims over places of material, strategic, and ritual significance to displaced Khoisan.[31] Being denied access to sites of ritual importance was a devastating blow delivered to Khoisan at the same time they were being forced onto more marginal land or into colonial service.

A PERMANENT SETTLER PRESENCE

The earliest settler occupation of land in the Olifants River Valley quickly became permanent. One advantage of the loan farm system from the tenant's perspective was that a farming family was not bound to a given piece of land and so could easily relocate if springs dried up or the land proved to be less productive than anticipated. By far the majority of the first loan farms registered in the region were renewed, however, and many were maintained throughout the VOC period. A good number of those farms were then converted to the quitrent system under British administration of the Cape.[32] Several of the original farm names still exist today, though the boundaries have changed numerous times in the interval. Figure 3.5 is a chronological list of the permits issued in the first five years of settlement in the area and gives an indication of the extent to which the first land claims were quickly renewed.

The surviving loan farm records are incomplete and the indexing system in the Cape Archives is only partial. Nevertheless there is abundant—though imperfect—information upon which to base firm conclusions about the nature of early colonial land tenure.[33] The loan farm system provided long-term stability in conjunction with ease of transfer, despite the fact that leases needed to be renewed each year. The practical functionality of loan farms enabled colonial settlement in the Cedarberg, since tenure was secure enough to encourage farmers to make permanent improvements to their land. Moreover, those improvements were readily transferable, which allowed a farmer options for the future: either to sell and move on, or to bequeath and build family wealth.

Lange Valleij, the first loan farm granted in the region, is typical of settler land tenure patterns in the Cedarberg (see Figure 3.6). Johannes Ras held the first permit from 1725 to 1728.[34] He subsequently transferred the farm to Andries Kruger, who held a series of consecutive permits from 1728 until 1734.[35] Then Cornelis Heufke took the farm and kept the title for 25 years.[36] In 1759, Heufke transferred Lange Valleij to Lucas and Class Visagie, who stayed on the land another twenty years.[37]

Fig 3.5. First Five Years of Cedarberg Loan Farm Claims

Source: CA: Receiver of Land Revenue series and L. Guelke RLR data

First Five Years of Cedarberg Loan Farm Claims

Permit Holder	Year	Farm
Johannes Ras	1725	Lange Valleij
Francois Smit	1725	Klein Valleij
Jurgen Hanekoom	1725	Modder Fontein
Arnoldus Johannes Basson	1725	Groote Valleij
Willem Burger	1726	Misgunt
Pieter Willemsz van Heerden	1726	Ratel Fontein
Daniel Pfeil	1726	Zeekoe Valleij
Alewijn Smit	1726	Thien Rivieren
Jan Steenkamp	1726	Groene Valleij
Jan Dissel	1726	Renoster Hoek
Daniel Sr. Pfeil	1727	Brakkefontein
Johannes L. Pieters Putter	1727	Halve Dorschvloer
Jochem Koekemoer	1727	Hendrik van der Wats Gat
Hendrik de Vries	1727	Zeekoe Valleij
Andries Kruger	1728	Lange Valleij
Jan Andries Dissel	1728	Groote Zeekoe Valleij en Klein Valleij
Hendrik Cloete	1728	Klein Valleij
Alewijn Smit	1728	Thien Rivieren
Francois Smit	1728	Lange Fontien
Jacob Mouton	1729	Berg Valleij
Andries Krugel	1729	Lange Valleij
Johannes Bota	1729	Breede Rivier
Guilliam Visagie	1729	Gonjemans Kraal
Juff Anna de Coning	1729	Sonquas Cloof en het Kley Gat

Fig. 3.6. Cedarberg Loan Farm Tenure Patterns

Long-term stability is also evident in other land claims, as I show regarding land ownership among the Lubbe family in chapter 7. The ownership genealogy of Groote Valleij continues in that chapter. To see the locations of farms mentioned in this table, consult the maps Early Cedarberg Settler Farms, Burger Family Farms, and Lubbe Family Farms.

Source: CA: Receiver of Land Revenue series and L. Guelke RLR data

Fig. 3.4. Early Cedarberg Settler Farms

Fig. 6.3. Burger Family Farms

Fig. 7.4. Lubbe Family Farms

Fig. 7.6. Continuity of Land Tenure in Lubbe Family Loan Farms

Cedarberg Loan Farm Tenure Patterns

Dates	Claimant	Length of Claim
BRAKKEFONTEIN		
1727–1758	Daniel Pfeil	31
1758–1791	Barend Fredrik Lubbe	33

Cedarberg Loan Farm Tenure Patterns

Dates	Claimant	Length of Claim
HENDRIK VAN DER WAT'S GAT		
1727–1750	Jochem Koekemoer	23
1750–1761	Martha Mouton	11

Period	Name	Number
	Wed. Barend Lubbe	-
1794–1801	Paul Willem Lubbe Barendsz.	7

CARTOUW

Period	Name	Number
1731–1745	Wed Paul Jourdaan	14
1745–1753	Christiaan Lievenberg	8
1754–1756	Joh Hend Blankenberg	2
1756–1788	Willem Burger	32
1788–1791	Barend Fredrik Burger	3
–1804	Willem Burger	

GROENE VALLEIJ

Period	Name	Number
1709–	Arie Kruijsman	
1711–1724	Arnoldus Kruijsman	13
1723–1724	Arnoldus Willemsen Basson	1

Period	Name	Number
1761–1779	Lucas Visagie	18
1779–1781	Johannes Liebenberg	2
1787–1790	Jan van Schoor	3
1800–1807	Cornelis C. Mostert	7

KLEIN VALLEIJ

Period	Name	Number
1725–1743	Francois Smit	18
1743–1786	Pieter Gous	43
1786–1790	Barend Vorster	4
1790–	Alewijn Jacobus Vorster	

LANGE VALLEIJ

Period	Name	Number
1725–1728	Johannes Ras	3
1728–1734	Andries Kruger	6
1734–1759	Cornelis Heufke	25

Fig. 3.6. (*continued*)

Groene Valleij b

Period	Name	Value
1726–1727	Jan Steenkamp	1
1730–1750	Jan Steenkamp	20
1754–1776	Andries Hobregt	22
1786–	Johannes Marthinus Deppenaar	
1792–	Johannes Marthinus Deppenaar	
GROOTE VALLEY		
1725–1728	Arnoldus Johannes Basson	3
1730–1736	Johannes Basson	6
1736–1785	Barend Lubbe	49

Period	Name	Value
1759–1779	Lucas en Claas Visagie	20
1779–1785	Hendrick Johannes Louw Jacobsz	6
1785–1791	Adriaan Louw Adriaanz	6
Lange Valleij b		
1757–1786	Andries Lubbe	29
MISGUNT		
1726–1727	Willem Burger	1
1730–1760	Wed Willem Burger	30
1760–1780	Schalk Willemsz Burger	30
MODDERFONTEIN		

GROOTE ZEEKOE VALLEY EN KLEIN VALLEY

1728–1732	Jan Andries Dissel	4
1732–1761	Jacob Cloete	29
1761–1773	Hendrik Cloete	12
1773–1789	Coen Hendrik Feith	16
1725–1746	Jurgen Hanekoom	21
1747–1762	Pieter Lourensz Stokvliet	15
1762–1764	Jan Abr Meyer	2
1764–1776	Wed Gerrit Hendrik Meyer Jansz	12
1782–1787	Hend Albertusz van Zyl	5

HALVE DORSCHVLOER

1727–1742	Johannes Lodewijk Putter	15
1742–1742	Hendriek Krieger	0
1744–1763	Schalk Willemz. Burger	19
1797–1804	Jacobus Stephanus Burger	7

PAKHUIS

1743–1744	Christiaan Liebenburg	1
1744–1794	Cornelis Koopman	50
1794–	Jacobus Redelinghuizen	
1800	Johannes Jacobus Botha	

Whether an individual chose to transfer a loan farm away or to keep the land within a kin network made little difference in the use of the land. Except for the years of particularly violent conflict between Khoisan and settlers leading up to the frontier war of 1739, few of the Olifants River loan farms remained unclaimed or unoccupied by Europeans during the eighteenth century. Once land formally came within the realm of colonial occupation it was not readily given up, despite armed Khoisan resistance. Initially, claimants used outlying loan farms as seasonal livestock stations, providing grazing areas for sheep and cattle that could not be accommodated at the owner's principal farm. Within the first three years of permits being granted for the Olifants River Valley, settlers began to establish a permanent presence. More affluent colonists with access to productive arable land elsewhere tended to keep living at their principal farm, using the Cedarberg only for grazing. Those with fewer means took advantage of the access to land, in spite of its remote location, to establish farmsteads.

Daniel Pfeil, for example, was a prominent and wealthy burgher. His Cedarberg farms Zeekoe Valleij (1726) and Brakkefontein (1727) were undoubtedly grazing land and not residential locations. According to the opgaaf, or census, in 1725 his primary residence was in the Cape district, where he lived with his wife, three daughters, a knecht (in this case, an overseer), 36 slaves, 16 horses, 100 head of cattle, 400 sheep, and 40 pigs. His farm produced wine, wheat, and barley. On a Stellenbosch district farm he kept an additional 100 cattle and 400 sheep.[38] Two years later his primary farm was still in the Cape district, and he was blessed now with another daughter, three more knechten, fewer horses, more pigs, and no other livestock. He claimed 100 cattle and 200 sheep at a secondary farm in Voor Stellenbosch.[39] He pastured more cattle at Brakkefontein.[40] Pfeil had other loan farms during the 1720s in Tulbagh and Elsenberg, suggesting that he acquired grazing land when and where it was convenient. Alewijn Smit, in contrast, did not claim a loan farm outside the Olifants River area in the 1720s, so he must have been counted for the opgaaf while living on Thein Rivieren.[41]

The census was taken geographically and reported according to *wyk*, administrative subdivisions within districts, so it gives a rough indication of who people's neighbors were.[42] Since farms were not laid out in any systematic way, no serial list can be completely representative of spatial relationships, but lists organized according to wyk are strongly suggestive.[43]

Having title to more than one farm was relatively common, and not just among men of substance like Daniel Pfeil. Farmers of more moderate means like Putter also had multiple farms, typically more regionally concentrated. Within a given area, multiple farm ownership provided one basis for the tight social network that connected people, land, and labor across relatively long distances. Regular movement of people and livestock from one farm to another permitted the exploitation of seasonally available water and vegetation. This movement, driven by economic and environmental imperatives, provided an opportunity for people to form and strengthen social relationships. This process was true for farmers—who often worked in partnership with extended family members—as well as for slaves, who moved among the properties of their masters, as well as to farms belonging to others.[44]

Settlers and slaves moved through the region along a network of farms linked by family ties and reciprocal obligations, which must have disrupted Khoisan society to an even greater extent than the mere presence of competing pastoralists. The movement of people and livestock strengthened settler society because it facilitated the flow of information and enhanced people's knowledge of the local terrain, thereby more firmly entrenching settler presence in the Olifants River Valley. The relationships formed among farms, farming families, and their slaves linked the valley to the surrounding mountains, the coastal plains, and the interior. The settler network thus spanned topographical and climatic divisions with a frequency and intensity unprecedented before the eighteenth century.

Putter, for example, had one farm in the mountains and another in the valley. Though the properties were less than twenty kilometers apart, the variation in surface water would have permitted advantageous seasonal exploitation. Putter would graze his small herd of 14 cattle and 60 sheep in the Piekeniers Kloof during the rainy winter months and move to the farm Halve Dorschvloer along the river for the hot, dry summer.[45]

Dissel and his wife Maria Vosloo were more prosperous in terms of agricultural production and land title than Putter; they exploited environmental differentiation across their farms. They grew wine grapes and wheat on their principal farm, while their livestock moved among three locations: Drakenstein, the coastal plain between the Cedarberg and the Atlantic, and over a ridge near the Olifants River. [46] This arrangement permitted Jan and Maria to spread out a relatively large flock to avoid overgrazing, and also provided access to water during the driest months of the year.

The fact that the Dissel household slaves moved regularly among these farms, as well as to neighboring farms, comes through in the trial of four of Dissel's slaves who ran away in the company of seven others.[47] Testimony from other cases against deserters suggests there must have been regular contact among slaves of different households and that the movement of slaves and Khoisan servants among farms was a regular, unremarkable occurrence.[48]

The evidence for reconstructing the bonds that forged colonial society across great distances and linked settlers to the land tends to be androcentric, though not exclusive of women. Loan farm permits, rent payment registers, freehold titles, auction records, the opgaaf, and even court documents obscure the extent to which women participated in the economic life of this agricultural society. Although Roman-Dutch law stipulates community property within marriage, only men were listed as titleholders, unless the woman was a widow. There are instances of unmarried women having property, but they are unusual. Women do, however, make it into the official records of the eighteenth century Cape, though in a subordinated way that masks the extent of their influence.

Links to extended families, intricate property networks, marriage patterns intended to optimize inheritance, and local alliances turned on women's participation. Maria Vosloo's case, for example, shows that she brought more to her third marriage than livestock, slaves, and access to land. When some of the Dissel household slaves ran away, they fled with some of Jan Botma's slaves. From the court documents, their flight together might seem coincidental. The fact that Botma was Maria's son-in-law is not included in the trial record, obscuring the family link between him and Dissel. The relationships among their slaves, the proximity of their farms, and the fact that Dissel and Botma must have shared more than discontent among their slaves is implied in the evidence presented to the Council of Justice, but Maria and her role in linking the two men is absent altogether.[49]

CHANGING KHOISAN LAND TENURE OPTIONS

Despite the deep division between Khoisan and colonial land use in the Cedarberg, land tenure patterns were not racially-based in the eighteenth century. There were no statutes limiting land title to whites or Europeans, although in practice those people with formal property rights under VOC administration were predominantly colonists. Predominantly is not exclusively, however, and the few exceptions to the prevailing pattern of colonial land tenure are important to note. Although not numerically significant, the fact that twenty loan farm permits in the Cedarberg area were held by individuals identified as being Bastaard or Bastaard-Hottentot indicates that the barriers to indigenous people claiming land under colonial authority were likely economic and social rather than racial.

The list of Khoisan and mixed race farmers in Figure 3.9 is not exhaustive. Unlike later nineteenth- and twentieth-century land registration practices, eighteenth-century titles were not categorized according to race, so the racial identity of landholders features only incidentally. In most cases, loan farm records identify claimants as being either a burgher or a widow, Bastaard or Hottentot. Further research in other regions is likely to uncover more examples of Khoisan land tenure in colonial terms. This initial sampling from the

Fig. 3.9. Khoisan and Mixed-Race Loan Farm Claimants

Source: CA: Receiver of Land Revenue series and L. Guelke RLR data

Loan Farms Claimed by Khoisan and Mixed-Race Individuals

Permit Holder	Year	Farm
Willem Koopman		Klip Rug
Cornelis Koopman	1754	Doornbosch
Jan Nicolaasz Swart	1770	Holle Rivier
Hendrik Koopman	1771	Twee Fonteinen
Cornelis Kok	1776	Elandsfontein
Matthys Scheffer	1776	Wagendrift
Matthys Scheffer	1777	Onrust
Bartholomeus Koopman	1782	Questberg
Engela Koopman	1782	Twee Fonteinen
Franciscus	1784	Douwenos
Paul Meyer	1784	Kweek Rivier
Fredrick Diederiksz	1784	Twee Fontynen
Frederik Diederiks	1786	Kogelfontein
Jan Jansz. Swart	1794	Holle Rivier
Willem Fortuijn	1794	de Valleij
Cornelis Koopman	1794	Pakhuis
Jan Koopman	1794	Honing Valleij
Cornelis Kok	1800	Olyven Fonteyn

Cedarberg, however, is sufficient to show that settled farming and formal title to land were not restricted to colonists of European origin. The Dutch "legal hegemony over the landscape" was not as complete as Guelke and Shell assert.[50]

Granted, if Khoisan wanted to claim land in areas where European settlement had begun in earnest, then they needed to make that claim in colonial terms, thereby participating in the orthodox society. The fact that Khoisan could pursue formal land title implies that they were not excluded from participation, as previous scholarship suggests.[51] According to Guelke and Shell, "There is only one example in the Dutch period of a Khoikhoi laying claim to property, namely Adam Kok, described in the source as a 'Hottentot' . . . "[52] This new evidence makes it clear that people other than Adam Kok chose to make claims to land and a place in colonial society. Although these individuals were not numerous, we should not overlook them.

Their presence as property holders in colonial documents further indicates that people of mixed or indigenous descent did not have to appear European or be identified as European in order to participate in colonial society. These few loan farm holders suggest that at least in terms of land tenure, Khoisan did not have to "pass unobtrusively" in Cape society.[53] Assuming they could pay the rent, they could participate as property owners.

Khoisan landholders in the Cedarberg were clustered in the last quarter of the eighteenth century. Perhaps it took a generation of sustained contact until individual Khoisan perceived there might be a benefit to claiming land according to VOC tenure practice. Perhaps it took that long until the land on which those individuals were living fell under an acquisitive colonial gaze, prompting an individual to preempt claim by another. Perhaps it was not until the 1770s that participating as a colonial landholder was a preferable option to further retreat from an advancing settler frontier.

Did people like Cornelis Koopman, Frederik Diederiksz, and Jan Swart Jansz use their land as household farmsteads, like frontier colonists? Or were their permits rather to secure access to grazing ground before all the better lands were claimed by settlers? Did they hold the land in the name of a group who lived communally, as their forebears did? If so, where did these people go when they were not in residence on the loan farm? The *Oud Wildschutte Boeke* do not specify land use on loan farms. The volumes record permits for hunting, grazing, and wood collecting, but do not otherwise define the terms of occupation. Consequently, we can only continue to speculate about what actually happened when colonial land tenure and Khoisan land use met on the same terrain.

CONTESTED LAND, ENDURING LANDSCAPE

The locations of the earliest loan farms granted in the Olifants River Valley coincide with points of intensive previous use as suggested by the frequency of Late Stone Age evidence, both rock paintings and stone tool assemblages. Based on the loan farms granted between 1725 and the 1740s, it is clear that farmers were competing with hunters and herders for use of the same places. This argument is intuitive: the land is unequally endowed, so people and animals gravitate toward areas with the best quality or highest concentration of natural resources.

Jan van Riebeeck understood that conflict between colonists and the indigenous population had to do with contested resources—cattle, pasturage, water. The archaeological record read in conjunction with documentary evidence gives specific, tangible substance to struggles in the Cedarberg. In the face of expanding colonial settlement, the indigenous inhabitants of the Western Cape fought not only for access to the means of economic subsistence independent from colonial service, but also to maintain the integrity of their social structures and belief system.

From the 1740s, the colonial presence became more entrenched in the Cedarberg. Earlier farms were maintained and permits in the region continued to be granted at a steady rate, once the region recovered from the frontier war of 1739, as shown in Figure 3.6. By the last quarter of the eighteenth century, some Khoisan began to claim land under colonial authority, indicating the extent to which the loan farm system determined land tenure. Despite long distances and rugged terrain, the settlers established a tightly woven social network that that was instrumental in maintaining colonial land claims, since it facilitated transportation, communication, and seasonal land use. This network also linked the region to the wider colony.

Increasing colonial presence disrupted the seasonal mobility of indigenous hunters and herders. However, the introduction of fixed boundaries, exclusive access to land, and permanent settlement did not alter the landscape fundamentally. The arid climate and low carrying capacity of the land meant that colonial settlers, like Khoikhoi, relied on pastoralism for sustenance, supplemented by hunting. Although arable agriculture did not begin to figure prominently until the introduction of citrus at the end of the eighteenth century, from the 1730s the permanent nature of European settlement challenged both hunting and herding lifestyles to the point that Khoisan either retreated further from colonial presence or entered into the service of frontier farmers. In the last quarter of the eighteenth century, however, a few Khoisan managed an alternative to retreat or subservience and established an independent presence on the land in colonial terms.

NOTES

1. Tony Manhire, *Later Stone Age Settlement Patterns in the Sandveld of the South-Western Cape Province, South Africa* (Oxford: BAR, 1987); John Parkington, "Time and Place: Some Observations on Spatial and Temporal patterning in the Later Stone Age Sequence in Southern Africa," *South African Archaeological Bulletin* 35 (1980), 73–83.

2. Andrew Smith, Karim Sadr, John Gribble and Royden Yates, "Excavations in the South-Western Cape, South Africa and the Archaeological Identity of Prehistoric Hunter-Gatherers Within the Last 2000 Years," *South African Archaeological Bulletin* 46 (1991), 71–91; Richard G. Klein, "The Prehistory of Stone Age Herders in the Cape Province, South Africa," *Prehistoric Pastoralism in South Africa* (South African Archaeological Society Goodwin Series 5, June 1986), 5–12.

3. Mary Louise Pratt, "Narrating the Anti-Conquest," in *Imperial Eyes: Travel Writing and Transculturation.* (London: Routledge, 1992), 38–68; J.M. Coetzee, "The Picturesque, the Sublime, and the South African Landscape," in *White Writing: On the Culture of Letters in South Africa.* (New Haven and London: Yale University Press, 1988), 49–54.

4. Gyan Prakash, "Subaltern Studies as Postcolonial Criticism," *American Historical Review* 99:5 (1994), 1475–90; Laura J. Mitchell, "Material Culture and Cadastral Data: Documenting the Cedarberg Frontier, South Africa 1725–1795," in *Sources and Methods in African History: Spoken, Written, Unearthed,* Toyin Falola and Christian Jennings, eds. (Rochester: University of Rochester Press, 2003), 16–32.

5. CA: VC 3 *Dagregister. Anteyckenning gehouden by Jan Danckaert, Journael van een tocht na Monomotapa,* 12 Nov. 1660–20 Jan. 1661.

6. For example, Pieter Cruijthoff in 1661, Pieter van Meerhoff in 1661, Cruijthoff again in 1662–63, Jonas de la Guerre in 1663–64, and Olof Bergh in 1682–83. For an account of the major seventeenth- and eighteenth-century expeditions that traveled to the Olifants River, see P.S. Scholtz, "Die historiese ontwikkeling van die Onder-Olifantsrivier, 1660–1902," *Archives Yearbook for South African History* (Cape Town: Staatsdrukker, 1966), 7–28.

7. Manhire et al., "A Distributional Approach," 29–30.

8. Parkington, "Late Pleistocene and Holocene Climates as Viewed from Verlore Vlei," *Palaeontology Africa* 23 (1980), 71.

9. Manhire et al, "A Distributional Approach," 29.

10. Parkington, "Soaqua: Hunter-Fisher-Gatherers of the Olifants River, Western Cape," *South African Archaeological Bulletin* 32 (1977), 150–57.

11. Manhire, et al, "A Distributional Approach," 30.

12. Klein, "The Prehistory of Stone Age Herders," 9; J. Deacon, "Later Stone Age People and Their Descendants in Southern Africa," in *Southern African History and Paleoenvironments,* ed. R. Klein (Rotterdam: A.A. Balkema, 1984), 221–38.

13. J.E. Parkington, R.J. Yates, A.H. Manhire and D.J. Halkett, "The Social Impact of Pastoralism in the South-Western Cape," *Journal of Anthropological Archaeology* 5 (1986), 313–329.

14. J.D. Lewis-Williams, *Believing and Seeing: Symbolic Meanings in Southern San Rock Painting* (London: Academic Press, 1981); Royden Yates and Anthony Manhire, "Shamanism and Rock Paintings: Aspects of the Use of Rock Art in the South-Western Cape, South Africa," *South African Archaeological Bulletin* 46 (1991), 3–11; Royden Yates, Jo Golson, and Martin Hall, "Trance Performance: The Rock Art of Boontjieskloof and Sevilla," *South African Archaeological Bulletin* 40 (1985), 70–80.

15. Smith, "Competition, Conflict and Clientship," 39; A.H. Manhire, J.E. Parkington, and T.S. Robey, "Stone Tools and Sandveld Settlement," in *Frontiers: Southern African Archaeology Today,* eds. D. Avery et al. (Oxford: BAR, 1984), 111–20.

16. Smith, "Competition, Conflict and Clientship," 39.

17. Klein, "The Prehistory of Stone Age Herders," 5.

18. Nigel Penn, "Pastoralists and Pastoralism in the Northern Cape Frontier Zone During the Eighteenth Century," *Prehistoric Pastoralism in South Africa* (South African Archaeological Society Goodwin Series 5, June 1986), 62–68.

19. Martin Legassick, "The Griqua, the Sotho-Tswana, and the Missionaries, 1780–1840: The Politics of a Frontier Zone." (PhD diss., UCLA, 1970); Nigel Penn, *The Forgotten Frontier: Colonist and Khoisan on the Cape's Northern Frontier in the Eighteenth Century* (Cape Town: Double Storey Books, 2005).

20. Elphick, *Kraal and Castle.*

21. Parkington, "Follow the San," (PhD diss., Cambridge University, 1977).

22. For example, the well-known rock painting *Veg en vlugte* in the Cedarberg. See also Tony Manhire, John Parkington, and W. J. van Rijssen, "A Distributional Approach to the Interpretation of Rock Art in the South-Western Cape," in *New Approaches to Southern African Rock Art* (The South African Archaeological Society, Goodwin Series, June 1983), 30–32 and figure 2.

23. Manhire, "Late Stone Age Settlement Patterns."

24. CA: RLR 6:58, *Oude Wildschutte Boeke*, 18 Oct. 1725. Lange Fontein granted to Johannes Ras. I am extremely grateful to Leonard Guelke for sharing his computerized Receiver of Land Revenue records with me. The Cape Archives has renumbered the RLR series since he cataloged the loan farm data. Unless noted otherwise, my references are also to the old numbering system.

25. The Castle of Good Hope was the home of the VOC government at the Cape. Local authority was represented by landdrosts, or magistrates. Throughout the eighteenth century the Olifants River was under the jurisdiction of the landdrost in Stellenbosch.

26. CA: 1/STB 11/18 and 1/STB 11/19, *Register Grootboek van Leningsplase,* 1793 and 1794.

27. Jan de Vries and Ad van der Woude, *The First Modern Economy: Success, Failure and Perseverance of the Dutch Economy, 1500–1815* (Cambridge: Cambridge University Press, 1997), 160–62.

28. P.J. van der Merwe, *Trek: Studies oor die Mobiliteit van die Pioniersbevolking aan die Kaap* (Cape Town: Nasionale Pers Beperk, 1945).

29. Leonard Guelke and Robert Shell, "Landscape of Conquest: Frontier Water Alienation and Khoikhoi Strategies of Survival, 1652–1780," *JSAS* 18:4 (1992), 803–24.

30. Manhire, et al, "A Distributional Approach," 29–33.

31. Mitchell, "Material Culture"; Megan Biesele, "Interpretation in Rock Art and Folklore," *New Approaches to Southern African Rock Art* (South African Archaeological Society, Goodwin Series 4, 1983), 54–55; Lewis-Williams, *Believing and Seeing.*

32. The quitrent system initiated after 1813 entailed an annual rent based on a valuation of the property, limited mineral rights, and a stronger sense of perpetuity of ownership than the previous loan farm system. Botha, *Early Cape Land Tenure,* 15–17.

33. From the Receiver of Land Revenue series (*Oude Wildschutte Boeke*), I identified 353 permits for 136 farms that lie in the Olifants River valley and the surrounding mountains. Several farms from the flats behind the Piketberg are also incorporated because they had clear links to farms and farmers in the initial sample. Because they are a part of the narrative, they are included in the numbers.

34. CA: RLR 6:58, 18 Oct. 1725.

35. CA: RLR 7:45, 8 Mar. 1728; 8:223, 1 Mar. 1729; 9:153, 1731.

36. CA: RLR 38:134, 22 June 1734.

37. CA: RLR 15:136, 9 Mar. 1759.

38. ARA: VOC 4096 *OBP*, 1725 opgaaf; Cape district; Stellenbosch district f. 6.

39. ARA: VOC 4103 *OBP*, 1727 opgaaf, Cape district f. 14; Voor Stellenbosch.

40. In the 1731 opgaaf, Daniel Pfeil reported 16 cattle and 300 sheep in the Cape district, and another 40 cattle and 150 sheep in the Drakenstein district, which encompassed Brakkefontein.

41. ARA: VOC 4103 *OBP*, 1727 opgaaf, Drakenstein district f. 7

42. Robert Shell, personal communication, Jan. 1998; Ad Biewinga, personal communication, July 1998.

43. Ross, *Beyond the Pale* 145–47, esp. n34, which points out that Newton-King disagrees with the opgaaf's utility for household analyses.

44. The practice of loaning or hiring out slaves is well documented for the Cape district, see Robert C.-H. Shell, *Children of Bondage: A Social History of the Slave Society at the Cape of Good Hope, 1652–1838* (Hanover and London: University Press of New England for Wesleyan University Press, 1994), 13–14. Anecdotal information from the Cedarberg fits this pattern, though more work remains to be done to confirm the extent of short-term slave transfers and temporal variations in outlying districts.

45. ARA: VOC 4130 *OBP*, 1727 opgaaf, Drakenstein district f. 10.

46. ARA: VOC 4130 *OBP*, 1727 opgaaf, Drakenstein district f. 9. CA: RLR 6:85, permit for Renoster Hoek, 15 July 1726. CA: RLR 7:54, permit for Groote Zeekoe Valleij, 14 Apr. 1728.

47. CA: CJ 785.28, *Crimineel Sententie*, 10 Jan. 1732.

48. Nigel Penn, "Fugitives on the Cape Frontier" and "Droster Gangs of the Bokkeveld and Roggeveld," both in *Rogues, Rebels and Runaways: Eighteenth-Century Cape Characters* (Cape Town: David Philip, 1999), 73–100, 147–66.

49. CA: CJ 785.28, *Crimineel Sententie*, 10 Jan. 1732.

50. Guelke and Shell, "Frontier Water Alienation," 811.

51. Malherbe, "Diversification and Mobility"; Russel Viljoen, "Khoisan Labor Relations in the Overberg Districts During the Later Half of the Eighteenth Century, c. 1755–1795," (MA thesis, University of the Western Cape, 1995).

52. Guelke and Shell, "Frontier Water Alienation," 811.

53. Penn, "Fugitives on the Cape Frontier," 94.

4. TRACES OF COMMUNITY

Cornelis Koopman, Frederik Diederiksz, and Jan Swart Jansz left few traces of their lives on the Cedarberg landscape or in the VOC's ledgers. In scattered land claims, a clerk categorized them as *gedoopte Bastaard* (baptized bastard), Bastaard-Hottentot, and Bastaard, respectively. Such labels marked these men as different from their neighbors, typically recorded as burgher or *landbouwer* (farmer). This taxonomy—evident in the loan farm permits of the *Oud Wild-schutte Boeke* and in the Stellenbosch landdrost's accounts of annual rent payments—reveals social differentiation at work.[1]

Social practice at the Cape relegated people into four overarching groups: settlers, free blacks, slaves, and Khoisan. This construction reflects hierarchies of power while masking indigenous sensibilities, instances of resistance, and individual preference. For example, Adam Kok was categorized as Hottentot in the landdrost's loan farm accounts; he was in fact a freed slave whose mixed-race sons established the Griqua community.[2] Cornelis Koopman was a mixed-race farmer who baptized his children in the Dutch Reformed Church.[3] When these men arrived at a Company post to pay rent for their loan farms, did they introduce themselves as a "full-blooded indigene" and a "mixed-race Christian," the strict descriptions implied by the labels they acquired in the landdrost's reckoning? Probably not—but within the "mutually constitutive colonial hierarchies" of identity, Kok, Koopman, and the Company's record-keeper understood themselves to have different social positions.[4]

Eighteenth-century social categories were subjective, the boundaries porous both within and among the four general groupings, which were unequally represented in colonial archives. Surviving documents provide the most details about settler society; they pay less attention to African and Asian identities. Moreover, this evidence was filtered through colonial eyes that often were not able or did not care to see fine-grained detail in other cultures.[5] Consequently, we have to excavate carefully, looking for signs of Khoisan, slave, and other colonial identities beyond the settler purview.[6] For example, Peter Kolb's careful ethnographic observations differentiated between Khoikhoi and San practices, but Kolb was a particularly attentive European observer.[7] It seems that for many farmers and officials, San were simply Khoikhoi without livestock, or alternatively, that describing attackers as San was most likely to elicit support for a reprisal commando.[8]

Although such archival descriptions are imperfect, often using labels in place of well-rounded identities, colonial records do offer ways to infer connections, reconstitute relationships, and sketch elements that enabled people to form meaningful communities. Settler society quickly established economic, social, religious, and political dominance, but indigenous characteristics persisted alongside the languages, artisanal skills, culinary practices, and Islamic traditions imported with slaves from around the Indian Ocean, providing a basis for individuals to forge alternative identities.

Evidence of such subaltern communities is fragmentary and sometimes conflicting, but no group identity was static. It is clear that the better-documented settler society continually renegotiated the terms of belonging; the outlines of indigenous, creole, mixed-race societies changed, as well. This social diversity has yielded a rich literature that establishes the general contours of various communities and maps their interactions.[9] The history and ethnography of Khoikhoi and San communities,[10] glimmers of Asian and nascent creole cultures,[11] characteristics of dominant settler society,[12] and a detailed picture of slavery and emancipation at the Cape are well documented.[13] Currents of identity formation and collapse run through this scholarship, pointing toward the more recent work that explicitly interrogates identity and its categories.[14]

IDENTITIES, CONTINGENT AND PERFORMED

Variously described as imagined, invented, and created, the intellectual framing of identity has been as malleable—and as effective—as its many lived experiences.[15] Identity is not a fixed analytical concept, but rather is relational and contingent—like race, class, gender, and generation which are some of its constitutive elements.[16] This theoretical emphasis on dynamism and purposeful construction does not mean that identity is only a fabrication of hindsight, or the imposition of control by dominant groups. On the contrary, even the deprecating categorization "Pygmy" has deep organic roots buried under layers of dispossession and power disequilibrium.[17] Despite colonial "inventions," identities that surfaced during periods of contested interaction were, in fact, based on preexisting communities—not fabricated from whole cloth.[18] This observation is as true for African societies as it was for settlers and slaves at the Cape.

Historically, then, identities have been both imposed and self-fashioned. The creation of distinct communities at the Cape shows that these processes were not mutually exclusive; individuals categorized into subordinated identities transcended social boundaries, and in some cases carved out alternative space for themselves. Amin Malouf emphasizes such agency, describing the self-conscious adoption or manipulation of identity in order to "belong" in a community. He sees the need to belong as motivation strong enough to explain shocking violence.[19] Malouf's insights, though aimed at explaining more recent history, correlate with scholarship on earlier periods that casts identity as performative—a conscious choice with both material and intangible outcomes.[20] The metaphor of performance implies both flexibility and selectivity: to perform or not; to adopt one role or another; to change roles midstream.[21]

Of course, there were significant constraints on such performances. Freed slave Angela van Bengal could perform the role of burgher Arnoldus Basson's housewife in a community of settlers, but she could no more perform the role of Governor than could her son-in-law Olof Bergh, though he was male, European-born, and high-ranking in the VOC bureaucracy. Gender, race, and class were not fixed, but there were limits on the extent to which individuals could puncture those categories in pursuit of belonging at the Cape.

IDENTITY AND THE CONTROL OF LABOR

The prevailing taxonomy—determined by dominant norms but manipulated across the social spectrum—was embedded in paper: labels applied in the pages of the landdrost's reports; relationships implied in criminal investigations; social status noted in auction rolls; wealth accounted for in the opgaaf. This evident differentiation served fundamentally to control labor.

Although legally explicit, the line between indenture and slavery blurred in practice. Company edicts protected Khoisan from enslavement from the earliest days of VOC settlement, but Jan van Riebeeck employed local servants, including Krotoa, whose incorporation into colonial society as Eva was never complete.[22] Her liminal status was a harbinger of things to come for Khoisan, whose own family connections or sense of belonging were often no match for the colonists' insatiable demand for labor and the dominant society's concomitant ability to construe subordinate identities as subordinated labor.

Legal slaves, imported by VOC ships from the east African coast, Madagascar, and across the Indian Ocean basin, were a significant segment of the Cape colonial population and a vital part of the economy as both commodities and labor. Valued and regulated, slaves left a paper trail through the eighteenth century that Khoisan labor did not. The formal registration of *ingeboekt* or indentured Khoisan workers did not begin until 1775, but the evidence for de facto bondage is strong enough to use the term to describe Khoisan labor throughout the eighteenth century.[23]

Commando raids yielded captive women and children who were indentured on settler farms. Although the Company discouraged settlers from antagonizing independent Khoisan, officials did not actively inhibit impressing local labor. On the frontier, captives were a significant percentage of the labor force, so Khoisan workers and slaves were much more interspersed than in the more settled areas.[24] Though there were fewer slaves in frontier areas, colonial settlement was still strongly a slave society, in which both chattel slaves and other impressed laborers filled the lowest social and economic niche—a role many Khoisan sought to avoid or struggled to leave. Penn argues that there was "little difference between the condition of being a slave and the condition of being a servant."[25]

It is important not to gloss over that "little difference" between slaves and servants, however. Working conditions were sometimes more harsh for Khoisan than for slaves, since it was in an owner's best interest to keep his capital investment alive, whereas there was no incentive not to work a Khoisan captive to death. Contemporary observers remarked on the degradation of those in servitude, and both the VOC and the British state took an interest—though largely an ineffectual one—in Khoisan welfare. A British summary of labor relations observed:

Although the polici [sic] regulations which have been given until the year 1803 are silent on the reciprocal rights and obligations which subsisted between the masters and the Hottentots who according to the already cited publications had engaged in the service of the Inhabitants, it is sufficiently known that the masters exercised the same discretionary power over their Hottentots which other Laws had granted them over their slaves, and that this has been the source of numerous well founded complaints on the part of the Hottentots since neither motives of self interest, the Hottentots not being saleable property, nor the superintending power of the Magistrates, could restrain the masters, who resided in the distant parts of the Colony, from tyrannising the Hottentots who happened to be under their control, and keeping them in a state worse than slavery itself.[26]

Despite such an expression of concern, neither law nor custom effectively protected Khoisan from brutal servitude.

The report does, however, reiterate the point that Khoisan were not "saleable property," a crucial distinction between them and slaves. Economic imperatives or brute force pushed countless Khoisan into service, but those who could survive without working for settlers were not compelled to do so in the eighteenth century.[27] Perhaps the notation of Adam Kok as a Hottentot in the landdrost's ledger was a conscious manipulation of identity on Kok's part, a move away from a connection to chattel slavery, rather than a misreading of identity by a colonial record-keeper. Even the minimal documentation of Adam Kok's life makes him admittedly more legible than most enslaved, Khoisan, and mixed-race individuals of his time. However, his cameo archival appearances cannot firmly connect Kok to a specified colonial role; they can only point to the multiplicity inherent in performance.

INITIAL SOCIAL PERMEABILITY

The greatest range of performance undoubtedly existed at the intersection of identities, where colonial categories overlapped or collided. Subordinated women—slaves, freed slaves, or Khoisan—with European husbands, whether church sanctioned or common-law, could live as settler wives.[28] Their children were often included, unremarked upon, in settler family networks.[29]

The Basson family, for example, descends from one of the first Dutch immigrants to the Cape and his wife, Angela van Bengal. Angela had children before she married Basson in 1669. Her illegitimate daughter, Anna de Koning, married Olof Bergh, a Company soldier who eventually commanded the Cape garrison. Both Basson and Bergh became prominent landowners; their many children married across the ranks of settler society—wealth and status evidently outweighed race to determine belonging in settler society at the end of the seventeenth century.[30]

When Angela and Basson's eldest grandson, Arnoldus Willemsz married in 1722 or 1723, he chose a wife of substantial property. Maria Vosloo, recently widowed, had only two daughters, both already married, so she must have been at least ten years older than her new husband. As a widow, Maria controlled a fortune: three farms, each with a furnished house and resident slaves; a blacksmith's shop; and outstanding loans due to the estate. Kruijshoff, her principal farm, had a dairy, a wine cellar, and a wagonmaker's shop in addition to the house and farmyard. Maria or her late husband, Arnoldus Kruijsman, owed Arnoldus Basson Willemsz 13 rixdollars—half a year's rent on a loan farm, but a paltry sum in an estate worth 79,436:11:4 rixdollars, certainly not enough leverage to broker a marriage if Maria had not been willing.[31]

From uncertain origins, Maria had secured both wealth and status with her first marriage. Her union with Basson certainly cemented an alliance to another notable family, but given the members of the nascent gentry with whom Maria and Kruijsman had business dealings, she likely married Basson for his ability to manage the estate or for affection.[32] As the Widow Kruijsman, Maria had money and connections of her own.

Both Kruijsman and Maria must have worked hard to achieve their position. In all likelihood, Maria's father was the Company's woodcutter, Johannes Vosloo—a man with money and status, but without acknowledged children.[33] Kruijsman arrived at the Cape as a midshipman. In 1699 he was seconded as a farmhand to Vosloo, for whom he worked until at least 1703. The following year he applied for and received his burgher papers in Drakenstein. He must have married Maria shortly thereafter.

Vosloo himself never married; in his will he declared that he had no lawful heirs.[34] However, he made bequests to Johannes van de Caab, Caspar van de Caab, Helena van de Caab, and to Christina and Anna Maria Kruijsman, Maria's daughters. Although Vosloo did not recognize his paternity, Maria made a bequest to "her father, Jan Vosloo of Drakenstein" in both of the wills she prepared in conjunction with her third husband, Jan Andries Dissel.[35] Kruijsman's estate owed 6,163:1:4 rixdollars to Jan Vosloo the Elder, and another 272:5:0 rixdollars to Jan Vosloo the Younger, indicating Kruijsman's relationship with his former employer continued for two decades after he left Vosloo's service.

Surely it was not pure coincidence that Maria married a man who worked for her putative father. It seems more likely to assume she had some sort of relationship with Vosloo and that she was at least an occasional visitor—if not a resident—on his farm prior to her marriage. If she did not meet Kruijsman on Vosloo's farm, then Vosloo must have taken an active part in arranging the match, or at least facilitating their introduction.

Given that Vosloo chose to make bequests to Caspar, Johannes, Helena, and to Maria's daughters (she died before Vosloo did), he must have had a particular relationship with these six people. Johannes Vosloo the younger, Caspar Vosloo and Maria Vosloo all appeared in the opgaaf, which indicates their place among their neighbors in the Drakenstein district.[36] The reference of a debt to "Jan Vosloo the Younger" in Kruijsman's inventory implies that Maria's brother was part of the local economy and was recognized by gentlemen appointed to oversee the administration of estates.[37] Both Helena and Maria made good marriages, despite being illegitimate and probably of mixed race. As Penn notes, "Favoured children of respected colonists probably passed unobtrusively into the ranks of colonial society, suffering no discrimination on account of their mixed blood."[38] Vosloo may not have legitimated his Cape-born children as Arnoldus Basson the Elder and Olof Bergh did, but they were part of settler society nevertheless.

COLONIAL PERSONAS: KHOISAN
AND MIXED-RACE COMMUNITIES

Other indigenous and mixed families, however, were clearly described outside the settler orbit. Cornelis Koopman and his younger brother Bartholomeus were sons of Albertus Koopman, an immigrant from Utrecht, and Francina Wina van de Caab.[39] Although the loan farm ledgers do not comment on Bartholomeus's social status (gedoopte Bastaard), Cornelis's mixed-race heritage and Christian conformity were noted along with his loan payment records. Both sons shared parents of the same origins as the Bassons and the Berghs: a European-born father and a slave or Cape-born mother. Cornelis Koopman, born after 1720, was categorized differently from the mixed-race children born around the turn of the century, and differently from his own brother. It is not possible to reconstruct an identity based on a few lines in the landdrost's loan farm payment ledgers, but the fleeting appearances of individuals like Cornelis Koopman and Jan Swart Jansz testify to the presence of individuals who did not "pass unobtrusively" as settlers or forge an alternative colonial identity such as Griqua.

The different experiences of Albertus Basson Willemsz and Cornelis Koopman might simply have been due to class position. Basson's grandparents acquired wealth that Koopman's parents did not, and the richer family more easily navigated nascent settler family networks. This explanation leaves Bartholomeus out of the equation, though. He had the same modest parents as Cornelis, yet was not described as mixed race. More likely, the Koopmans exemplify the gradual reification of social identities taking place over the course of the eighteenth century. Fluid social boundaries slowly ossified, limiting the range of possible identity performances—but not eliminating choice completely. It is possible that Cornelis chose to emphasize his connections to one part of his family, while Bartholomeus claimed another. Since both men registered loan farms, nascent racial categories—whether asserted or imposed—did not inhibit their access to land claims, which were the basis of subsistence and a fundamental signifier of social identity. Whatever the Koopman's particular circumstances, it became less common for individuals to "pass unobtrusively" into settler society during their lifetimes (though transitions among other groups may have remained more permeable). By the middle years of the nineteenth century, Christianity, education, and social connections would not be criteria enough for full inclusion in the dominant social order, as the mixed-race family of missionary James Read learned with dismay. For them, the color bar descended painfully in the 1830s.[40]

Other people excluded from settler society—or who chose not to belong to the dominant group—forged alternate possibilities. In addition to well-documented examples such as the Griquas and the Basters, limited independent

Khoisan presence persisted within the settler orbit.[41] Increasing colonial land claims along the Olifants River and the surrounding Cedarberg changed the movement and distribution of indigenous communities. Penn documents violent resistance through the 1790s, but not everyone took up arms. References to Hottentot servants in settler households document one path to survival.[42] Limited loan farm registration in frontier areas indicates another strategy for working within encroaching colonial economic structures. Although Khoisan and their colored descendants in the Clanwilliam district ultimately were excluded from independent land tenure in the nineteenth century, the option remained viable for over a hundred years.[43] Other sporadic archival appearances show people from the Olifants River area who moved to the heart of colonial settlement in search of opportunities. Some found work on settler farms, and one household of three adults and a toddler lived as tenants—not servants—on a Franschoek farm.

Like the fleeting references to Hottentots and Bastaards among loan farm records, the notations in the "Hottentot Register" cannot describe identities, only hint at their existence. The landdrost captured their presence near Stellenbosch in the newly-implemented "Hottentot Register."[44] In 1812, individuals categorized as Hottentot originally from the Olifants River were living in Drakenstein and Franschoek, far from the frontier. Their journeys and the frequency with which they returned home, if at all, lie beyond the ambit of the archives, despite greater documentation in the nineteenth century. The coming of British rule to the Cape in 1806 changed colonial administration; forms of registration proliferated and the 1809 Caledon Code increased the regulation (and exploitation) of Khoisan labor.[45] Even with these additions to colonial record-keeping, evidence of individual Khoisan lives remained sporadic.

The traces that survive suggest a Khoisan population inclined toward mobility—much to the chagrin of colonial farmers trying to secure subordinated labor.[46] The extent of that mobility, whether from one farm to the next or from the Salt River to the Orange, varied widely. The few individual stories preserved and resuscitated exhibit a great range of motion.[47]

The experience of Titus Valentyn and the others recorded by the landdrost in the early nineteenth century are embedded in the wider experiences of indigenous and mixed-race communities coming to terms with expanding colonial dominance.[48] Some people pushed off the land near the Olifants River, rather than retreating further from the colonial orbit, went to the heart of it. The format of the "Hottentot Register" that captured their presence indicates colonial administrators thought they were dealing with a stable population—people who had perhaps already moved a great distance, but who had come to stay, not people who were simply passing through.[49] Repeated attempts by masters to keep laborers on their farms suggest that assumption was wrong at the turn of the century. Legislation passed in the first two decades of the nineteenth century ultimately succeeded in immobilizing Khoisan labor, but the "Hottentot Register" of 1812 does not suggest permanence.[50] Only five of the 120 entries made between 1812 and 1823 represent a second appearance by the same family group or individual.

The form of the "Register" asks for a list of the men, women, and children living on a settler farm. The "Register" also asks for details about dwelling places and kraals. Some veldkornets making inquiries on behalf of the landdrost commented on family relationships, but most did not, and very few responded to the request for information about residences. Perhaps the veldkornets could not be bothered to collect all the information the state requested, or perhaps they simply did not see houses and kraals they thought merited notation. Although the level of detail is uneven across the "Register," it does document mobility.

One of the individuals identified as hailing from the Olifants River was 16–year-old Anna. She lived on Willem Louw's farm in the Moddergat with her mother, Mietje, and another mother-daughter pair, Efa and Klara. According to Veldkornet Roos, Efa hailed from the Sneeuwberg, but bore her 10-year-old daughter in Hottentots Holland, suggesting that Efa had been living near Stellenbosch for at least a decade. Mietje was born in Hantam, but bore Anna near the Olifants River, suggesting that Mietje had made (at least) two major moves in her life. Only little Klara lived within a day's travel of her birthplace when the "Register" was compiled.

Jacob Rens, also originally from the Olifants River, lived with his wife Caatje Dikkop on J.P. van der Merwe's farm in Franschoek. Though they were born at different places on the frontier, Veldkornet de Villiers described Jacob and Caatje both as Goijman, but whether the couple shared a clan identity prior to marriage or showed a united front in the face of colonial inquiry is impossible to tell. They had three daughters, Roset, 14; Annaat, 12; and Jacomijn, 10. Six years later, de Villiers documented the family still on van der Merwe's farm, but without Caatje and Roset. He recorded the younger daughters now as adult women, aged 18 and 16, without commenting on the death, marriage, or migration that might have taken the other two women from the household.[51]

The farm-by-farm compilation in the "Register" shows mostly small groups of laborers, typically two or three adults along with their children. In cases where two or more adult women lived on a single farm, their respective children were usually identified, as we saw with Mietje and Anna. The "Register" rarely clearly indicates a family; Jacob, Caatje, and their daughters were an exception. Most adult relationships—siblings, other kin, or sexual partners—went unnoticed or unrecorded, so the links binding scattered groups of Khoisan together or the tensions pulling them apart are lost.

Was it only a desperate need for work that kept five adult laborers on a farm in Franschoek? The four men hailed from different parts of the colony: Gert van der Horst was from Gourits River; Arnondusmatijs was from Elandsfontein; Carolus from the Zwartskop River; and Africaander was identified as Goijman, but his birthplace was not mentioned.[52] The lone woman, Caatje Libergete was from the Roggeveld. Were the five children ranging in age from 7 to 14 all hers? What was their relationship to the men on the farm? Did these ten people share a hearth and a household? The "Register" is taciturn, telling us only that they lived, but not how.[53]

The "Register" is equally selective about the residents on Andries Zieman's Franschoek farm. Though careful to note them as tenants, not laborers, the veldkornet's brief report stops short of explaining their situation. Thirty-year-old Titus Valentijn was born near the Olifants River, the child of a slave and a Goijman woman, as was Elsje Abrahamse, 23. Twenty-year-old Lijs Titus was born on van Schoor's Olifants River farm, the child of a Bastaard father and Goijman mother.[54] Valentijn, Elsje, and Lijs were born near each other; they each had a Goijman mother. Was she the same woman? Or were the three related in some other way? Was Valentijn the father of Elsje's year-old baby Anna? The colonial state, concerned with the registration and regulation of labor, was not interested in life histories beyond ascertaining whether individuals were eligible for labor contracts or other forms of bondage.

COLONIAL PERSONAS: SETTLER COMMUNITIES

Colonial settlers, regulated by both church and state, left a wider paper trail than Khoisan and slaves, though their paths remain littered with ambiguity. As a Christian congregation, the Dutch Reformed Church recorded marriages and baptisms, thereby documenting family relationships. As a merchant company, the Dutch East India Company assiduously filed land claims, tallied annual economic production, and recorded the transfer of assets—including slaves—thus documenting possessions. Significant elements of dominant settler identity emerge in this nexus of belonging and belongings.

Class stratification was evident in settler society, but the distinctions were not rigid.[55] While the legal and economic difference between a soldier and a burgher were clear, in practice both men could work for wages as artisans or farm hands. The soldier, contracted as a bouknecht to a landowner, might apply for his burgher papers and in due time head his own household, thus erasing any previous difference in legal status. In a society continually augmented by migration, this transition from soldier to burgher was common. Hard work or a propitious marriage could narrow or reverse any gap in wealth between these two hypothetical men. In fact, marriage to a propertied woman was the most certain route to fortune for an immigrant man. Three stories detailed in subsequent chapters document immigrant men creating or joining settler family networks and thus establishing themselves firmly within the dominant colonial society. Willem van der Merwe, Barend Burger, and Barend Lubbe d'Oude married women of modest wealth. They survived, some of their children prospered, but none of them approached the levels of wealth attained by Martin Melck and Jan Andries Dissel, men who through marriage became among the richest at the Cape.[56]

Dissel's case is relevant to the history of the Cedarberg because he was one of the first settlers to claim land along the Olifants River. His presence in the region, though brief, was significant enough to leave his name on a small watercourse, the Jan Dissels River, which joins the Olifants. Until Governor Cradock renamed the village in 1814, Clanwilliam was called Jan Dissels Vlei.

When Dissel claimed Renoster Hoek as grazing land in 1726, he undoubtedly lived with his new bride, the twice-widowed Maria Vosloo, on her farm Kruijshoff. Two years later, Dissel took out another permit near the Olifants River.[57] Shortly thereafter, Maria died, but Dissel's quest for land continued, which is understandable. By 1731 he had 1,500 sheep, 280 cattle, and 24 horses.[58] In terms of livestock, vines, and wheat production reported in the 1731 opgaaf, Dissel's return placed him among a small economic elite. Guelke and Shell reckoned there were 882 census households in 1731.[59] Dissel, at this point a childless widower, ranked seventh among them in numbers of sheep and tenth in terms of cattle. He owned one of the twenty largest vineyards, and was among the top fifty grain harvesters. Given the extensive agricultural production at Kruijshoff, it is no wonder he sought additional land for grazing.

Dissel and the others who pioneered claims at the outer limits of colonial territory in the years between 1725 and 1730 were not struggling *veeboere* (cattle farmers) trying to make a go of it in marginal country. Dissel, Daniel Pfeil, and Jacob Mouton were wealthy men with freehold farms and significant agricultural production. In contrast, Johannes Ras, Johannes Lodewyk Putter, and Jochem Koekemoer had more modest means, but even Ras, the poorest among them, surpassed Guelke's estimate of a household's minimal needs for survival, and he grew a little wheat.[60] In between, men like Willem Burger, Alewijn Smit, and Pieter van Heerden expanded their established households and farming enterprises into the Cedarberg. They had residential farms in more settled areas, and though their first farms were not bursting to capacity as Dissel and Pfeil's appear to have been, they took advantage of the availability of more land. Gentry, common landed farmers, and poorer stock farmers all participated in the process of expanding colonial territory, but it was the families in the middling tier who shouldered the brunt of conquest. Men like Dissel and Pfeil used the Olifants River region only for necessary grazing, while the Burgers and Smits built on their early claims. They and their children actively settled the Cedarberg frontier.

The gentry's frontier interactions nevertheless shed light on the process of identity formation. Dissel's case is particularly provocative. His exceptionally large herds and flocks, along with evidence presented against two of his slaves who ran away in 1731, raises significant questions about how absentee ranchers like Dissel and Pfeil managed their outlying farms. Although Dissel had abundant agricultural produce, he did not have as many slaves as others with similar opgaaf returns. Pfeil, for example, had less livestock than Dissel, though he reported more vines and a larger grain harvest. But Pfeil had three knechten and 41 slaves, while Dissel claimed to work without an overseer and with only 14 slaves.[61] Dissel was childless; his wife's daughters and sons-in-law were busy running farms of their own. As many as 76 households at the Cape had more slaves than Dissel did, but only nine had more cattle. Who besides Dissel and his 14 slaves did the work implied by his opgaaf return? He clearly relied on labor he did not report.

Another source mentions several of these servants without comment, however, accepting as commonplace that a man of Dissel's wealth would have many subordinates.[62] When Dissel's slaves Moses van Angola and April van Bengal ran away in the company of nine other slaves from two neighboring Drakenstein farms, a commando pursued them and confronted the gang near the Olifants River. One deserter was killed in the melee; one commando member was shot for his trouble. Two other deserters avoided capture, but Moses, April, and six others stood trial. The sentencing records provide a detailed account of the deserters' journey from Drakenstein to the Cedarberg, including encounters with two men described as knechten working for Dissel, and a Khoisan shepherd named Dol tending to Dissel's beasts on one of his Olifants River farms. The deserters recounted another interaction with an unnamed Hottentot on Dissel's distant farm. We will never know if this individual worked for Dissel, belonged to a nearby kraal, or was simply passing through, but his presence in the deserters' testimony is a gentle reminder that the Cedarberg frontier was a site of ongoing engagement among many communities. The deserters' testimony thus documents the presence of individuals not otherwise enumerated in other colonial sources, such as the opgaaf. This mention of an anonymous shepherd shows that significant labor evaded capture in the opgaaf, even if the workers themselves did not avoid the work.

The question of who provided labor is slightly less mysterious—though still opaque—for the households that settled in the Cedarberg. Among the early families who homesteaded along the Olifants River, only the Smits had many slaves at the time they made their first land claims there.[63] Alewijn also went on to have 24 children, another important source of labor for frontier families. Both single adult and married children circulated among their relatives' farms, staying and working with aunts, uncles, and cousins—a practice evident in the Burger, Lubbe and Campher family stories. And, of course,

these families would all have employed (or coerced) Khoisan labor. Although the details and disposition of that work were never recorded, oblique
references surface, a mention of Dol the shepherd or Hans the wagon-driver
taken in stride, not needing any explanation at the time their presence was
noted.

Although both gentry and ordinary families made early loan farm claims
in the Cedarberg, the more affluent farmers did not stay in the area. It was the
prosperous middling households whose initial claims anchored generations
of settlers, forming the basis of an identity that included neighboring families
but excluded subordinate laborers and independent Khoisan. The social network that sustained these early land claims and supported subsequent expansion from the Olifants River Valley into the mountains had important roots
in Stellenbosch and Drakenstein. Prior to making claims in the Olifants River
area, Alewijn and François Smit farmed together, as did brothers Willem and
Andries Burger. Willem Burger and Alewijn Smit also claimed neighboring
farms in the Twenty-four Rivers area. Surely it was no accident that two of Burger's sons married two of Smit's daughters. Johannes Lodwyk Putter and Jochem
Koekmoer were brothers-in-law, and Andries Kruger was Putter's stepfather.
François Smit's wife, Maria van Staden, was a cousin of Willem Burger's wife,
Elsje van der Merwe; Maria was also related to Jürgen Hanekom's wife, Maria
van den Bosch. The wealthy claimants like Dissel, Pfeil, and Jacob Mouton did
not feature in this web of overlapping relationships, though Mouton's children married into the network, firmly planting their family within the emerging orthodox settler orbit.

Family relationships entwined with land claims; both elements were significant components of settler identity. The ability to claim a freehold or a loan
farm was not in itself sufficient to assert membership in the settler community. Although land was an important precondition for economic production,
as well as a marker of social status, claiming one parcel of land was not the
same as claiming another.[64] In addition to resource considerations, social geography was a significant factor. Even the most geographically distant loan farms
were not "in the middle of nowhere," but were instead claims that complemented existing family land holdings. Nigel Penn shows seasonal connections
across five geographical and climate areas in the Northern frontier region.[65]
Farmers like Jan Dissel exploited multiple climate zones, not unlike the seasonal migration practiced by indigenous hunting and herding Khoisan. The
settlers' ability to make and sustain disparate claims depended on social relationships, so their decisions about when and where to claim land were predicated on both practical and affinal considerations.

Consequently, frontier land claims located settlers physically in the landscape and metaphorically within colonial networks. Land owning and family
connections were not the only signals that farmers shared a wider sense of

identity, however. Over time, families in the Cedarberg increasingly owned housewares, furniture, and specialized tools that represented increasing wealth, and, significantly, demonstrated conscious affiliation with dominant material culture, a process documented in Chapters 6 and 7. These tangible cultural markers, along with other traces of contested colonial communities, took many paths into the Cedarberg.

NOTES

1. CA RLR 14:3, Cornelis Koopman permit for Doorn Bosch, *over de Olifants en Doorn rivieren*, 25 Oct. 1754–25 Nov. 1777 (per L. Guelke data); CA: 1/STB 11/19, folio 5, LFL, Bastaard-Hottentot Frederik Diederiksz payments for Kogelfontein, *over de Olifants rivier*, 12 July 1787, 31 Aug. 1792; CA: 1/STB 11/18, vol. 3, LFL, Bastaard Jan Swart Janz payments for Holle Rivier, *in de Hantam*, 20 Feb 1795, 25 Apr. 1798.

2. CA: 1/STB/11/19 folio 10 p 5, LFL, Hottentot Adam Kok, for Stinkfontein, 31 Aug. 1792; Robert Ross, *Adam Kok's Griquas: A Study in the Development of Stratification in South Africa* (Cambridge: Cambridge University Press, 1976).

3. H.F. Heese, *Groepe sonder grense: Die rol en status van die gemengde bevolking aan de Kaap, 1652–1705* (Bellville: Institute for Historical Research, 1985; translated by Delia Robertson as *Cape Melting Pot: The Role and Status of the Mixed Population at the Cape, 1652–1795*. Johannesburg: self-published, 2006), 137.

4. Pamela Scully, "Indigenous Women and Colonial Cultures: An Introduction," *JCCH* 6:3 (2005), http://muse.jhu.edu/journals/journal_of_colonialism_and_colonial _history/toc/cch6.3.html.

5. Mary Louise Pratt, *Imperial Eyes: Travel Writing and Transculturation* (London: Routledge, 1992). Though criticized by both Guelke and Penn for misunderstanding local conditions and South African history, her analytical insights show ways in which culturally embedded preconceptions shaped how European visitors could understand the people and landscapes they encountered in Africa and Latin America. Leonard Guelke and Jeanne Kay Guelke, "Imperial Eyes on South Africa: Reassessing Travel Narratives," *Journal of Historical Geography* 30:1 (2004), 11–31.

6. Gyan Prakash, "Subaltern Studies as Postcolonial Criticism," *AHR* 99:5 (1994), 1475–90.

7. Peter Kolb, *The Present State of the Cape of Good Hope* (New York: Johnson Reprint Corp., 1968).

8. Shula Marks, "Khoisan Resistance to the Dutch in the Seventeenth and Eighteenth Centuries," *JAH* 13:1 (1972), 55–80.

9. The clearest articulation of this premise remains Richard Elphick and Hermann Giliomee, eds. *The Shaping of South African Society, 1652–1840*, 2nd ed. (Cape Town: Maskew Miller Longman, 1989). Subsequent research has enriched the level of detail, but not overturned the conceptualization of Cape history as best understood through "intergroup relations."

10. Russel Viljoen, *Jan Paerl, a Khoikhoi in Cape Colonial Society, 1761–1851* (Leiden: Brills, 2006); Alan Barnard, *Hunters and Herders of Southern Africa: A Comparative Ethnography of the Khoisan Peoples* (Cambridge: Cambridge University Press, 1992); Richard Elphick, *Kraal and Castle: The Khoikhoi and the Founding of White South Africa* (New Haven: Yale University Press, 1977).

11. Kerry Ward, "Knocking on Death's Door: Mapping the Spectrum of Bondage and Status Through Marking the Dead at the Cape," in *Contingent Lives: Social Identity and Material Culture in the VOC World*, ed. Nigel Worden, 391–413 (Cape Town: University of Cape Town Press, 2007); James Armstrong, "The Estate of a Chinese Woman in the Mid-Eighteenth Century at the Cape of Good Hope," in *Contingent Lives: Social Identity and Material Culture in the VOC World*, ed. Nigel Worden, 75–90 (Cape Town: University of Cape Town Press, 2007).

Older literature includes: J.S. Marais, *The Cape Coloured People* (Johannesburg: Witwatersrand University Press, 1957); W.M. Macmillan, *The Cape Colour Question: A Historical Survey* (Cape Town: A.A. Balkema, 1968); I.D. du Plessis, *The Cape Malays: History, Religion, Folk Tales* (Cape Town: A.A. Balkema, 1972); F.R. Bradlow and Margaret Cairns, *The Early Cape Muslims* (Cape Town: A.A. Balkema, 1978).

12. Newton-King, *Masters and Servants*; Ross, *Status and Respectability*; Penn, *The Forgotten Frontier*.

13. James Armstrong, "The Slaves, 1652–1834," in *The Shaping of South African Society, 1652–1840*, eds. Richard Elphick and Hermann Giliomee. 1st ed. (London: Maskew Miller Longman, 1979); Robert Ross, *Cape of Torments: Slavery and Resistance in South Africa* (London: Routledge and Keegan Paul, 1983); Nigel Worden, *Slavery in Dutch South Africa* (Cambridge: Cambridge University Press, 1985); Robert C.-H. Shell, *Children of Bondage: A Social History of the Slave Society at the Cape of Good Hope, 1652–1838* (Hanover and London: University Press of New England for Wesleyan University Press, 1994); Elizabeth Eldredge and Fred Morton, eds., *Slavery in South Africa: Captive Labor on the Dutch Frontier* (Boulder: Westview Press, 1994); John Edwin Mason, *Social Death and Resurrection: Slavery and Emancipation in South Africa* (Charlottesville: University of Virginia Press, 2003); Pamela Scully, *Liberating the Family? Gender and British Slave Emancipation in the Rural Western Cape, South Africa, 1823–1853* (Portsmouth, NH: Heinemann, 1997).

14. The conference Contingent Lives: Social Identities and Material Culture in the VOC World, held at the University of Cape Town, 17–20 Dec. 2006 is a case in point; see the conference volume *Contingent Lives: Social Identity and Material Culture in the VOC World*, ed. Nigel Worden (Cape Town: University of Cape Town Press, 2007). Also see Herman Giliomee, *The Afrikaners: Biography of a People* (London: Hurst, 2003); Nigel Worden. "Forging a Reputation: Artisan Honour and the Cape Town Blacksmith Strike of 1752," *Kronos* 28 (2002), 43–65; Susan Newton-King, "For the Love of Adam: Two Sodomy Trials at the Cape of Good Hope," *Kronos* 28 (2002), 21–42; Ross, *Status and Respectability*; Viljoen, *Jan Paerl*.

15. Benedict Anderson, *Imagined Communities: Reflections on the Origin and Spread of Nationalism* (London: Verso, 1983); Eric Hobsbawm and Terrence Ranger, eds., *The Invention of Tradition* (Cambridge: Cambridge University Press, 1992); Leroy Vail, ed., *The Creation of Tribalism in Southern Africa* (Berkeley: University of California Press, 1991).

16. Thomas V. McClendon, *Genders and Generations Apart: Labor Tenants and Customary Law In Segregation-Era South Africa* (Portsmouth, N.H. Heinemann, 2002); Joan Scott, "Gender as a Useful Category of Analysis," *AHR* 91:5 (Dec. 1986), 1053–75.

17. Kairn Klieman, "(Re)Constructing Histories: Central African Societies and the Burden of Myth," Chap. 1 in *"The Pygmies Were Our Compass": Bantu and Batwa in the History of West Central Africa, Early Times to c. 1900 C.E.* (Portsmouth , NH : Heinemann, 2003).

18. David Gordon, "History on the Luapula Retold: Landscape, Memory and Identity in the Kazembe Kingdom," *JAH* 47 (2006), 21–42.

19. Amin Malouf, *In the Name of Identity: Violence and the Need to Belong* (New York: Arcade, 1996).

20. Rachel Sarah O'Toole, "Castas y representación en Trujillo colonial, " in *Más allá de la dominación y la resistencia: Estudios de historia peruana, siglos XVI–XX*, eds. Paulo Drinot and Leo Garofalo (Lima: Instituto de Estudios Peruanos, 2005), 50–51; Cecilia Morgan, "'A Wigwam to Westminster': Performing Mohawk Identity in Imperial Britain, 1890s–1990s," *Gender and History* 15:2 (Aug. 2003), 319–41. On mimicry, see Homi Bhabha, *The Location of Culture* (London and New York: Routledge, 1994).

21. Julia Wells, "Eva's Men: Gender and Power in the Establishment of the Cape of Good Hope, 1652–74," *JAH* 39 (1998), 417–37. Though not couched in the language of performance, Wells evaluates Eva's choices in fulfilling colonial or Khoisan social expectations.

22. Pamela Scully, "Malintzin, Pocahontas, and Krotoa: Indigenous Women and Myth Models of the Atlantic World," *JCCH* 6:3 (2005), http://muse.jhu.edu/journals/journal_of_colonialism_and_colonial_history/toc/cch6.3.html. Wells, "Eva's Men;" V.C. Malherbe, "The Life and Times of Cupido Kakkerlak," *JAH* 20:3 (1979), 365–78.

23. Russel Viljoen, "Khoisan Labor Relations in the Overberg Districts During the Later Half of the Eighteenth Century, c.1755–1795" (MA thesis, University of the Western Cape, 1993), 41–43; Fred Morton, "Slavery and South African Historiography," in Eldredge and Morton, eds., *Slavery in South Africa*, 3; Susan Newton-King, *Masters and Servants on the Eastern Cape Frontier* (Cambridge: Cambridge University Press, 1999), 57–59.

24. Newton-King, "The Enemy Within," 233.

25. Penn, "Droster Gangs," 147.

26. CA: M 142(a), *Laws Respecting Hottentots and Bastards at the Cape of Good Hope, 1652–c.1823*, Art. 9.

27. On Khoisan forced labor in the nineteenth century, see Wayne Dooling, "The Origins and the Aftermath of the Cape Colony's 'Hottentot Code' of 1809," *Kronos* 31 (Nov. 2005), 50–61; Barry Morton, "Servitude, Slave Trading, and Slavery in the Kalahari," in Eldredge and Morton, *Slavery in South Africa*, 167–88.

28. Viljoen, "'Till Murder Do Us Part': The Story of Griet and Hendrik Eksteen," *SAHJ* 33 (1995), 13–32.

29. On the incorporation of mixed-race children into "white" colonial society, see Heese, *Groupe sonder grense*. Scant information suggests that settler women did not have as much mobility across social groups as slaves or Khoisan. Maria Mouton com-

mitted adultery along with transgressing race and class boundaries when she had an affair with her slave, so it is difficult to untangle the implications of her punishment. For an account of this case, see Nigel Penn, "The Wife, the Farmer, and the Farmer's Slaves: Adultery and Murder on a Frontier Farm in the Early Eighteenth-Century Cape," *Kronos* 28 (2002): 1–20.

30. O.F. Mentzel, *A Geographical and Topographical Description of the Cape of Good Hope (1787)*. Trans. G. V. Marais and J. Hoge, ed. H. J. Mandelbrote (Cape Town: Van Riebeeck Society, 1925), Vol. II: 114.

31. CA: MOOC 8/4.48, Estate Inventory of Arnoldus Kruijsman, 5 Dec. 1722.

32. Leonard Guelke and Robert Shell, "An Early Colonial Landed Gentry: Land and Wealth in the Cape Colony 1682–1731," *Journal of Historical Geography* 9:3 (1983), 265–86; Ross, "The Rise of the Cape Gentry," *JSAS* 9:2 (April 1983), 193–217.

33. J. Hoge, "Personalia of Germans at the Cape, 1652–1808," *AYB* 9 (1946), 442. dv&P,1966, 1082.

34. *"geen kinderen nog maagde . . . an wie hij volgens regte iets behoofd vermaken."* CA: CJ 2650:118, *Testamenten*, 1714; CA: CJ 2652:71, *Testamenten*, 1726.

35. CA: CJ 2603:9, *Testamenten*, 23 Aug. 1725. CA: CJ 2603:28, *Testamenten*, 18 Mar. 1726.

36. ARA: VOC 4096 *OBP*, 1725 opgaaf; VOC 4100 *OBP*, 1726 opgaaf; VOC 4103 *OBP*, 1727 opgaaf; VOC 4152 *OBP*, 1742 opgaaf.

37. Carohn Cornell and Antonia Malan, "Household Inventories at the Cape, a Guide for Beginner Researchers" (Cape Town: UCT Historical Studies Department, 2005), 25–26.

38. Penn, "Fugitives on the Cape Frontier," 94.

39. H&L IV, 408, 410.

40. Elizabeth Elbourne, *Blood Ground: Colonialism, Missions and the Contest for Christianity in the Cape Colony and Britain, 1799–1853* (Montreal: McGill-Queen's University Press, 2002), 368–70. Racial identity did retain a measure of fluidity, however; some of Read's family members regained white status in the twentieth century. Robert Ross, personal communication, April 2007.

41. On independent mixed-race communities, see Ross, *Adam Kok's Griquas*; Elbourne, *Blood Ground*.

42. CA: CJ 785.28, *Crimineel Sententie*, Case against Moses van Angola and others, 10 Jan. 1732; ARA: VOC 4158 *OBP*, 1743–1744, Vol. 2. Testimony in the case against Willem van Wyk, 1743, ff. 928–43; Viljoen, "Khoisan Labor Relations."

43. Dawn D'Arcy Nell, "Land, Land Ownership and Occupancy in the Cape Colony During the Nineteenth Century With Special Reference to the Clanwilliam District," (BA Honours thesis, University of Cape Town, 1997).

44. CA: 1/STB 16/139, *Hottentot Register* 1812. This register records Anna, Jacob Rens, Titus Valentijn, Lijs, and Elsje Abrahamse all as Hottentots originally from the Olifants River area then residing in the Stellenbosch magisterial district.

45. Wayne Dooling, "The Origins and the Aftermath."

46. Viljoen, "Khoisan Labor Relations;" Malherbe, "Diversification and Mobility of Khoikhoi Labor in the Eastern Cape Districts of the Cape Colony Prior to the Labor Law of 1 November 1809," (MA thesis, University of Cape Town, 1978).

47. Viljoen, *Jan Paerl*; Malherbe, "Cupido Kakerlack." In addition, relevant archival material remains unexploited, for example CA: CJ 785.28, *Crimineel Sententie*, Case against Moses van Angola and others, 10 Jan. 1732; and other cases of desertion, including ARA: VOC 4010, f. 88r, 16 Aug. 1673. ARA: VOC 4011, f. 69v, 16 Nov.1674. ARA: VOC 4013 f. 164v, 16 Jan.1677; f. 245; f. 252; f. 318v–319r. ARA: VOC 4014, f. 537r, 1 Sept.1678; f. 386, Dagh 14 Mar. 1678; f. 391 Dagh 25 Mar. 1678. ARA: VOC 4015, f. 225, Dagh 16 Jan.1679; f. 227, 228, f 235. I am grateful to Jim Armstrong for sharing his seventeenth-century references with me.

48. This process persisted for a century; for a later version, see Charles van Onselen, *The Seed is Mine: The Life of Kas Maine, a South African Sharecropper, 1894–1985* (New York: Hill and Wang, 1995).

49. CA: 1/STB 16/139, *Hottentot Register*, Compiled According to Proclamation of 23 Apr. 1812.

50. Dooling, "Origins and Aftermath," 51.

51. CA: 1/STB 16/142, *Hottentot Register*, 1818.

52. Elandsfontein was Griqua elder Cornelis Kok's farm in the Copperberg (CA: 1/STB 11/18, LFL; 1/STB 11/19, LFL, f. 8, p 25; RLR 24:144, 5 May 1776 new permit). A possible connection to Arnondusmatijs, though tantalizing, is probably coincidence, since Elandsfontein was a common name, given to at least eight other farms in addition to Kok's (L. Guelke RLR data).

53. CA: 1/STB 16/139, *Hottentot Register*.

54. Jan van Schoor held the permit on Hendrik van der Wat's Gat from 1778 to 1790 (CA RLR 35:116 4 Apr. 1787–30June, 1790, per L. Guelke data), and on De Caffres Kraal from 1790 (RLR 6:231, 29 June, 1790, per L. Guelke data). Both farms were near the Olifants River.

55. Mentzel II:107.

56. For a brief discussion of Martin Melck's life, see Shell and Guelke, "Landed Gentry," 279–80.

57. CA: RLR 6:85, Renoster Hoek to Jan Andries Dissel, 15 July 1726–16 Aug. 1728. Renewed through 31 Oct. 1732, CA: RLR 7:54, Groote Zeekoe Valleij to Jan Andries Dissel, 14 Apr. 1728–14 Apr. 1729. Renewed through 5 July 1732, CA: RLR 9:205 (per L. Guelke data); ARA: VOC 4100, *OPB*, 1726 opgaaf, Drakenstein p. 8.

58. ARA: VOC 4100 *OPB,* 1731 opgaaf, Drakenstein p. 11.

59. Guelke & Shell, "Landed Gentry," 265, 273–75.

60. Ras reported 30 cattle and 70 sheep in the 1731 opgaaf. Guelke's minimum estimate is 20 cattle and 50 sheep, see "Freehold Farmers and Frontier Settlers, 1657–1780," in *The Shaping of South African Society, 1652–1840*, eds. Richard Elphick and Hermann Giliomee, 2nd ed. (Johannesburg: Maskew Miller Longman, 1989), 87.

61. Daniel Pfeil's 1731 opgaaf return: 30 horses, 156 cattle, 450 sheep, 60 swine, 30,000 vinestocks, 350 *muid* wheat harvested, 10 *muid* rye, and 90 *muid* barley.

62. CA: CJ 785.28, *Crimineel Sententie*, 10 January 1732, the case against Moses van Angola and others.

63. ARA: VOC 4118 *OBP*, Francois Smit's return, 1732 opgaaf, Drakenstein p. 6.

64. Ross, *Status and Respectability*, 80–83. Moreover, the social and symbolic importance of the ability to claim land is embedded in South Africa's colonial history

and historiography: P.J. van der Merwe, *Trek: Studies oor die mobiliteit van die pi-onersbevolking aan die Kaap* (Cape Town: Nasionale Pers Beperk, 1945); Guelke, "Early European Settlement of South Africa," (PhD diss., University of Toronto, 1974); Norman Etherington, *Great Treks: The Transformation of Southern Africa, 1815–1854* (London: Longman, 2001).

65. Penn, *Forgotten Frontier,* 19 back

III

Mechanics of Conquest

A river only flows one way, not so the traffic of a colonial frontier: expanding land claims, contracting Khoisan kraals; advancing commandos, receding herds of game. Even settler moves into the Cedarberg were not unitary marches northward, but rather a series of roundtrips, orbits rather than trajectories. Part III examines this undulating process one family at a time. It looks in detail at marriage strategies, household formation, material culture, the circulation of wealth, and the many, overlapping relationships that linked settler farms to one another while connecting the frontier back to the heart of the colony.

These four family histories illustrate how colonial settlement expanded from Cape Town to the Cedarberg, demonstrating the importance of women-anchored family networks to settler land claims, documenting the gradual dominance of settler orthodoxy, and highlighting the centrality of coerced labor even when the laborers themselves were effaced from the archives.

Each chapter is also a methodological essay that plumbs the possibilities of a particular documentary source. The van der Merwe story challenges the presumptions of patrilineal genealogies, revealing the depth of multigenerational relationships traced through women. The Burger story pushes estate inventories to reveal frontier dynamics as well as to document material culture. The Lubbe story unpacks the elements of kin, community, and status embedded in an auction roster (*vendu rol*). The Campher and van Wyk saga interrogates criminal depositions, combing these documents for clues about social relationships, household composition, the circulation of land ownership and labor on the frontier, and travel between the Cedarberg and Cape Town—everything except the guilt or innocence of the accused. These source-specific inquiries amplify the struggles over land and identity reconstructed through an imaginative reading of lists in Part II.

Ultimately, frontier conquest took shape in the nexus between belonging and belongings. Communities claimed, created, and exploited socioeconomic networks; colonial settlers used the ownership of land, slaves, and material things to assert a position of dominance within those networks. Aggregated and in hindsight, this process looks imperial. Its practice was local and ordinary, though, negotiated in churches and kitchens, over porcelain plates and by campfires, and, at least once, in the back of an ox wagon.

5. KINSHIP AND IDENTITY

A Van Der Merwe Story

An Atlantic crossing, drought, frontier warfare, a smallpox epidemic: Anna Prevot survived them all. Most surprising for a woman who lived through the turn of the eighteenth century, Anna Prevot survived childbirth 17 times. Her second child, it seems, died in infancy. Against all odds, his 16 brothers and sisters lived to adulthood and married. The most obvious question, after mere survival, is how a settler family of modest means managed to feed and clothe so large a brood. One answer is that the eldest siblings married before the youngest were born, so it is unlikely all 16 children ever lived together. Moreover, the older children, even before marriage, would have been able to contribute labor toward household production, alleviating some of the material strain on a large family.

So perhaps the more pressing question is how Anna and her husband, Schalk van der Merwe, helped all their children find spouses, particularly the ten boys. The Cape's population, excluding the garrison, was only 7,306 in 1731; more than half of those people were slaves.[1] Company shipping assured the ongoing immigration of single men, who arrived as soldiers and sailors, some of whom applied for permission to stay. Yet none of the van der Merwe girls married one of these newcomers, and the family found more than ten brides for the ten brothers, since two remarried as widowers.

Kin and community connections are evident in all 19 marriages solemnized by Schalk and Anna's children between 1716 and 1752, a pattern prevalent among settler families of the eighteenth century. These marriages alone did not generate settler identity, but looking at the nexus between marriage strategies and emerging social distinctions highlights the importance of kinship in both creating a cohesive colonial society and enabling its expansion into frontier regions. Equally important, understanding these unions as choices emphasizes the contingent, constructed, permeable nature of settler identity.[2] A self-proclaimed "white," European-derived colonial identity was created, not inherent.[3] The process of its creation established the preconditions of dominance so strongly associated with South African history, but the forms of that domination, like the identity of the group that became hegemonic, was not foreordained. How and when some individuals and their families were described within the settler orbit, while others were excluded from it, therefore bears careful scrutiny.

ESTABLISHING A BEACHHEAD AT THE ALTAR

Endogamous marriage strategies emerged in the first generation of colonists born at the Cape and intensified with subsequent generations. Exogamous unions with newly-arrived immigrants, with locally-born settlers from previously unrelated families (including free blacks), and with manumitted slaves coexisted with endogamy, suggesting that parents and/or cohorts of siblings sought to reinforce existing connections and to make new alliances in every generation.

These marriage strategies moved with colonists from the more densely settled areas around Cape Town and Stellenbosch into the colonial hinterland. Pioneers took alliances, material culture, ideas about status and civility, and a notion of permanent, bounded, alienable land tenure with them into frontier areas. Of course, others fled to the frontier precisely because social norms—or at least enforcement mechanisms—were pliable, if not openly contested.[4] Over the course of the eighteenth century, though, the majority of colonists in frontier regions increasingly tied their lot—and their identity—to the society anchored in Cape Town. (This argument about the increasing orthodoxy of the Cedarberg frontier is developed more fully in Chapter 6.)

In frontier regions, family networks enabled colonists to establish households, physically settle on the land, and maintain their initially tenuous foothold in the landscape. It was the very function of marriage and land ownership that enabled eventual settler dominance in frontier regions. Moreover, it was through family connections and material culture that frontier settlers demonstrated not just their connection, but also their allegiance, to the dominant colonial society centered on Cape Town. Whether colonists lived near the harbor or hundreds of kilometers inland, their identity was tied to marriage and kinship—who they belonged to—and to wealth—what belonged to them.

Ideas about marriage—including the characteristics of desirable or eligible spouses—and expectations about family, both nuclear and extended, must have traveled with the soldiers, sailors, and officials of the VOC. Isolating precisely which traditions they took from a culturally heterogeneous Europe is difficult to accomplish, however. Immigrants came from across northwestern Europe, speaking versions of French, Dutch, German, and Scandinavian languages. The Company filled its ranks with the sons of farmers, artisans, and unskilled workers from rural and urban homes. The VOC insisted upon Protestant practice, accepting Lutherans among the Calvinist majority. Whether in the first years of settlement—when the choice of partners was especially limited—or later in the eighteenth century when both natural increase and ongoing immigration had swelled the ranks of the free population, neither home language nor confessional preference appeared to preclude marriage. Individuals chose spouses for reasons other than place of origin or theological persuasion.

Although their theological revision dispensed with many other impediments to marriage ingrained in Catholic doctrine, both Luther and Calvin upheld the existing prohibition on marriage between first cousins.[5] In spite of this religious restriction, and the importance subsequently accorded to it by some scholars,[6] it is reasonable to suppose that a number of German-speaking and Dutch-speaking immigrants to the Cape thought close-cousin marriages were unexceptional, as the practice was common in their home region.[7]

At the Cape, repeated endogamous marriage was undoubtedly rooted in the transfer of wealth through partible inheritance, since marriage to relatives kept property within an extended family. Children of both wealthy families and those of more modest means regularly married their cousins, so in-marriage was not a strategy only to preserve elite social status.[8] While Julia Adams and Jean Gelman Taylor argue convincingly for the social insularity among political elites achieved through strategic marriages in the Netherlands and the Dutch East Indies,[9] similar marriage practices at the Cape were diffused across a broader economic spectrum.[10] Marriage across a nebulous, permeable boundary between gentry families and other farmers happened often. Thus endogamy, rather than being used to create or sustain a narrow elite, was instead a component of a more general settler identity that embraced landed gentry, middling stock farmers, and households of modest means. Whatever their class position, and regardless of ethnic, regional, or racial origin, a significant marker of settler identity was marriage within recognized family networks.

Bachelor immigration initially sustained the free population of the Cape settlement. The colonists did not recognize or seek to marry into indigenous elite (or merchant) families as they did in parts of Southeast Asia, so the notion of kin, or of extended family, could not have been paramount in the first years of the settlement, or among the first marriages at the Cape. Family connections were in play by the time the first Cape-born generation married, though. Kin networks, endogamy, and repeated affinal marriages were evident by the second generation, establishing patterns that persisted throughout the eighteenth century. A detailed look at the extended family started by two seventeenth-century immigrants illustrates the process.

COLONIAL MARRIAGE STRATEGIES: CONSIDER THE VAN DER MERWES

As one of South Africa's early settlers and the *stamvader* (forefather) of an abundant family, Willem van der Merwe has something of an iconic status in South Africa's collective memory, or at least the name van der Merwe does. So it is convenient that van der Merwe marriage patterns over three generations reflect strategies that were typical of many colonial families throughout the eighteenth century.

I do not want to establish the van der Merwes as a normative baseline to which some families conformed or from which others deviated. Instead, I want to argue emphatically that a family's marriage strategies were not isolated or unitary, but rather resulted from decisions made by many individuals from a variety of ethnic, linguistic, religious, and class backgrounds in Europe, eventually creating specifically colonial networks of overlapping kin groups and self-conscious strategies for consolidating and transferring landed wealth.

If we accept "van der Merwe" as an icon of "Dutch" settler society, and if we understand some of the van der Merwes' motivations for choosing marriage partners, then we can see that the early van der Merwes were unsurprisingly typical—though they were not particularly "Dutch." They were also not all men; and most significantly, they were not all van der Merwes in name, though they were important members of the family.

"My name is van der Merwe," proclaims the title of a history and genealogy of this prolific colonial family.[11] Clearly, in this context, the surname is an integral part of individual and family identity. Descendents of van der Merwe sons, those who carry the family name, belong to the group. Because their name is van der Merwe, we know who they are—at least in a historical context. Oud Hendrik van der Merwe (1698–1762), for example, did not leave traces of a personal, interior identity. However, extant records reveal what his society thought was relevant to Hendrik's place in it. We can also see what subsequent generations have preserved, perpetuated, emphasized, and, significantly, what they have forgotten.

Hendrik was the youngest child of Elsie Cloete and Willem, the stamvader. He married three times and was the father of eight children. When he came of age he married his first cousin, Catharina Cloete.[12] They were both 19 years old. After Catharina's death, Hendrik married Aletta Keyser, thirty years his junior. She died in childbirth, or shortly thereafter, and within a year Hendrik took another bride, Maria Fick. At his death, Hendrik had six farms, 29 slaves, and considerable material wealth.[13]

Such is the outline of a life, broad strokes without a lot of detail. Even with this limited sketch, though, we know more about Hendrik van der Merwe than we do about most of the residents of the Cape in the eighteenth century. We could, of course, create fuller biographies of other colonists, even of other van der Merwes. Hendrik, however, is an ideal place to start looking at a van der Merwe family portrait, even with the limited perspective we have on him.

A member of the first generation born in South Africa, Hendrik was one of only two brothers to have sons of his own. Consequently, his contribution to the founding of a settler family with a name still recognizable in South African society seems, at first glance, straightforward. In fact, the details revealed in a close focus on Hendrik highlight the importance of women and emphasize the major role played by individuals not named van der Merwe in perpetuating a discernable family identity.

Though already fifty when he entered his second marriage, Hendrik had six of his eight children after that point. Apparently Catharina was a weak reproductive link in an otherwise fecund chain; she had only two children in nearly thirty years of marriage. I assume she lived until a year or two before Hendrik's second marriage because it does not seem likely that a young, prosperous farmer raising two daughters would have remained a widower for long.[14] Hendrik's second wife, Aletta, like so many settler women, had her first baby within a year of marriage and her second two years later. Unfortunately, she did not live long after that. Hendrik promptly married again, undoubtedly needing help with 2-year-old Hendrik Junior and baby Aletta Sibella.

The years from 1747 to 1750 were particularly eventful—and undoubtedly emotional—for Hendrik. Assuming that he lost his first wife shortly before his second marriage, Hendrik and his surviving daughter, Catharina Margaretha, left some of their grief at the altar. They both married in 1747. Hendrik became a father and a grandfather within a year; within the next two years, however, both his wife and his daughter passed away. The widowers, one only 23 years old, the other 52, promptly remarried. Catharina Margaretha's husband took his second bride in September 1750, three months before Hendrik wed Maria

Fick. Both men were members of families with social status and significant land holdings in Cape Town and Stellenbosch.[15] They seemed to have no trouble finding wives, in spite of the imbalanced sex ratios that left some settler men bachelors (though not necessarily celibate or childless).[16]

Hendrik's third marriage seems to have been motivated by procreation. With only two of his four children still living, he remarried soon after Aletta's death and continued fathering children. Just two of Hendrik and Maria's four children married, though. They were both sons, who, along with Hendrik Junior, Aletta's firstborn, were able to pass on the van der Merwe name. Just one of Hendrik's four van der Merwe grandsons married, however, and it does not appear that he had children.[17] One of those grandsons, Theodorus, was the son of Hendrik's daughter, Aletta Sibella. She married her first cousin once removed, Nicolaas van der Merwe Isaaksz.[18] Aletta Sibella and Nicolaas's children were, of course, called van der Merwe. Theodorus did not marry, though, so all of Hendrik's great-grandchildren appear in the family trees of the Myburghs, the du Toits, and the de Villiers, among others.[19] Whatever their surnames, these descendants' material circumstances were undoubtedly influenced by the material legacy Hendrik bequeathed.[20] His children were not poor; those who lived long enough married into families possessed of landed wealth in Stellenbosch and Drakenstein.

WOMEN'S ROLE IN PATRILINEAL DESCENT

In a patrilineal society with patronymic conventions, record keeping has been organized around men and their male offspring. South Africa's early colonial landed gentry, its dynasties of wealth and power, and even the accumulation and transfer of more modest properties in frontier regions have all been recognized according to family names determined by relationships to men.[21] The procreation of those families was, naturally enough, equally dependent on women's participation, which is starkly evident on Hendrik's branch of the van der Merwe tree. Without Aletta Keyser and Maria Fick, the branch would have ended. Even with Aletta's and Maria's van der Merwe sons and son-in-law, Hendrik's van der Merwe offspring ended with his grandchildren, reminding us of how important it is to consider both halves of a matrimonial union, since the transfer of wealth and kin relationships were not defined only according to family name or male descendants.

Hendrik's succession of three wives underscores the importance of women and men in reproduction. Five of his children married cousins, thus reinforcing family relationships. Hendrik's daughter Aletta Sibella, through her marriage to Nicolaas van der Merwe, was as important in creating the next generation of van der Merwe sons as her brothers were. The random distribution of Y chromosomes and the fate of those who did not live long enough to have children of their own determined that none of Hendrik's van der Merwe grandsons reproduced, meaning family connections assumed other names.

Preferences for marrying within certain families, the advantages of marriage between cousins, and the significance of natal family relationships for both men and women hinted at in Hendrik's case are more clearly evident when the van der Merwe portrait is expanded to include his siblings. Petronella, one of Hendrik's elder sisters, married Johannes Cloete—her first cousin and the elder brother of Hendrik's first wife, Catharina. The parents must have influenced the selection of spouses, since the marriage of two van der Merwe siblings to their first cousins reinforced the relationship between their family and the Cloetes first forged between Willem and Elsie.

IMMIGRATION AND ENDOGAMY

For the early years of European settlement at the Cape, when most settlers were immigrants, portraying marriage as a relationship between families is, perhaps, overstating the case. By the time the first generation of Cape-born children married, though, familial relationships were striking. For example, Oud Willem van der Merwe came to the Cape from the Low Countries as a bachelor, a man without local family connections. A midshipman, he arrived aboard the *Dordrecht* serving as an arquebusier. The following year the Company released him from service and granted him burgher rights. Seven years after that, in 1668, he married Elsie Cloete, daughter of Jacob and Fytje, both from Cologne. Elsie was born in Europe and came to the Cape with her parents and brother, Gerrit.

Jacob Cloete first arrived at the Cape in 1652; he was one of the first free burghers and received a farm on the Liesbeeck River in 1657. Though repatriated to Europe in 1761, he eventually returned to the Cape as a corporal. His third and fourth children were born at the Cape; all of his children came of age and married locally. He was killed two months before his youngest child, Coenraad, married. The governor's official journal entry of 23 May 1693 describes his murder and acknowledges the respect Cloete commanded as one of the men who helped to found the colony.[22] Given that European men outnumbered European women by more than two to one in the late seventeenth century,[23] Cloete's daughters Elsie and Catharina would have had their pick of single men as husbands. That Elsie married Willem van der Merwe suggests his seven years as a free burgher were both respectable and financially promising.

Despite having an illegitimate child with a slave,[24] Willem van der Merwe married into the Cloete family, thus linking his fortune to a prominent local landowner and his future to a nascent colonial dynasty.[25]

As an immigrant settler, Oud Willem van der Merwe also founded a colonial legacy of his own. Of the 13 children he and Elsie had, only three did not marry. Surely it was not coincidence that two of the ten who did—Petronella and Hendrik—wed first cousins, children of Elsie's brother Gerrit. Both Elsie and Willem were immigrants to the Cape; Elsie as a daughter in her natal family, Willem as a single young man. Two of their children's marriages reinforced the couple's only significant family relationship—to the Cloetes. The fact that Elsie's children married Gerrit's children and not the offspring of her other brother and sister may have had to do with lack of opportunity rather than a plan to create particular affiliation only with her brother Gerrit. Catharina Cloete and her husband Jan van Brienen did not have children; only one of Coenraad's two sons married, and both of them were a bit too young to be ideal matches for the van der Merwe daughters. Gerrit's children were the only option.

Moreover, marriage among multiple siblings made sense in the context of partible inheritance.[26] In the case of a large family dividing an inheritance that included landed property, the ability to exchange interests in particular farms, or to have a roughly equivalent inheritance from a spouse's family available to buy out a sibling's share, meant that farms could be transmitted across generations without being subdivided into parcels too small to be useful. In a family with six children, at the death of a parent the surviving spouse would inherit half the estate; the children would split the other half equally. One-twelfth of a farm was not enough to offer subsistence, let alone a stepping-stone to prosperity. If, however, a pair of siblings was willing to cooperate with siblings from another family, an equitable exchange was possible that would put both couples on a better footing. Assume that two siblings from family A married two siblings from family B. For argument's sake, presume that the A siblings inherited one-twelfth of their parents' estate, and the B siblings inherited one-tenth of their parents' estate. If the portions were roughly equivalent, or if modest credit could be arranged to make up any difference, the first couple could exchange a share of the A family inheritance for a share in the B family estate, an equation re-stated in Figure 5.3.[27] Thus one couple would have received two portions of the A estate, while the other couple received two portions of the B estate. One-fifth of an interest in a farm was closer to viable, and could have provided enough collateral to buy out other siblings, thus leaving the farm intact. Given the frequency with which sets of siblings made multiple marriages between families, negotiating inheritance certainly played a prominent role in marriage decisions.[28]

Fig. 5.3. Inheritance Advantages of Close Cousin Marriages

Inheritance Advantages of Close Cousin Marriages

Without exchanging inheritance portions:	If exchange is possible:
A1 1/12 + B1 1/10 = insufficient land on two farms	Couple 1: 2/12 of farm A
A2 1/12 + B2 1/10 = insufficient land on two farms	Couple 2: 2/10 of farm B

The unions between van der Merwes and Cloetes show that this strategy was in use from the first generation of settlers born in South Africa. Marriage served to reinforce relationships as well as to consolidate landed property. However, in a recently established colony with growth fueled by ongoing immigration, marriage only within existing relationships was not possible. Elsie, for example, did not have enough nieces and nephews to marry her children. Nor would complete insularity have been desirable, since marriage to other families or to immigrants was a potential source of new wealth, not to mention an opportunity to cement alliances with neighbors and strengthen relationships with politically powerful individuals.

Willem and Elsie's Cape-born children entered into 17 marriages with partners from 16 different families. Five of those unions were second (or third) marriages after the death of a spouse. Of the 17 spouses, two were Cloete cousins born at the Cape, three other partners were locally born, and 12 were immigrants. Hendrik alone accounts for three of the five Cape-born partners: Catharina Cloete, Aletta Keyser, and Maria Fick. His first marriage to his cousin was likely both a familial and a financial advantage. His second marriage, when he was 50 years old, and his third, when he was 52, were to younger women whose fathers were less prosperous than Hendrik himself. Already established, Hendrik does not appear to have sought wealth or status through his marriages later in life. It seems he wanted children, not material or political gain. However, he was alive when his eldest daughter chose a husband—her first cousin, Albert Myburgh Albertsz. This marriage both reinforced familial alliances and connected Catharina Margaretha to a family with property.[29] Although Hendrik may have used other criteria for his subsequent marriages, he influenced his daughter to make the same kind of choices his parents undoubtedly helped him make in deciding on his first bride, favoring existing family connections and wealth.

In Hendrik's generation, locally born spouses were the minority. His three elder sisters, who married Cape-born men, appear to have chosen their partners with family, prestige, or wealth in mind. Petronella got all three with Jan Cloete, her first cousin, the son of an influential family who was eventually named a heemraad himself, and a property owner who amassed significant wealth by the time he died.[30] Helena's first husband, Jacob van As, was already a widower when they married. At his death, she inherited a farm in Drakenstein, a farm in Paarl with a large stand of timber, 11 slaves, and enough tools and livestock to indicate a successful, though not particularly wealthy, farm.[31] Elsie married Albert Myburgh Senior, the only son of a Dutch immigrant. Over the course of their marriage the couple accumulated property, vineyards, livestock, and slaves; their children certainly numbered among the nascent gentry.[32] It is unclear whether Albert already had significant wealth at the time of their marriage, or if their material success was due to the combined forces of van der Merwe and Myburgh energy and resources.

Oud Willem and Elsie Cloete's other children married immigrants, meaning that family connections could not have been a factor in their attractiveness as spouses. Not all of them were well-established when they married, suggesting that although financial resources were important, they were not a defining feature for a potential bride or groom. Whereas some members of the first South African–born generation of van der Merwes appear to have had logical material or familial reasons for their choice of spouse, other siblings married for their partner's potential, or for mutual attraction, or for any of a host of reasons beyond speculation.

Among the immigrant partners, three came from the Netherlands, six from German-speaking regions, and one was a Huguenot who came to the Cape as a child with her parents. Three of those immigrant men—Barend Burger, Pieter Willem van Heerden, and Nicolaas Janse van Rensburg—clearly married into the van der Merwe clan. As immigrants without incumbent family obligations, they were absorbed into their wives' social world. Their children carried their fathers' surnames, but their eventual marriages were van der Merwe–driven relationships. The first two generations of Burgers, van Rensburgs, and van Heerdens born at the Cape showed a striking propensity to marry van der Merwes, which created a multiply-intersecting extended family.

Marietjie, the third van der Merwe child born at the Cape, married Barend Burger, a blacksmith from Lübeck. They had five children before he died in 1705. She remarried a year later, but did not have children with her second husband, German immigrant Lambert Smit. After Barend's death, Marietjie owned two farms near Paarl and another near the grain mill at Drakenstein. Though their house was minimally furnished, the couple had acquired 11 slaves, 600 sheep, and 80 head of cattle.[33] Financially, Marietjie was an attractive widow. With three farms to manage, a baby still at her breast, and her eldest child only 7 years old, we can imagine Marietjie's motivations to remarry, and to choose a man without children or other family obligations of his own. When it came time for her children to marry, however, none of them chose immigrant partners. The three eldest married first cousins, children of Marietjie's two elder siblings. The choice of which of their many cousins to marry may have had to do with affinities among the siblings, or with attraction between the cousins, or simply the logistics of age and availability. Perhaps Marietjie's sons married the children only of their mother's elder siblings because the daughters of her younger siblings were just too young. Even the inheritance advantage of a first-cousin marriage might not have been worth waiting for.

Aletta, ten years younger than Marietjie, married Nicolaas Janse van Rensburg. Already a widow with three young children; she had seven more with van Rensburg. One of Aletta's van Staden children married an immigrant; one of her van Rensburg children married a locally born but unrelated partner. The rest of her children married individuals already connected to the van der Merwes by birth or marriage. Her children with Nicolaas van Rensburg married within a much tighter orbit than her children with van Staden. It is impossible to assess the degree to which Aletta's husbands influenced their children's choice in marriage partners. Since van Staden had been dead for nearly two decades before his children married, he probably did not impart words of wisdom directly into their ears, but he might have made his wishes known to Aletta. Did Nicolaas van Rensburg actively support the marriage of most of his children to their van der Merwe cousins? Did he passively observe matrimonial alliances being crafted by his wife and her siblings? Or did five van Rensburg siblings just fall for their cousins? Given the number of van der Merwe–van Rensburg marriages in subsequent generations, there must have been strategy as well as affinity in play. Moreover, the degree of consanguinity in these cases was particularly close.

Three of the seven van Rensburg children married first cousins. A fourth married Anna Sophia Burger, his first cousin once removed. Hendrik van Rensburg married his niece.[34] The eldest van Rensburg child, Johannes, married Anna Maria Botha. Theirs was the third union of their generation between the Botha and van der Merwe families, a practice that continued in subsequent generations. The van Rensburg family fortunes and social alliances were clearly bound tightly to the van der Merwe network.

Unlike her sisters Marietjie and Aletta, Magdalena van der Merwe was not widowed early, so she married only once—Dutch immigrant Pieter Willem van Heerden. The proportion of endogamous marriages among their 11 children was not as high as among their Burger (three of five marriages) and van Rensburg (five of seven marriages) cousins, but among the three van Heerdens who did marry van der Merwes, the practice of intermarriage remained strong across subsequent generations. Only eight of Madgalena and Pieter's children married. Two of them married Jordaan siblings, two more married unrelated local men, and Aletta van Heerden married German immigrant Christian

Ernst in 1735. Aletta's marriage to an immigrant was atypical of the van der Merwe clan in the period.

The prevalence of familial endogamy evident in the second and third generations of van Heerden marriages was more common. Eleven of Magdalena and Pieter's grandchildren married their van der Merwe cousins, including the daughter of Jacob van Heerden and Anna Jordaan, which suggests that the continued van Heerden link to the van der Merwes was not influenced only by those who themselves had married their first cousins. The practice applied broadly.

Among the first Cape-born generation, marriage to both local and immigrant spouses established parameters for repeated intermarriage in subsequent generations. The first-generation van der Merwes looked to their siblings' families when suggesting or helping to arrange mates for their children. The next generation could turn to the offspring of both siblings and cousins, and they did.

SPECTACULAR PROLIFERATION:
SCHALK VAN DER MERWE AND ANNA PREVOT

This expanded van der Merwe family portrait would not be complete without Schalk, the eldest son, and his wife, Anna Prevot. A Huguenot refugee, Anna came to the Cape as a child. She sailed with her family, including older brother Abraham and younger sister Elisabeth, on the *Schelde* in 1688. She was seven years old when the Prevots arrived, and 15 or 16 when she married. Shell's data shows that the Huguenot arrivals overwhelmingly contributed men to the colonial population, suggesting that Anna (or her parents) could have found a suitable French-speaking partner, had marriage within the Huguenot community been of primary importance.[35] Her sister Elisabeth's first husband was, in fact, a fellow Huguenot.[36] Schalk, son of Dutch and German immigrants, was part of a large brood. At the time of his marriage, his youngest siblings were not yet born, but adding a child or two to the partible inheritance equation would not have changed his prospects substantially. The opgaaf suggests his parents could sustain themselves, but they were not wealthy,[37] so his attractiveness as a husband was not likely financial.[38] Perhaps, though, even a few head of breeding stock from his father looked more promising than the lot of many Huguenot sons in the 1690s: landless, in debt, and still dependent on support from the VOC.[39]

Schalk's marriage to an immigrant woman was unusual simply because there were few female migrants. His coming-of-age coincided with the demographic bubble of Huguenots. Although only a small percentage of them arrived as families, Schalk nevertheless benefited from this influx of European-born women. Given the small size of the settler population at the end of the seventeenth century, a new face may have been reason enough to marry.[40]

Whatever their respective motivations, the couple proved long-lived and prolific. Anna had her first child at 16 and her seventeenth at 44. She survived 28 years of childbearing, a feat remarkable enough in itself to merit historical notice. Sixteen of these children found spouses. Imagine Anna, pregnant with Gerrit (her fourteenth child) giving marital advice to Elsje, her eldest. *Think about your cousin, Willem Burger. He's just turned 20. He and his brother Andries have started running sheep out by the Twenty-four Rivers. Your cousin Margaretha is homesteading with their older brother Barend in the Land van Waveren, so they'd be close by. In three years, when your sister Maria turns 16, she could marry Andries, and you'd all be neighbors. Think about Willem. He's a good match.*

In fact, Elsje and her younger sister Maria did marry their first cousins, the Burger brothers. The two couples claimed neighboring loan farms; their cousin, Margaretha Pasman, and her husband, the eldest Burger brother, claimed Twee Jonge Gezellen in the Tulbagh valley.[41] We are not likely ever to know how much choice the young people exercised in selecting their marriage partners, or how much enthusiasm they had for sharing the work of opening previously unclaimed land for colonial settlement, but this pattern happened often enough to look like conscious strategy rather than repeated coincidence. Whether their parents engineered the matches or the couples made their own plans, the prevalence of relationships sustained by women poses a challenge to the assumption that "patriarchal" fathers controlled marriage choices.[42] Women—mothers, aunts, sisters, and cousins—linked families across the landscape, and across generations.[43]

Of course, male relationships and male relatives were important, too. The van der Merwe sisters were related to their Burger cousins/husbands through their father, Schalk *and* his sister, Marietjie. Schalk's relationship to his siblings was also key to other unions by his children. Willem, Martha, and Gerrit married van Heerden first cousins (children of their Aunt Magdalena). David, Pieter, and Izaak married van Rensburg first cousins (children of their Aunt Aletta).

Since Schalk and Anna had so many children, the preference for marriage to first cousins and the practice of multiple sibling unions is particularly resonant. Despite ongoing Christian injunctions against endogamous marriage with close relatives and affines, including a prohibition of first-cousin marriages reiterated by Calvin,[44] there were always exceptions in early-modern Europe.[45] In general, though, familial restrictions and the limits of geography meant that a proportion of Europeans remained unmarried, since they observed the injunctions.[46] Whether because of the relatively small population, because of material considerations of partible inheritance, or simply a question of preference, colonial society at the Cape bent these Christian, European norms. Consequently, consanguineous unions were a significant proportion of the consecrated marriages.

SOME ELEMENTS OF SETTLER IDENTITY

Schalk and Anna's 16 surviving children made 19 marriages; those unions were to only 10 families, three of which were already related. With 16 progeny to marry off, Schalk, Anna, or the children themselves made alliances with only seven new families, five of which were Huguenot.

Anna Prevot seems to have played as important a role as Schalk in identifying, suggesting, or arranging mates. All but one of their children who did not marry one of Schalk's nieces or nephews married a child descended from a Huguenot refugee, though none of these families was related to Anna. Other Huguenot-descended families did make first-cousin marriages (the du Toits and Moutons, for example), so it is not possible to make a blanket statement about the refugees having a different understanding or application of Calvin's precepts than the Dutch-speaking Reformed Church members.

Patricia Romero recently categorized the Huguenot population as liminal and hybrid, on one hand,[47] and as distinct bearers of a "diaspora identity" trying to "cling to their Frenchness," on the other.[48] She argues against an older literature that points to a fairly rapid dissolution of a separate Huguenot identity.[49] Romero admits her initial assumption—that the Huguenots sought to maintain a distinct community through endogamy—was not born out by her research, yet she nevertheless argues that the refugees "tried to maintain their Frenchness in their choice of marriage partners and patterns of name giving."[50]

The problem with her argument is that the families of Huguenot refugees were not markedly more or less endogamous than settler families descended primarily from Dutch- or German-speaking immigrants.[51] The practice of naming children after their grandparents, aunts, and uncles was also widely used; sets of first names tended to circulate within families, regardless of the stamvaders' and stammoeders' places of origin. Most importantly, the marriages of Anna Prevot's children suggest that traces of unions among Huguenot-descended colonists should be pursued with equal vigor through matrilineal ties, and not just through patrilineal descent formalized with patronymic conventions. Though there is no evidence to suggest that Anna Prevot and Schalk van der Merwe's children thought of themselves as Huguenot, or part Huguenot, little more than French surnames link other descendents of the refugees to a particular Huguenot identity among the colonists at large. Given the extent to which families with Dutch and German surnames married in close circles, and the numerous van der Merwe spouses with Huguenot names, we need more than marriage patterns to define a specific settler identity such as Huguenot.[52] Marriage as a component of social identity is useful to differentiate in broad strokes between settlers and other colonial inhabitants. Marriages also can determine the scope of family networks, but as an analytical tool it is not fine-grained enough to differentiate one kin group from another, since settlers married across class and other differences. Consequently, the question of sustained Huguenot identity or community affiliation remains open to more investigation.

In spite of a romanticized notion of persistent Huguenot identity,[53] the lack of pervasive Huguenot endogamy when traced only through descendants of men in the first two generations of marriages suggests that French-speaking colonists—like their Dutch and German descended neighbors—considered a variety of factors important in a prospective spouse. Language, religion, and community figured alongside family relationships, wealth, property claims, geographical proximity, and social status.[54] Among these considerations, family relationships were prominent.

INCREASING ENDOGAMY

Unlike the diversity of partners seen in the first Cape-born generation of van der Merwe marriages (17 unions to 16 different families), second-generation spouses came from a more circumscribed pool. Oud Willem and Elsie had 118 grandchildren who solemnized 73 marriages. Those 73 spouses came from

Fig. 5.8. Declining Marriage to Immigrants in Three Generations of Van der Merwes
Hendrik van der Merwe Willemsz's second and third marriages happened late in his life, extending the closing dates for marriage in his generation by more than thirty years, and extending the latest dates for birth and marriage among his children and grandchildren up to forty years. I excluded those dates from this table, since those marriage and birth events represent a small proportion of their generation and serve to conflate the chronologies of the c and d generations.

dV&P; H&L, Hoge

Declining Marriage to Immigrants in Three Generations of van der Merwes

	gen b	gen c	gen d
no. of children	13	118	385
birth date range	1670–1698	1697–1727	1717–1762
no. of marriages	17	73	303
marriage date range	1684–1717	1717–1770	1741–1782
no. of immigrant spouses	12	6	22
as percentage of total spouses	70.59%	8.22%	7.26%

only 36 families; 25 of those marriages were to first cousins, and another four were to other close relatives, meaning that 40 percent of second-generation partners were close kin. In contrast, only six spouses were immigrants, making marriages like those of Aletta van der Merwe, mentioned previously in this chapter, rare in this family. Fourteen of those 73 marriages were the second consecutive unions between families. The Burgers, Cloetes, van Heerdens, Myberghs, Pasmans, and van Rensburgs established multiple relationships with the van der Merwe family that spanned generations and helped to sustain colonial social networks into expanding frontier regions.

Colonial families at the Cape and the multiply-intersecting alliances among them were local manifestations of kinship patterns also present in Europe and the Dutch East Indies. The connections forged or reinforced through marriage at the Cape were predominantly local, rooted in the colony rather than a wider imperial orbit. There were, however, a few exceptions in which a Cape marriage reflected European or Asian connections among elite Company officials. Moreover, some of the Huguenots who immigrated as a group made local marriages that reflected family relationships transplanted from Europe or made during the long Atlantic passage. Even families that honored such external connections also made marriage alliances within local networks, indicating the importance of local kinship in creating Cape colonial identity that differentiated settlers from indigenous Africans and Asian slaves.

The van der Merwes alone were not responsible for establishing a pattern of repeated in-marriage. Rather, they were part of an early colonial population in the process of adapting European, Asian, and African cultural practices to their local circumstances. These early colonists created new norms to meet the particular exigencies of life under VOC rule as they moved from the shores of Table Bay into an increasingly colonized hinterland. Family alliances, marriage strategies, marital expectations, social status, inherited wealth, gendered social roles, ideologies of race, and enslaved or subordinated labor all emerged in concert in the settled areas of the Cape, Stellenbosch, and Drakenstein districts at the turn of the eighteenth century. This complicated bundle accompanied the van der Merwes, Burgers, van Rensburgs, Moutons, Lubbes, Smits, and their compatriots northward to the Cedarberg frontier, where, in search of available land, the growing colonial population began to associate a settler, or dominant, identity specifically with connection to established families and with the ability to make specific, demarcated, alienable claims to land.

Understanding the extent of these family networks, their repeated reinforcement across generations, and the centrality of women to these relationships complicates prevailing assumptions about both race and patriarchy in South African history. Belonging in settler society was not necessarily about being "white," or being descended only from Europeans, but rather about claiming relationships in kin networks, which could be accomplished by marriage. Those kin networks, in turn, were determined through both maternal and paternal ties, making extended families larger than the list of male-descended heirs typically reconstituted in genealogies. Understanding settler identity thus starts with family relationships. Placing individuals in overlapping and multivalent kin networks is an important step toward moving beyond taxonomic labels.

NOTES

1. ARA: VOC 10481, *Inkomende stukken van de kantoren*. Letter from Jan de la Fontaine (verbatim copy), 2 Aug. 1731.

2. Amin Maalouf, *In the Name of Identity: Violence and the Need to Belong* (New York: Arcade Publishing, 1996).

3. The "white" population at the Cape was, of course, not entirely comprised of Europeans and their descendants. For examples, see H.F. Heese, *Groepe sonder grense: Die rol en status van die gemengde bevolking aan die Kaap, 1652–1705* (Bellville: Institute for Historical Research, 1985; translated by Delia Robertson as *Cape Melting Pot: The Role and Status of the Mixed Population at the Cape, 1652–1795* Johannesburg: self-published, 2006); R. Viljoen, "'Till Murder Do Us Part': The Story of Griet and Hendrik Eksteen," *South African Historical Journal* 33 (1995), 13–32; Richard Elphick and Robert Shell, "Intergroup Relations: Khoikhoi, Settlers, Slaves and Free Blacks, 1652–1795," in Elphick and Hermann Giliomee, eds., *The Shaping of South African Society, 1652–1840*, 2nd ed. (Cape Town: Maskew Miller Longman, 1989), 184–239.

4. Leonard Guelke, "The Making of Two Frontier Communities: Cape Colony in the Eighteenth Century," *Historical Reflections/Reflexions Historiques* 12: 3 (1985), 419–48. Hermann Giliomee articulates an open and closed frontier model in "Processes in Development of the Southern African Frontier," in *The Frontier in History: North American and South Africa Compared*, eds. Howard Lamar and Leonard Thompson, (New Haven: Yale University Press, 1981), 19–26. For the frontier space for lawlessness, see Nigel Penn, "Fugitives on the Cape Frontier" and "Droster Gangs of the Bokkeveld and Roggeveld, 1770–1800," both in *Rogues, Rebels and Runaways: Eighteenth-Century Cape Characters* (Cape Town: David Philip, 1999), 73–100, 147–66.

5. Jeffrey R. Watt, *The Making of Modern Marriage: Matrimonial Control and the Rise of Sentiment in Neuchâtel, 1550–1800* (Ithaca: Cornell University Press, 1992), 43–44.

6. Jack Goody, *The European Family: An Historico-Anthropological Essay* (Oxford: Blackwell Publishers, 2000); Roderick Phillips, *Putting Asunder: A History of Divorce in Western Society* (Cambridge: Cambridge University Press, 1988).

7. For example, see David Warren Sabean, *Kinship in Neckarhausen, 1700–1879* (Cambridge: Cambridge University Press, 1998).

8. The prevalence of first-cousin marriage among elite Amsterdam burghers as well as among farmers and artisans in Neckarhausen raises questions about the class dimension of endogamous marriage. Julia Adams, *Ruling Families and Merchant*

Capitalism in Early Modern Europe (Ithaca: Cornell University Press, 2005); Sabean, *Kinship in Neckarhausen.*

9. Adams, *Ruling Families;* Jean Gelman Taylor, *The Social World of Batavia: European and Eurasian in Dutch Asia* (Madison: University of Wisconsin Press, 1983).

10. Thanks to Kerry Ward for a particularly fruitful conversation about the non-elite characteristics of many endogamously-marrying families of the Western Cape.

11. C.P. van der Merwe, *Van der Merwe Gedenkboek,* 1952.

12. Unless otherwise noted, marriages, marriage dates, and birth or baptism dates are those complied in H&L and/or dV&P. The Heese and Lombard genealogies are more accurate and complete than de Villiers and Pama. In cases of significant discrepancies between H&L and dV&P, I have, where possible, verified the information through other sources. For example, dV&P show both Aletta Keyser and Maria Fick married to Hendrik van der Merwe Schalksz, rather than to his uncle, Oud Hendrik Willemsz the Heemraad. In terms of age, the younger Hendrik does seem a more likely partner for Aletta and Maria, but the women did, in fact, marry the elder Hendrik. Both men died in 1762, leaving widows and minor children. Their estate inventories clearly identify spouses and children that correspond to the H&L genealogy. CA:MOOC 8/10.32a, Estate Inventory of Hendrik van der Merwe (and Hester Pienaar), 21 Sept., 1762. The estate inventories in the MOOC collection are now available online at http://www.tanap.net/content/activities/documents/Orphan_Chamber-Cape_of_Good_Hope/index.htm

13. CA: MOOC 8/10.38, Estate Inventory of Hendrik van der Merwe and Maria Tik, 8 Dec. 1762.

14. Leonard Guelke and Robert C.-H. Shell point out that most remarriages happened within a year of a spouse's death; "An Early Colonial Landed Gentry: Land and Wealth in the Cape Colony 1682–1731," *Journal of Historical Geography* 9:3 (1983), 279.

15. Catharina Margaretha married Albert Myburgh, son of a Cape Town burgher, himself a burgher in Stellenbosch, and the younger brother of Johannes Albertus, who established the Myburgh dynasty at Meerlust farm.

16. For specifics on sex imbalance at the Cape, see Robert Ross, "The 'White' Population in the Eighteenth Century," in *Beyond the Pale: Essays on the History of Colonial South Africa* (Johannesburg: Witwatersrand University Press, 1993), 127; and Robert C.-H. Shell, "Immigration: The Forgotten Factor in Cape Colonial Frontier Expansion, 1658–1817," *Safundi* 18 (Apr. 2005), 3. For documentation of settler men having illegitimate children with slaves, free blacks, and mixed-race women, see H.F. Heese, *Groep sonder grense.*

17. Schalk Willem van der Merwe, born 1791, married Regina Jacoba Steyn, H&L.

18. Cape settler patterns of naming children after parents, grandparents, aunts and uncles—depending on birth order—means there were frequently two or more individuals in the same family alive at once with the same name. Nicknames were common but typically do not appear in official documents such as loan farm records or the opgaaf. Designation as a father's son often appears, for example, Nicolaas van der Merwe Isaaksz. This convention is particularly helpful to differentiate cousins, such as Barend Burger Barendsz or Barend Burger Willemsz, discussed in Chapter 6. Unfortunately, these appellations were not applied consistently in eighteenth-century sources.

Moreover some contemporary records as well as subsequent transcriptions sometimes confuse abbreviations of the *zoon* appellation with abbreviations of middle names, which further obscures individual identities

19. Marriage partners of Hendrik's children: Myburgh, du Toit (both in Ross's 1983 list of 19 major vine-cultivating families), Hauman, van Heerden. Marriage partners of Hendrik's grandchildren: Le Roux, du Toit, du Plessis, de Villiers, Theron, and Minaar (all from vine-growing gentry families), and Bruwer, van der Vyver, Viljoen, Opperman, Steyn, Enslin, van der Merwe.

20. At his death, each of Hendrik's children received RxD 631, 14 stuivers, and one slave. His two eldest surviving children (those he had with Aletta Keyser) received an additional RxD 1040:16 from the estate settlement agreed upon at their mother's death. CA: MOOC 8/10.38, Estate Inventory of Willem van der Merwe, 8 Dec. 1762.

21. Guelke and Shell, "Early Colonial Landed Gentry"; Robert Ross, "The Rise of the Cape Gentry," *JSAS* 9:2 (Apr. 1983), 193–217; Wayne Dooling, "The Making of a Colonial Elite: Property, Family and Landed Stability in the Cape Colony, c. 1750–1834," *JSAS* 31:1 (Mar. 2005), 158–61.

22. Hoge, "Personalia of Germans at the Cape, 1652–1808," *AYB* 9 (1946), 61.

23. Shell, "Immigration," 4; Ross, "The Rise of the Cape Gentry," 127.

24. Heese, *Groep sonder grense* (Robertson trans.), 55.

25. The material and moral consequences of illegitimacy at the Cape in the eighteenth century remain underexplored. The pioneering study is Gerald Groenewald "Parents, Children and Illegitimacy in Dutch Colonial Cape Town, c. 1652–1795," unpublished paper, 2006. For illegitimacy in the nineteenth century, see V.C. Malherbe, "*In Onegt Verwekt*: Law, Custom and Illegitimacy in Cape Town, 1800–1840," *JSAS* 31:1 (2005), 163–85.

26. Robert Ross, "The Development Spiral of the White Family and the Expansion of the Frontier," in *Beyond the Pale*, 139–44.

27. On credit and mortgages, see Wayne Dooling, "Agrarian Transformation in the Western Districts of the Cape Colony, 1838–c.1900," (PhD diss., St. John's College, Cambridge, 1996).

28. Dooling, "The Making of a Colonial Elite."

29. ARA: VOC 10481, *OBP*, 1731 opgaaf; Leonard Guelke, Robert C.-H. Shell and Anthony Whyte, compilers, "The de la Fontaine Report," (New Haven: Opgaaf Project, 1990). CA: MOOC 9/8.20, Estate Inventory of Albert Meijberg, 11 Feb. 1756; Ross, "The Rise of the Cape Gentry," 207.

30. CA: MOOC 8/5.52, Estate Inventory of Jan Cloete, 20 Mar. 1732.

31. CA: MOOC 8/2.89, Estate Inventory of Jacobus van As, 30 Nov. 1713.

32. Ross, "The Rise of the Cape Gentry," 207. Their son Johannes Albertus bought Meerlust in 1757. The farm continues to produce wine and is still owned by Myburgh descendants.

33. CA: MOOC 8/2.3, Estate Inventory of Barent Burger, 1 Oct. 1705.

34. Hendrik's sister, Sophia van Rensburg, was David van der Merwe's second wife. Anna van der Merwe, Hendrik's wife, was a child of David's first marriage, thus Sophia's stepdaughter. Given that marriage conferred a degree of relationship close enough to warrant the prosecution of incest for sexual transgressions (ARA: VOC

4158, ff. 928–43, 1743. *OBP,* Notes on criminal inquiry against Landbouwer Willem van Wyk in case of incest with Jacoba Alida Campher), it seems reasonable to consider Anna van der Merwe as Hendrik van Rensburg's niece; see Phillips, *Putting Asunder,* 6 for proscribed degrees of consanguinity. Even if an actual familial relationship is disavowed in this case, the social relationship between the two families remains evident.

35. Shell, "Immigration," 3–4.

36. M. Boucher, *French-Speakers at the Cape in the First Hundred Years of Dutch East India Company rule: The European Background* (Pretoria: University of South Africa, 1981), 271. He asserts that the Prevot and des Pres families became close on the Cape-bound voyage.

37. Heese, *Groep sonder grense* (Robertson trans.), 54.

38. Susan Newton-King, "In Search of Notability: The Antecedents of David van der Merwe of the Koue Bokkeveld," Collected Seminar Papers (University of London, Institute for Commonwealth Studies), No. 48, The Societies of Southern Africa in the Nineteenth and Twentieth Centuries, vol. 20, p. 32; Newton-King, personal communication, 2 Nov. 2006.

39. Pieter Coertzen, with Charles Fensham, *The Huguenots of South Africa 1688–1988,* (Cape Town: Tafelberg, 1988), 84–85.

40. The "gross free 'white' population" of the colony in 1700 was 1,245 people, including 418 men and 222 women, Ross, "The 'White' Population," 127. Heese calculates that there were only 268 free burghers in the Cape district, 164 in Stellenbosch, and 130 in Drakenstein in 1700, making his male population figures slightly higher than Ross's; Heese, *Groep Sonder Grense* (Robertson trans.), 30. Guelke and Shell tallied 567 census households at the Cape in 1705, "Early Colonial Landed Gentry," 265, 270. Presumably women would have headed some of those "census households," so the number should not be taken as a source of sex-differentiated population figures.

41. Barend Burger's claims to the farm at Twee Jonge Gezellen, CA: RLR 6:19, 6 Feb. 1725. RLR 8:218, 19 Feb. 1729 (to 1731 per L. Guelke data); Willem and Andries Burger's claims to farms in the Twenty-four Rivers: CA: RLR 6:123, 16 Apr. 1727 to 30 Apr., 1728; RLR 3:308, to 15 Nov. 1717, RLR 4:24, 15 Nov. 1717 to 16 Nov. 1718, RLR 4:106, 16 Nov. 1718 to 20 Nov. 1719; RLR 4:174, 20 Nov. 1719 to 20 Nov. 1720; RLR 5:18, 20 Nov. 1720 to 17 Nov. 1721, RLR 8:148, 25 Nov. 1728 to 25 Nov. 1730; RLR 8:237, 30 Mar. 1729 to 30 Mar. 1731 (per L. Guelke data).

Leonard Guelke graciously shared his compilation of RLR data with me, allowing me to cross-check my own archival references and to easily search and sort voluminous loan farm records. I am grateful for his generosity with raw data and for his published scholarly interpretations of colonial land claims and frontier farming life.

42. Patricia Romero, "Some Aspects of Family and Social History Among the French Huguenot Refugees at the Cape," *Historia* 48:2 (Nov. 2003), passim, and esp. 45.

43. Women also anchored extended families in Batavia; Taylor, *The Social World of Batavia,* 71–77. Sabean similarly argues for the importance of women in anchoring kin networks in early-modern Germany, *Kinship in Neckarhausen,* 379–97.

44. Goody, *The European Family,* 27–30.

45. Goody, *The European Family,* 11.

46. ". . . the Ecclesiastical impediments of consanguinity and affinity . . ." Phillips, *Putting Asunder,* 7.

47. Patricia Romero, "Encounter at the Cape: French Huguenots, the Khoi, and Other People of Color," *JCCH* 5:1 (2004), http://muse.jhu.edu/login?uri=/journals/journal_of_colonialism_and_colonial_history/voo5/5.1romero.html.

48. Romero, "Some Aspects of Family History," 32.

49. Boucher, *French Speakers at the Cape.*

50. Romero, "Some Aspects of Family History," 47.

51. My assessment comes from comparing Romero's marriage statistics among nine Huguenot families with my own work on frontier-based families. This initial impression certainly warrants further specific comparisons. The existing literature is contradictory. Heese asserts, "Most [Huguenots] arrived as family groups and the chances of unions with other cultural groups were, to begin with, minimal." (*Groupe*, Robertson trans, 53). This statement puts him at odds with Shell's demographic study, "Immigration," 3–4. Moreover, numerous marriages by Huguenot arrivals and their Cape-born children also seem to challenge this assumption. See Romero, "Some Aspects of Family History," 46.

52. Thera Wijsenbeek usefully considers other markers of community identity such as education, separate worship, and material culture in "Identity Lost: Huguenot Refugees in the Republic and its Former Colonies in North America and South Africa, 1650–1750: A Comparison," in *Contingent Lives: Social Identity and Material Culture in the VOC World*, ed. Nigel Worden, 91–109 (Cape Town: University of Cape Town Press, 2007), though I am not convinced by the portions of her argument that rely on the absence of recognizably "French" pieces of material culture at the Cape.

53. Romero, "Some Aspects of Family History;" Boucher, *French Speakers at the Cape*; Heese, *Groupe* (Robertson trans.), 53.

54. See Philips, "Putting Asunder," 355–57 for a discussion of changing marriage considerations in Europe, especially in the eighteenth century.

6. DOMESTICATING THE CEDARBERG

A Burger Family Story

One rented farm, a distant grazing permit, 100 cattle, 600 sheep, six horses, six slaves, one old ox wagon, an old plow, a wooden harrow, and assorted housewares.[1]

After 15 years of marriage lived on the frontier, Elsje van der Merwe faced widowhood with few creature comforts. She did, however, have access to land and labor, adequate farming implements, and enough livestock to sustain her household.[2] Whether through good management or good luck she prospered, as did her sons.

Elsje's story of economic success connects the van der Merwes and the Burgers in a tale of complicated accumulation. Farms, families, cattle, and housewares increased along the Olifants River over the course of the eighteenth century, while the growing community progressively displayed more signs of colonial orthodoxy. The Burger family history—including many van der Merwe wives—is emblematic of the ways in which allied households gradually established settler dominance in the Cedarberg. Although violent land alienation was admittedly a crucial feature of colonial settlement, the daily mechanics of conquest happened in homes. The intimate, quotidian structuring of daily survival in an uncertain landscape enabled gradual settler success. Its incremental progress was marked by increased creature comforts from one generation to the next, including the proliferation of European signs of status and civility. From a few iron cooking pots and pewter plates to copper tart pans and porcelain tea cups, the material success of frontier farmers was not just about extensive land claims and fat livestock, it was significantly about furniture, crockery, and other symbols that connected scattered homesteads to the heart of colonial society in Cape Town, and thus to European-derived cultural norms. Both women and men forged these connections, creating households

Fig. 6.1b. Willem Burger's Inventory, Transcribed
The entirety of Willem and Elsje's material possessions were summarized on one page.

Courtesy of the TANAP transcription project.
http://databases.tanap.net/mooc/

Inventories of the Orphan Chamber
Cape Town Archives Repository, South Africa

Reference no.: MOOC8/5.35

Testator(s):
Willem Burgert
12 Julij 1731

Inventaris en taxsatie van alle soodanige goederen als er naegelaeten en met er dood ontruijmt is, door den landbouwer Willem Burgert, door ons ondergeteekende Jacob van der Merwe voor de weeduwe, en Andries Burgert voor de kinderen, gedaen aen de 24 Rivieren den 12 Julij 1731, namentlijk

1 opstal geleegen over de 24 Rivieren gen:t Hauw Constant	100
6 mansslaeven rx: 70 t stuk	1260
100 runderbeesten rx:7 t stuk	2100
600 schaepen 2 t stuk	1200
6 paerden waeronder is eenige veulens 50 ied:r	300
1 oude osse waegen	100
huijsraed	50
1 oude ploeg met zijn toebehooren	15
1 houte egh	6
Somma	5131

Deezen boedel is niet te quaet ook heeft die niets te goet.

Vijff kinderen met naemen Barent, Schalk Willemsz:, Martje, Anna Sophia en Maria Magdalena Burgert. Komt ieder kint voor haer vaeders erfportie 509:1

Dat aldus geinventariceert datum den 12 Julij 1731

Als boedelhouster: Elsie van der Merwen weduwe Willem Burger

Jacobus van der Merwen

Andries Burgher

Publication is only permitted if the name of the repository and the reference number are mentioned.

and domestic space that came to mark their sites of settlement as colonial—not entirely European but rather distinctively "of the Cape."

Evidence of a colonial material culture, redolent of European aesthetics but regularly inflected with local character, emerges in household inventories. The frontier was a place of cross-cultural contact; some consequences of this interaction surface alongside the more obvious markers of European customs embedded in lists of household possessions. Estate inventories thus offer a way to examine settler households and their material culture. Read in conjunction with property records, tax rolls, and travelers' accounts, the inventories offer a unique, if partial, view into the domestic life of colonial settlers. These records describe material circumstances, evaluate wealth, enumerate children, suggest close relationships among other family members or neighbors, and hint at settlers' ideas about domesticity and class.

These inventories let us see, however darkly, inside settler homes, revealing aspects of what emerged as hegemonic over the course of 350 years of contested cultural interactions. Moreover, by looking inside the homes of a frontier region in the eighteenth century we begin to see how that hegemony was established. We can also see traces of subordinated people and their contributions to a creole society that colonists subsequently claimed as "Afrikaner." A focus on the domestic emphasizes the colonial, hybrid characteristics of South African history while it reveals the power latent in claiming connections to European culture. As Antoinette Burton and Ann Stoler eloquently argue, the colonial was created in the quotidian; power was embedded in the intimate. Thus, we need to challenge a presumed distance between state politics and family life and explore those tangled linkages. In this context, the personal and its records are an invaluable source for explaining how one society exercised political, economic, and social control over another.[3]

HOUSEHOLD INVENTORIES, HISTORICAL SOURCES

There is poignancy in a life represented by a list of things, an existence documented by assets, whether meager or abundant. Although the Burger family history is greater than the sum of its possessions, the probate remnants from three generations of family members illustrate trajectories—both geographic and economic—of frontier settlement. The Burgers' history is representative of patterns of land acquisition, material accumulation, marriage strategies, and household composition typical of frontier settlers.[4] Their inventories also reveal aspects of generational change and cast light on shifting frontier dynamics.

In a family's lifecycle, death was a moment of reckoning that produced a specific set of records, overseen and subsequently preserved by the state. Dutch practices of community property in marriage and partible family inheritance assured a surviving spouse half the couple's wealth and an equal portion for each child. When a marriage partner died and minor children survived, the government required an official tally of the couple's assets in order to ensure a fair accounting of the minors' portions.[5] The resulting household inventories are evidence of families' lived experience entwined with imperial power. Since colonial law only required an inventory if minors survived, they do not exist for all members of a family or for every frontier household. Consequently, inventories are particular relics of the state's regulation of inheritance, providing partial but valuable details about mundane daily life across class lines.[6]

There are important limits, though, to what these eighteenth-century records can say about colonial domesticity and household intimacy. The inventories show a proliferation of beds, for example, but do not comment on who slept in them. Successive generations of colonists owned increasing numbers of slaves, but the available sources unfortunately do not locate their labor. Typically slaves herded distant livestock (thus slept in the fields) or did agricultural work on the farm (and slept in the barn) or performed household chores (and slept in the kitchen or at the foot of the master's bed).[7] Archived documents identify specific families and put their households into a general colonial context, but do not provide enough concomitant detail to reconstruct all the facets of domestic relationships.

A historical reconstruction based on inventories skews the story toward European-descended settlers at the expense of the slaves and Khoisan indentured servants (*inboekselinge*) who were a fundamental part of colonial households, and whose ideas and actions were integral to colonial dialogues.[8] Without consistent prodding, these records tend to obscure Asian and African presence, but this disparity reminds us of the obstacles faced by subordinated peoples.

There is not yet enough scholarship on families, domesticity, and gender for eighteenth-century South Africa to locate specific labor or categorize it according to gender, class, race, or generation. Without egregious speculation, I cannot populate a house and farmyard with women and men at different, complementary work as Laurel Thatcher Ulrich does so well for colonial New England.[9] These records of quotidian existence do, however, symbolize the state's ability to regulate the material consequences of death,[10] showing just how powerful a merchant company acting like a prince could be, both in Cape Town and on the colonial frontier.

FRONTIER HOUSEHOLDS

After a half century of land claims, the Cedarberg—though still governed from a distance—was within the colonial orbit to the extent that travelers like Swedish botanist Carl Thunberg visited the region in 1773–74. He noted,

> Hospitality is carried to a great length among the farmers throughout all this coun-
> try, insomuch that a traveller [sic] may, without being at any expense either for board
> or lodging, pass a longer or shorter time with these people, who with the greatest
> cordiality receive and entertain strangers.[11]

The available range of that hospitality varied greatly, though. European visitors were alternately pleased and dismayed by the domesticity of frontier
settlers.

By the 1770s the Burger family could graciously host European visitors, a
capability that was not evident in the 1730s. Barend Burger and Helena Smit,
both born on the frontier, grew up to have more outward signs of conformity
to European-based norms than their parents did. This phenomenon is not ex-
plained by a wave of migrant stock farmers opening a region to settlement; subsequently surviving relative isolation and warfare; engaging in cross-cultural
contact with their slaves, indentured Khoisan servants, and indigenous Khoisan
inhabitants; eventually winning the fight; and finally claiming more land. Such
a conception of frontiers as serially opened then closed assumes rather than
explains the terms of conquest. Looking instead at the Cedarberg through Leonard Guelke's formulation of heterodox and orthodox frontiers brings into relief specific aspects of conflict and elements of identity formation. Starting from
this perspective also emphasizes that people variously contested this process,
both across colonial social boundaries and within groups of colonists, Khoisan,
and slaves.[12] Finally, exploring the dynamics of orthodoxy reveals the extent
to which conquest had a significant domestic component.

In the Cedarberg, we can measure colonial conquest by the proliferation of
tenable settler land claims, which were made household by household; increasing signs of European-inflected domesticity is tangible evidence of their success.
Thus the Cedarberg—which encompassed sites of violent conflict and provided
a harbor for runaway slaves and criminal fugitives in the 1730s and 1740s—was
by the end of the eighteenth century home to established farms supported by
families living according to norms that were more European than African.[13]

The most basic unit of settler social and economic organization, whether
in town or the frontier regions, was the household.[14] Frontier households centered on a married couple and their children, and included slaves, Khoisan
indentured servants, and other settlers, usually relatives.[15] Neighboring homesteads helped to sustain each other.[16] Linked by relationships determined by
women as much as by men, they were the locus of colonial frontier conquest.[17]

The clerks of the Dutch East India Company apparently did not need to de-
limit households. Recognizing marriages, land claims, and the annual agricultural production of married couples as well as individual adult men was sufficient
for their purposes. Beyond marriage and slave ownership, the settlers' organization of social and productive relationships went unrecorded by the VOC. So the

specific composition of frontier households is not documented in the colonial archives, but there is enough evidence from which to infer generalizations.[18]

These households were stable but fluid. Long-term loan farm claims, and an increase in the value of farm buildings listed in inventories indicates that leaseholders maintained a domestic base and improved the permanent structures on that land. The question of who actually lived in the farmhouse—and how many houses might have graced a single farm—remains unanswered, for now. Here I offer well-reasoned assumptions about who comprised households based on inventories and the annual census and taxation rosters (the opgaaf), a reconstruction in accord with contemporary travelers' descriptions.[19]

The opgaaf recorded first and foremost adult men. Free Chinese, emancipated slaves, and mixed-race individuals all appeared in its pages, though the preponderance of entries were for European-descended settlers. Each adult man merited a line in the annual register. Next to his name was space for his wife's, which in Dutch custom remained her maiden name. Then there were columns for enumeration: minor children separated into boys and girls, overseers, followed by slaves, livestock, crops, and weapons.[20] When boys reached adulthood, their names appeared in the register directly below their parents' names. Thus, a careful reading of the opgaaf shows a family's lifecycle. A young man appeared first in his father's household with possessions limited to some permutation of a horse, a pistol, a musket, and a sword. Sometimes he acquired livestock and/or slaves before a wife, but not always. After marriage, adult sons often stayed for several more years listed below their parents. Daughters typically went from unnamed tally marks to some other place in the opgaaf, recorded as someone's wife, starting the process again.

Grouping people into households according to the list presented in the opgaaf is speculative but tenable. Genealogies describe consanguineous relations, while estate inventories name spouses and children, both minor and adult. Freehold and loan farm records attest to land claims, but most stock-farming families had multiple permits, so property records alone do not necessarily indicate where people lived. And none of these sources is explicit about which people lived together. Nevertheless, repeated patterns in the opgaaf mirror documented family relationships and offer reasonable assumptions about neighbors.[21]

The opgaaf also enumerates slaves; household inventories name them individually, but neither source shows relationships among slaves or assigns labor. More importantly, these sources mask the presence of Khoisan indentured servants, or inboekselinge. Framing the Burger family history with sources focused on possessions consequently renders opaque the presence of subordinated members of the household, though the Burgers' dependents undoubtedly resisted encroaching colonial dominance.[22] There is ample evidence of desertion by slaves and Khoisan, as well as violence against masters in Cape colonial history.[23] Although specific instances of such action do not emerge in these household records, the inventories do suggest ways that slaves and Khoisan shaped colonial practice, but did not ultimately undermine colonial power.

The issue is not whether European-derived norms of household organization, family authority, and state governance prevailed, but how. One mechanism of dominance was the control of labor. Settler households composed of European-descended property owners and their dependents—slaves, Khoisan servants, and children—commandeered labor for domestic and agricultural tasks. Neither the work nor the workers emerge clearly in colonial sources, but the resulting surplus does—converted to material possessions that masters and mistresses decided to buy. So those who controlled labor also determined forms of social orthodoxy expressed in household goods.

MEET THE BURGERS

The history of the Burger family sheds light on this process of creating orthodox conformity and illustrates changing material circumstances from one generation to the next. The family's economic production remained focused on stock farming; their land-claim strategies, marriage patterns, and fundamental household composition remained consistent across two generations, but the standard of living as expressed in creature comforts rose significantly. What is more, markers of social status absent in one generation were clearly present in the next. The Burgers' growing livestock wealth and expanding land claims, ever further from the center of colonial authority, were accompanied by increasing displays of domestic niceties associated with social status in the metropole and in the colonial heart of Cape Town.[24]

GENERATION 1: BAREND BURGER AND MARIETJIE VAN DER MERWE

The Burger family's three-generation trek to the Cedarberg actually started in Lübeck, present-day Germany, with Barend Burger, a blacksmith who came to the Cape in the service of the VOC sometime toward the end of the seventeenth century. Around 1690 he married Marietjie van der Merwe. She was the third of 13 children born to Willem van der Merwe and Elsie Cloete.[25]

Barend and Marietjie settled in the Drakenstein district near present-day Paarl. The couple prospered, perhaps in part due to Barend's smithing skills; it is not likely that Marietjie brought a large inheritance to their marriage.[26] By the time of Barend's death in 1705, the couple owned three farms in freehold plus slaves, livestock, tools, and household goods.[27] Unfortunately, Barend's inventory is not very detailed. It appraises household and other goods together and assigns this collection the same worth as the farming equipment, each valued at 200 guilders, or the same as a single slave. Perhaps the tools included iron-working implements for Barend's trade. The bundle must also have included farming implements such as a plow and a harrow, a wagon, and tack for their 15 horses. Significantly, the inventory also shows the couple entwined in local credit networks, solvent despite large outstanding debts.

On paper, the Burgers were prosperous and embedded in the community at Drakenstein. Yet all five of their children moved north with the expanding frontier and settled on distant farms. Did Marietjie sell the Landskroon farm to settle her debt to the Drakenstein colony? When the children came of age, did they decide to liquidate the remains of the estate and take their inheritance in cash, livestock, or slaves rather than as a share of a land title? Whatever the reasons, Barend and Marietjie's children struck out for the frontier without visible signs that their parents had owned significant property. The eldest son, Barend, settled in the Land van Waveren (now Tulbagh).[28] Daughter Helena and her husband Jan Olivier also held loan farms there, as did the youngest sibling Jacobus.[29]

GENERATION 2: WILLEM BURGER AND ELSJE VAN DER MERWE; ANDRIES BURGER AND MARIA VAN DER MERWE; BAREND BURGER (THE ELDER) AND MARGARETHA PASMAN

Middle brothers Willem and Andries ventured farther afield, going as far north as the Twenty-four Rivers (present-day Porterville) to establish a farm. Though only a nominal 50 kilometers apart, the Twenty-four Rivers and the Land van Waveren are separated by mountains and are consequently distinct from one another.[30] The brothers made their first land claim jointly, which was an unusual documentary practice. Shared tenancy, shared residences, and the circulation of labor were common among frontier farmers and have precedent in European peasant farms, but the fact of jointly registering a farm was not typical at the Cape.[31] These farms remained registered to both brothers even after Willem branched out and made individual claims. It is unclear whether the brothers maintained separate households during this period or not, though they both married and had children.

Their mother, Marietjie van der Merwe, must have been close to her own brother, Schalk, and his wife Anna Prevot. As parents, they obviously influenced their children's selection of spouses. Willem and Andries married sisters Elsje and Maria van der Merwe, Marietjie's nieces (thus first cousins to their husbands). Their brother Barend's wife, Margaretha Pasman, was another cousin, the daughter of Marietjie's sister Sophia. [I consider these marriages from the van der Merwe's perspective in Chapter 5] Three of Marietjie's five children thus reinforced the connection between Burgers and van de Merwes first forged with her own marriage.[32] There were other available partners, so marriage to first cousins was not the result of a sparsely populated district, but rather a strategy chosen by many families that could, instead, have chosen mates from a wider circle. In the context of partible inheritance, marriage to close kin was one way of keeping farms from being parceled into tracts too small to be productive.[33]

The spatial relationship among the farms claimed by these three sons, the shared tenancy of Willem and Andries, and the geographical proximity of the farms they subsequently claimed individually suggest that the brothers and their wives maintained close ties. These bonds influenced where they claimed land, where they lived, and helped to sustain their presence on an often hostile frontier.

In 1726 Willem was among the pioneers in the Cedarberg, making the first claim to Misgunt on the Olifants River. Four years later, he claimed Houd Constant in the Twenty-four Rivers, near the farms he shared with Andries. Willem and Elsje established a house there, where he died the following year. After Willem's death, Andries assumed sole ownership of their shared farms near the Twenty-four Rivers while widow Elsje maintained the claims to Houd Constant and the distant Misgunt.[34]

Before Willem and Elsje moved to Houd Constant, it is not clear where the two Burger–van der Merwe couples lived or the composition of their households—if indeed they lived apart. Regardless of housing arrangements, the brothers' lives and families were tightly interconnected; in addition to shared property claims and marriage to sisters, had Willem lived long enough, they would have shared grandchildren, too.[35] The eventual marriage of Andries's son to Willem's daughter indicates a continued alliance between the Burger brothers and the van der Merwe sisters. Although both Willem and Maria died before their children wed, their surviving spouses continued to live on neighboring farms and saw the third consecutive generation of Burger–van der Merwe unions.[36]

INHERITANCE IN GENERATION 2: ELSJE, ANDRIES, AND MARGARETHA

Elsje van der Merwe managed the Houd Constant farm for two decades as the Widow Burger, presiding over increasing prosperity for herself and her children. Even after her sons came of age and married they remained in their mother's household.[37] As a widow running a farm and heading a household, Elsje was not unique. Unbalanced ratios of men to women meant most women got married; but since men tended to marry later than women, many of those brides were widowed.[38] While there are numerous examples of women amassing significant wealth through serial widowhood, there are also cautionary tales like that of twice-widowed Maria Vosloo, whose resources dissipated during her third marriage to a propertyless former Company sailor.[39]

Fig. 6.6. Status and Relationships Among Early Loan Farm Claimants

Source: CA: Receiver of Land Revenue series and L. Guelke RLR data; dV&P; H&L, Hoge

Status and Relationships Among Early Loan Farm Claimants

Date	Permit Holder	Status	Spouse	Other Relationships	Farm
1725	Johannes Ras	Cape-born, 1698	Anna Magdalena Senekal		Lange Valleij
1725	Francois Smit	?	Maria van Staden	Maria was Elsje van der Merwe's first cousin	Klein Valleij
1728					Lange Fontien
1725	Jurgen Hanekom	immigrant (Germany)	Johanna van den Bosch	Johanna was related by marriage to Maria van Staden	Modder Fontein
1725	Arnoldus Johannes Basson	Cape-born 1702	Catharina Olivier	grandmother was Angela van Bengal, a freed slave; cousin Arnoldus was Maria Vosloo's 2nd husband	Groot Valleij
1726	Willem Burger	Cape-born 1696 burgher	Elsje van der Merwe		Misgunt
1726	Pieter Willemsz van Heerden	immigrant (Netherlands)	Magdalena van der Merwe	Magdalena was Elsje van der Merwe's aunt	Ratel Fontein
1726	Daniel Pfeil	immigrant (Sweden)	Anna Maria Six v. Chandelier, in Bengal		Zeekoe Valleij
1727					Brakkefontein
1726	Alewijn Smit	Cape-born, 1695	Hester Becker	two of Smit's daughters marry two of Willem Burger's sons	Thien Rivieren
1726	Jan Steenkamp	immigrant (Netherlands)	Gesina Visser		Groene Valleij
1726	Jan Andries Dissel	immigrant (Germany)	Maria Vosloo	Maria related by marriage to Arnoldus Basson	Renoster Hoek
1728					Groote Zeekoe Valleij en Klein Valleij
1727	Johannes Lodewyk Putter	Cape-born, 1696	Anna van der Swaan		Halve Dorschvloer
1727	Jochem Koekemoer	?	Maria Putter	Maria was Jan Lodewyk Putter's sister	Hendrik van der Wats Gat
1727	Hendrik de Vries	immigrant (Netherlands)	Johanna van Es		Zeekoe Valleij

Fig. 6.6. (*continued*)

1728	Andries Kruger	immigrant (Germany) [1734 owned *Weltevreden* (nr. Stellenbosch)]	Zacharia Jansz Visser; second marriage to Maria Ras	Zacharia was the mother of Maria and Jan Lodewyk Putter; Maria Ras was Johannes Ras' sister	Lange Valleij
1728	Hendrik Cloete	Cape-born, 1696	unmarried?		Klein Valleij
1729	Jacob Mouton	immigrant (Flanders)	Francina Bevernagie		Berg Valleij
1729	Johannes Botha	Cape-born, burgher Drakenstein	Anna van der Merwe	Anna was Elsje van der Merwe's sister	Breede Rivier
1729	Guilliam Visagie	Cape-born, 1674	Gerritje Prinsloo		Gonjemans Kraal
1729	Juff Anna de Koning	Cape-born; mother was freed slave Angela van Bengal	Olof Bergh (deceased)		Sonquas Cloof en het Kley Gat [agter Piquetberg]

A widow with land and assets was an appealing match, either for younger men who could help run the farm and share in its produce, or for men of property who could offer a propitious alliance that would increase both partners' wealth. Assuming that Elsje had any such offers, she turned them down and headed her own household for at least twenty years.[40] Her eldest son was 14 at the time of his father's death, old enough for hard work but not yet an adult. Elsje did not hire an overseer, or knecht, but instead managed with the labor of her six slaves, her own children, probably unregistered Khoisan servants, and possibly the help of her neighboring brothers-in-law and nephews. Willem's and Andries' long joint tenancy, the eventual marriage of cousins Maria Magdalena and Willem Andriesz, the regular movement of sons and nephews among various family households, and the existence of neighborly kin networks that spanned the countryside suggest that although Elsje may have been widowed, she was not alone.

At the time of Willem's death, the couple already appeared slightly better off than the majority of frontier farmers in terms of productive assets, though not in creature comforts.[41] Their household goods were valued at only half the worth of their old ox wagon. However, they husbanded sufficient livestock and had converted some of that wealth into slaves and horses rather than housewares. Elsje inherited six slaves—all adult men—and six horses, so she had an unusually high concentration of labor power on her farm, particularly for the Cedarberg in the 1730s.

In contrast, when Willem's elder brother Barend died in 1729, his estate had only two slave men and no horses.[42] Barend and his wife Margaretha Pasman had less livestock, but more housewares—and more debt—than either of the two younger brothers who shared land claims at this time. At Barend's death, the community property consisted of a farmhouse, two slaves, livestock, one old ox wagon, and weapons. The housewares were described and together totaled 78 Cape guilders—more than the value of housewares for the other two Burger couples combined. In addition to enough cattle and sheep to be viable, and practical items like a milk can and a butter churn, Margaretha's widowhood was graced by porcelain and pewter plates, serving dishes, some pewter cutlery, and a tea kettle. The total appraised value of Margaretha and Barend's possessions was less than those of those of the other two Burger brothers at about the same time, but the estate had more domestic niceties. In the early years of frontier farming, it seems that spending on markers of civility rather than maintaining larger herds diminished a family's actual prosperity.

The two Burger–van der Merwe households of this generation were frugal in their domestic consumption compared to Barend and Margaretha. When Elsje's sister Maria died in 1725 or 1726, Maria and Andries's household had a similar material profile to that of Willem and Elsje documented five years later: adequate cattle and sheep, four horses, four slaves, basic agricultural implements, and limited domestic possessions. As was the case at Willem's death, Maria's household goods were not enumerated, though we might imagine cooking pots, a butter churn, and some basic furniture.[43] Given the tenor of travelers' accounts from later in the eighteenth century regarding the domestic comforts and civilities of frontier homes, the twenty Cape guilders worth of housewares recorded for Maria and Andries was indeed very meager.[44] However, subsequent opgaaf returns show Andries Burger, like Elsje, prospering in the years after his wife's death.[45]

European visitors to the Cape did not appreciate this preference for livestock and tools over housewares. Anders Sparrman was particularly scathing in his appraisal of a frontier farming household.

> The distance at which they are from the Cape, may, indeed, be some excuse for their having no other earthenware or china in their houses, but what was cracked and broken; but this, methinks, should not prevent them from being in possession of more than one or two old pewter pots, and some few plates of metal; so that two people are frequently obliged to eat out of one dish, using it besides for every different article of food that comes upon table . . . Each guest must bring his knife with him, and they frequently make use of their fingers instead of forks.[46]

Sparrman further comments on the homespun clothes, the lack of furniture, and the absence of social refinement, all of which he saw as a stark contrast to the large herds of livestock possessed by these same people. This perceived disjuncture between material wealth and markers of social status clearly disturbs Sparrman's Swedish-formed sensibilities, which did not adjust to colonial realities.[47] As Newton-King convincingly shows, Cape stock farmers preferred to keep their wealth in animals; they were likely to spend any surplus on agricultural implements before household goods.[48]

Having only rudimentary domestic possessions does not seem to have hampered Elsje van der Merwe, though. A decade after her husband's death, the Burgers' herds and flocks continued to flourish and the household acquired more slaves and horses. It appears from the census that both of Elsje's adult sons and her youngest daughter, Maria Magdalena, lived at the farm at Houd Constant. Their sister Anna Sophia and her husband lived either in the house or adjacent to it. Willem Janse van Rensburg did not have a loan farm claim in the 1740s or 1750s, so I assume the livestock that he and Anna Sophia declared in the 1743 opgaaf grazed at Houd Constant or Misgunt.[49]

Unfortunately there is no way to assess the changes in Elsje's domestic possessions over the course of two decades as a widow. The opgaaf shows her increasing prosperity in terms of land, slaves, and livestock and suggests she headed a large, thriving household as her children matured. The inventories of her sons indicate that they had more furniture, kitchen implements, farming tools, and slaves than she did. Since Elsje's household included her adult children, any indication of the pace and timing of housewares accumulation would reveal a great deal about generational transitions. When and how did a family go from having something on the order of a few pewter plates and a butter churn to *five dozen* porcelain plates and a coffee grinder?[50] Did Elsje see any of those niceties, or did her children acquire them only after her death?

GENERATION 3: BAREND BURGER (THE YOUNGER) AND HELENA SMIT; SCHALK WILLEM BURGER AND HESTER SMIT

Elsje's children Barend the Younger, Schalk Willem, Anna Sophia and Maria Magdalena all lived in her household after their marriages, but not all at once. Her sons did not claim slaves or livestock of their own until 1750, after nearly a decade of marriage. At this point Barend the Younger and Schalk Willem were either still part of the household or were their mother's closest neighbors, and Maria Magdalena resided nearby.[51] After 1750 all the siblings except Anna Sophia lived on neighboring loan farms. Having established a solid economic footing in the Burger household at Houd Constant, Barend and Schalk Willem—married to sisters Helena and Hester Smit—along with Willem Andriesz and Maria Magdalena eventually turned distant grazing farms along the Olifants River into permanent residences.[52]

Brothers Barend the Younger and Schalk Willem, their wives, and their sister—married to first cousin Willem Andriesz Burger—continued the expansion into the Cedarberg begun with Willem's 1726 claim to the Misgunt farm. This third generation accumulated more wealth than their parents had.

Though they ended up living even farther from Cape Town, they used some of this wealth to acquire both creature comforts, like beds and chairs, and luxuries such as books and glassware.

When Barend the Younger died in 1770, he left Helena Smit with three adult and three minor children plus a significant estate. A farmhouse, six men and five women slaves, a wagon, building tools, carpenter's tools, a brandy still, cooking pots, chairs, a four-poster bed, shelves, cupboards and chests were among the goods inventoried. The opgaaf indicates their increased agricultural productivity; the estate inventories reveal what that meant for life at home.

Couples made choices about how to spend this accumulated wealth, though they did not leave records that reveal who, exactly, made which choices. Furniture, cookware, crockery, wagons, harnesses, milk cans, and brandy stills were not foregone conclusions, but had to be evaluated against other possible expenses such as grain or breeding stock.[53] Moreover, acquiring any material possessions meant selling or exchanging livestock, which many stock farmers were reluctant to do.[54] Showing a general increase in consumption over the course of the eighteenth century indicates the importance of the domestic realm for creating colonial identities and claiming territory, but it does not suggest why some families purchased more than others, or who in the household controlled the purse strings.

CONSUMPTION IN GENERATION 3: AT HOME
ON HALVE DORSCHVLOER

Even without details of domestic decision making, we can see the results preserved in the property claims and inventories of the third generation of Burgers. At the time of Schalk Willem's death, he and Hester Smit were firmly established in the Cedarberg with all of their 11 children still living. Schalk Willem had converted Halve Dorschvloer from a loan farm to freehold property in 1763; he maintained the adjacent Misgunt as a loan farm, and in 1782 claimed three additional loan farms.[55] The assessed value of Halve Dorschvloer was nearly the amount of his parents' entire possessions in 1731, but the farm was only about 15 percent of his estate (see Figure 6.7). In fact, Schalk Willem was owed more in outstanding loans than his parents had declared as assets in their report to the VOC.[56]

In addition to land, livestock, 25 slaves, and considerable credit due to them, Hester and Schalk Willem had the trappings of an industrious farm and a comfortable home. For working the land they had two plows and a harrow, for transportation three wagons, one of them new but still without a yoke or reins, suggesting they were in the process of equipping themselves to move more goods or people. They actively fermented wine and brewed beer, evidenced by the assortment of casks and barrels, some still full. They even

Fig. 6.7. Schalk Willem Burger's Estate, 1782

These categories are explicit in the inventory, though the subtotals are my calculations.

Source: CA: MOOC 8/49.25 Estate Inventory of Schalk Willem Burger, 24 Sept. 1782.

Schalk Willem Burger's Estate, 1782

Category	Value (in Rixdollars)
Land	2,166.32
Livestock	2,298.32
Labor (slaves)	4,000.00
Farm implements	572.00
Household goods	285.00
Outstanding loans	1,930.00
Subtotal	11,252.16
Arrears owed to VOC	-258.00
TOTAL ESTATE	10,994.16

had a specialized beer jug (*bierpyp*). Whereas the previous generation had one butter churn for each couple, Hester and Schalk Willem had two, along with two butter vats. They headed a large household, which undoubtedly supplied the labor to stir the churns as well as eager stomachs for the dairy products. Empty grain sacks, a vat with tar, a whetstone, carpenter's tools, and a used saddle all further attest to working life and the needs of agricultural production.

The largest proportion of the inventory, though it has the lowest total value, is devoted to household furnishings. Beds, a dining table, chairs, several chests and cupboards, a Bible and five other books, plus a daunting array of cooking and serving dishes attest to multiple markers of social status and civility. The Bible is significant, described in the inventory as "big," the kind of imposing tome from which the patriarch would have read to the rest of the household as part of regular devotional practice.[57] The Dutch Reformed Church did not establish a *gemeente* (congregation) in the Cedarberg until 1826, so evidence of religious devotion at home was an important part of claiming membership in a wider settler community. The extent to which that community met European expectations was uneven, though.

Eighteenth-century travelers' accounts, as well as especially descriptive depositions in a 1742 criminal investigation, variously describe slaves, servants, visitors, and family members sleeping by the kitchen hearth. The depositions, in particular, portray shared sleeping space on the floor of common rooms.[58] Sparrman, ever critical, corroborates the practice,

> Again, when we had an opportunity of taking a night's lodging at a peasant's house, we were for the most part rather worse lodged [than outdoors]. In most places the house consisted of two rooms only, with the floor of earth or loam. The interior one of these was used for a bed-chamber for the boor [sic] himself, with his wife and children. The outer one composed the kitchen, in a corner of which they spread a mat for us on the floor; and in this generally consisted of all the conveniencies [sic] the good folks could afford us. As for the rest we were obliged to make our beds of our saddles and great coats, together with a coverlet we brought with us. The Hottentots [Khoisan] of either sex, young and old, who were in the boor's [sic] service, always choose to sleep in the fireplace.[59]

When Schalk Willem died, Hester had six proper beds and only two minor children; though shared householding suggests that older children and/or nieces and nephews might well have been in residence, too.[60] Had Sparrman come to Halve Dorschvloer and Misgunt as Thunberg did, he might have been offered a bed and not a piece of floor by the hearth.

At Halve Doerschvloer, Hester would have served dinner at the table, using some of her 20 porcelain serving bowls and laying a place for each diner; she had 60 porcelain plates plus 16 pewter spoons, 12 knives, and 12 forks! The house had wine glasses, tea cups, and an earthenware tray with five ceramic wine cups, an item clearly meant for formal serving. Apparently guests at Halve Dorschvloer could anticipate coffee and tea. In addition to a coffee grinder, the household had both copper and pewter coffee pots, perhaps allocated for special occasions and daily use. Depending on who was present, a slave could have served tea in one of two porcelain or four metal teapots, bringing more hot water in the two pewter serving kettles.

What kind of tea was on offer, though? Did the Burgers drink black tea imported from Asia, or local *rooibos*, a plant still used to make herbal infusions and widely drunk in South Africa?[61] This unanswered question hints at Khoisan presence and at the transfer of local knowledge implicit in colonial domestic life. From the ambiguity of tea to the farmers' long-horned cattle and fat-tailed sheep originally bred from indigenous stock, these household inventories actually reflect African elements of colonial life, though they are listed in terms that might otherwise be read as strictly European, like crockery and farm animals.

The kitchen, too, suggests local adaptations lurking among the European cookware. There was an iron kettle for boiling water on the fire, in addition to a variety of practical cooking tools. Iron cooking pots, frying pans, griddles, and fire tongs were supplemented with a copper tart pan and a small copper saucepan. There were water buckets, assorted bottles and flasks, a saltcellar, and a mortar and pestle. Who used the mortar and pestle—a slave, a Khoisan servant, Hester, or one of her daughters? What did they grind there—local herbs, spices from the VOC trade, or medicinal *buchu* collected on the farm by Khoisan servants?

This kitchen was outfitted for more than just rudimentary cooking; did the copper tart pan get used every day? The kitchen was also equipped for bulk work. Were the ten "assorted iron pots" of great variety, or were they on hand for stewing big quantities of *breedie*, a Cape lamb stew inflected with Asian spices? What recipes went into making this and other food? What combinations of spices, flavorings, and cooking methods were most often invoked? With slaves from across the Indian Ocean, the cooking skills and food habits at Halve Dorschvloer were likely to be diverse.[62] Although some of the 25 slaves must have tended livestock on distant grazing claims, the farm's kitchen undoubtedly fed many mouths each day. The house had an abundance of porcelain plates and serving bowls, but none in metal. Did the slaves eat from porcelain, or did they have their own cooking and eating utensils? Even without answers to these questions, the inventory nevertheless shows that Schalk Willem and Hester's household was equipped to prepare a variety of food and serve it graciously.

Without clues about the daily disposition of labor, and without descriptions of household linens and clothing, it is tenuous (though tempting) to suppose the household allocated the most arduous domestic work to slaves, leaving Hester and her daughters sewing or tending fowl while Schalk Willem rode out to check on distantly pastured livestock.[63] Since some slaves were known for their fine needlework, perhaps subordinates shouldered this labor, too. This uncertainty emphasizes the need for more research on daily life at the Cape in the eighteenth century.[64] The artifacts of a household offer a way to begin.

In Hester and Schalk Willem's sitting room, guests and family members could warm up with copper coal holders, read by the light of candles held in copper candlesticks, and extinguish the flame with a copper snuffer. The extent and variety of these household goods suggests acquisition for function as well as for display. The furniture—beds and tables and chairs—provided basic comfort in a European-style house. Halve Dorschvloer, however, had more than basics. Six teapots and two coffee pots might simply be the number required in a family of 11 children and with close kin as near neighbors, but in that case an equal number of pewter pots would have served the same purpose. When the inventory was compiled, someone took great pains to differentiate among copper, porcelain, glass, earthenware, pewter, iron, and wood. The recorder saw both value and status in the material as well as the function of the items.

Schalk Willem and Hester had wine glasses and earthenware wine cups, porcelain teacups with saucers and ordinary teacups, iron kettles, earthenware kettles, and pewter serving kettles. This differentiation suggests a con-

scious appreciation of European attitudes about status and civility. Did the
Burgers see the graceful manor houses of the winelands gentry when they
took cattle to market? Were they entertained at tables more lavish and ornate
than their own? Did a *smous* (traveling salesman) present a coveted item with
a flourish—or suggest that it should be coveted in the first place?[65] Regardless
of how various domestic amenities made their way to Halve Dorschvloer, the
Burgers clearly possessed niceties that Sparrman saw lacking in other frontier
homes. Their consumption was limited, though: their candlesticks and candle
snuffer were copper, not silver.

HOUSEHOLD BELONGINGS, FRONTIER DYNAMICS: CHANGE OVER GENERATIONS

The second and third generations of Burgers were frontier families.[66] Despite
violent hostilities and the initially meager circumstances of Barend the Elder,
Willem, and Andries, the frontier became a place of increasing prosperity
for the brothers, their wives, and especially their children, dramatically illus-
trated by the difference in estate inventories from one generation to the next.

The differences between the inventories that marked the start of widowhood for Margaretha Pasman and Elsje van der Merwe in the second generation
are notable, but not nearly as dramatic as the difference between Elsje and her
daughters-in-law. In 1731 it appears that Elsje was barely literate. Her signature is
difficult to discern on the document, yet she subsequently made land claims,
paid rent, and appeared in the opgaaf as a head of a household for years. As with
the lump-sum declaration of her household goods, this documentary interface
thwarts the opportunity for a more complete picture of Elsje. We are left with
just a glimpse, retreating to interpretations of silence and absence. [67]

Elsje's brother Jacobus and brother-in-law Andries also witnessed the estate settlement; they both signed their names with difficulty.[68] Her sister-in-
law Margaretha signed Barend's inventory, but with a shaky hand. The third
generation, however, signed with a flourish. Both Hester and Helena Smit had
mastered handwriting—at least as far as their names. The opportunity for
some education came with other trappings of better living. Greater agricultural wealth, increased domestic comforts, some markers of European civility, and a few luxuries differentiate the Burgers living in the last quarter of the
eighteenth century from their forebears who died before 1750. The archival
records changed, too, making a transition from short, perfunctory lists to orderly pages of carefully described household and farmyard equipment.

Barend the Younger, Schalk Willem, and their mother Elsje were frontier farmers with sustained claims to a residential farm; their wealth derived
from running cattle and sheep at home and on more distant grazing permits. The brothers shared a significant transition, living in changed material

circumstances at the two moments when the state intervened to document the entirety of their family's possessions—when their father died and at the time of their own deaths.[69]

The third generation of Burger men lived longer than their predecessors, giving them more time to produce and accumulate before the state counted their assets. The simple fact of working longer and having more possessions does not explain what the families acquired, though. In variety and bulk, the ten pots, two griddles, and four frying pans of Halve Dorschvloer represent both a quantitative and qualitative change from the kitchen described in Barend Burger the Elder's inventory of 1729, which had but three iron pots and a kettle. Widow Margaretha Pasman's few goods were apparently more than those of her sisters-in-law, whose housewares were too paltry even to be itemized. Thus, we see a clear generational difference in the material circumstances of brothers Barend the Elder, Willem, and Andries compared to Willem's sons: Barend the Younger and Schalk Willem.

The difference is not only in the total value of the community property assessed at the death of a spouse, but in what that increased wealth meant in terms of daily living. The small lump-sum assessment of housewares reported by sisters Maria and Elsje van der Merwe in the 1720s and 1730s suggests a different class position than the more elaborate inventories of sisters Helena and Hester Smit in the 1770s and 1780s, yet all four women were Burger wives living in the contested zone of a colonial frontier. In spite of the sizable land claims and evident prosperity associated with Schalk Willem and Hester, they were no more a part of the Cape Gentry than their parents or grandparents.[70] They were, instead, affluent stock farmers who chose to display some of their wealth through domestic consumption, the description of which is detailed in household inventories that differ significantly from those of their parents' generation of frontier settlers.

This generational difference in inventories has several possible explanations. The first is clearly material: Hester and Helena owned more possessions than their mother-in-law Elsje or Elsje's sister Maria had, so it was not possible just to estimate the household contents and say "about fifty guilders," which was the value of a horse, and less than the value of an adult male slave.[71] An equitable inheritance process demanded a better accounting of the household for Hester and Helena. A second possible explanation is change over time: record keeping got more accurate in the half century between the inventories of two successive generations. This explanation, however, does not account for the careful, detailed inventories of other estates recorded in the 1720s and 1730s.

A third possible explanation is embedded in frontier issues. Perhaps Houd Constant was just too far from the Company's administrative gaze in 1731, and so a more lax standard of record keeping applied. However, other evidence suggests that although the Company may have tolerated long absences from formal reporting, officials did not tolerate a complete dereliction of the duty to account for production, and ultimately to pay.[72] Despite the greater distance between their farms and the magistrate, the Burger sons' inventories were more detailed than that of their father or their Aunt Maria, who died closer to the seat of colonial administration.

In this instance, the frontier was less about spatial relationships or geographic distance than about heterodox and orthodox connections to the Cape. Stock-farming families did not move to the Cedarberg with a homogenous bundle of European norms that they fought to impose in a hostile environment; they certainly did not move with many pieces of European material culture. Instead they gradually acquired furniture, serving ware, crockery, and utensils to complement necessary cooking and farming tools. Orthodoxy, symbolized by domestic markers of status and respectability derived from European customs, came a generation after initial colonial land claims.[73] Significantly, evidence of this cultural orthodoxy appears in archival sources after a period of contested frontier life. This eventual colonial conquest was not a monolithic, triumphal march toward a foreordained conclusion; rather context, contingency, and local detail shaped various colonial situations.[74]

This settler orthodoxy evident in household inventories was achieved through domestic relationships, not through military conquest, and not through direct state intervention.[75] Men and women formed families and maintained homesteads, transitioning from rudimentary survival based on raising livestock to a material culture that was recognizably rooted in European norms. Changing household possessions suggest changes in the ways people managed and experienced daily life. The material accoutrements owned by families and the monetary value assigned to these goods complicates our understanding of a colonial frontier as contact zone.[76] This reading of inventories enriches Guelke's presentation of orthodoxy, moving his characterization beyond the realm of law-abiding, church-going inhabitants to also describe people who ate off porcelain plates and slept in beds, people who in the mundane aspects of their life claimed affinity with the dominant colonial culture.

Guelke points out the significant difference between the frontier and the more settled areas near Cape Town, "Unlike the arable areas, where wealth became even more unevenly distributed and a small class of very rich farmers emerged, in the stock farming regions of the open frontier most people were rather poor, although they lived in rough comfort and were free of large debts."[77] Judging from household inventories, there was a wide range of "rough comfort," with household goods increasing in number, diversity, and refinement commensurate with increasing overall wealth measured in terms of land and livestock.[78] As this analysis of Burger family inventories shows, greater overall prosperity was displayed at home through markers of a European-inspired domesticity.

Late in the 1720s and in 1731 the inventories of Barend Burger, Maria van der Merwe, and Willem Burger depict the Land van Waveren and Twenty-four Rivers as regions of economic marginality, with stock farmers living in the roughest of comforts and reporting the minimum to the state. Within a generation the more distant and environmentally more marginal Cedarberg was transformed into a frontier of economic opportunity, affording the Burgers a material position that placed them among the most well-off frontier farmers.[79] The more affluent third generation certainly did not "live like beasts."[80] In fact, their domestic possessions solidly proclaimed their connection to colonial social order rooted in Cape Town. Moreover, their detailed estate inventories reflect a more responsible reporting to the state. Within the VOC archive, both Barend the Younger and Schalk Willem have properly formatted, formally constituted inventories as well as "rough drafts," written by a less-skillful hand and omitting details such as the individual names of children and slaves.[81]

This transition in one generation from a materially marginal, but economically viable, heterodox frontier to a prosperous, orthodox frontier located in a region of even greater geographic isolation suggests that we need to think about frontier as a temporal as well as spatial and cultural concept. For the Burgers, the frontier was a time as well as a place of accelerated change, exemplified by family choices to spend increasing wealth on domestic goods that provided both greater comfort and social significance.

Despite moving through the landscape at the pace of an ox wagon, successive generations of settlers likely experienced frontier life as a period of rapid transformation. The material circumstances of the Burgers and other families altered markedly from one generation to the next. For Barend the smith, life on a colonial frontier meant economic accumulation happened faster than if he either had remained in service with the VOC or continued living in Lübeck. His children and grandchildren experienced even greater shifts of fortune. For the Burgers, as for other settlers, the possibilities—and challenges—of accelerated change were not tied to specific dates, such as the 1680s, the late 1730s, or the 1780s—periods of significant transformation in early settlement history. Instead, particular families or individuals experienced dramatic changes throughout the eighteenth century. Those changes were tied to being part of frontier dynamics—their location in space—rather than being tied to a particular calendar.[82] Thus the periodization of intense transformation is contingent; the temporal aspects of the frontier figure as the pace of change rather than being ascribed to universal dates.

Throughout this prolonged period of transformation, colonial identity was contested—and in fact continues to be debated in present-day South Africa.[83] Frontier settlers were at pains to distinguish themselves from indigenous Khoisan and to establish affinities with the culture linked to state power in Cape Town.[84] Markers of European-derived status such as furniture, porcelain tableware, formal serving pieces, copper housewares, books, and the Bible all suggest that settlers with enough means strove to create domestic space recognizable to a Europeanized gaze. There is some irony in the use of porcelain—probably from Asia—as a status marker on a European scale. Sitting astride the trade route from the Indies, Cape Town had access to VOC imports; some of these luxury goods clearly made it from the port to the hinterland, permitting frontier people to eat in style.[85]

The presence on the farm of 25 slaves from places as diverse as Malabar, Timor, Madagascar, and Mozambique provides irrefutable proof that Halve Dorschvloer was far removed from polders of Zeeland or even the Baltic entrepot of Lübeck. This frontier farm was hybrid space. One of the adult slave women and all of the farm's nine slave children were born at the Cape, their toponym "of the Cape" an embodiment of their creole status. They were born in the colony, just like their masters, but unlike the Burgers, the slaves could not claim affinity to European-based hegemonic power through religion or shared material culture.

FRONTIER DOMESTICITY
AND COLONIAL IDENTITIES

A careful reading of three generations of Burger family estates illuminates domestic aspects of settler identity in the Cedarberg. From one generation to the next we see stock farmers claiming more territory and firmly establishing their presence in a frontier region through European-style houses respectably furnished. Along with porcelain teapots and copper candle snuffers, the inventories locate Indian Ocean slaves in frontier households, while collateral sources indicate the presence of Khoisan inboekselinge. As servants, they undoubtedly worked with these objects of European and colonial material culture; their labor certainly helped the Burgers to procure refined housewares. In a kitchen stocked with local herbs and exotic spices, these Africans and Asians contributed to a culture that excluded them from belonging. As subordinated laborers, they were consciously described outside the settler community, but their knowledge and effort supported their master's display of European-inflected domesticity.

For the Cedarberg, as for many other colonial frontiers, the "contact zone" needs to be rethought to include homes, hearths, and barnyards—places of quotidian encounter among Africans, Asians, Europeans, and their locally-born children. Colonists need to be conceptualized as families—women, men, and children—in addition to the male functionaries who created the official archives.[86] Trading posts, battlefields, and landdrosts' offices were undeniably crucibles of cross-cultural exchange. However, the norms claimed and recognizable as European that predominated in South Africa for three and half centuries were shaped as much in domestic as in civic realms. The history of the Burgers and their belongings powerfully proves this point.

In the records of their deaths, these South Africans disrupt the neat narratives of centralized power and state hegemony associated with European expansion in general and the history of the VOC in particular. The life histories revealed in the Burger family estate inventories firmly place women and domesticity at the center of colonial encounters. Their stories suggest the importance of settler household composition for frontier survival, the persistence of marriage strategies connecting men, women, and landed property across generations, and the conscious efforts of third-generation frontier people to demonstrate their connection to the locus of colonial power, authority, and respectability in Cape Town. Thus, we see not a frontier boundary making steady progress across the landscape, or a series of contested zones sequentially opened and closed, but rather a process of gradual conformity, a presence measured in generations and, in this case, marked by increasing displays of orthodoxy in homes. Margaretha Pasman's porcelain plates and Hester Smit's copper saucepan are symbols of frontier conflict, iconic representations of the culture they helped to forge, household by household, along the Olifants River.

NOTES

1. CA: MOOC 8/5.35, Estate Inventory of Willem Burger, 12 July 1731. CA: RLR 1/38/25, loan farm permit for Houd Constant, 16 Nov. 1730; CA: RLR 2/9/18, loan farm permit for Misgunt, 18 Sept. 1730.

2. Guelke estimates a stock farmer's minimum needs as a horse, a wagon, 20 cattle, and 50 sheep, amounting to about 1,000 Cape guilders in "Freehold Farmers," 87.

3. Ann Laura Stoler, *Carnal Knowledge and Imperial Power: Race and the Intimate in Colonial Rule* (Berkeley: University of California Press, 2002), 9, 12–14; Antoinette Burton, *Dwelling in the Archive: Women Writing House, Home and History in Late Colonial India* (Oxford: Oxford University Press, 2003), 5–7.

4. Trends in the Cedarberg-area inventories mirror those from Eastern Cape frontier households reported by Susan Newton-King, *Masters and Servants on the Eastern Cape Frontier, 1760–1803* (Cambridge: Cambridge University Press, 1999). Frontier inventories differ from the more detailed records of established colonial residences in Cape Town; for Cape Town, see Antonia Malan, "Households of the Cape, 1750 to 1850: Inventories and the Archaeological Record" (PhD diss., University of Cape Town, 1993). Complete transcripts of estate inventories in the Cape Archives have recently been made available online; see Toward a New Age of Partnership (TANAP) Web site: http://www.tanap.net/content/activities/documents/Orphan_Chamber-Cape_of_Good_Hope/index.htm (accessed 28 July 2006).

5. Secretary William Bird, *State of the Cape of Good Hope in 1822*, facsimile reprint (Cape Town: Struik, 1966); Robert Ross, *Beyond the Pale: Essays on the Histories of Colonial South Africa* (Johannesburg: Witwatersrand University Press, 1994), 139–40.

6. For practical guidance in working with inventories, auction papers, and other estate documents, see Carohn Cornell and Antonia Malan, *Household Inventories at the Cape: A Guide for Beginner Researchers* (Cape Town: UCT Historical Studies Department, 2005).

7. Robert C.-H. Shell, *Children of Bondage: A Social History of the Slave Society at the Cape of Good Hope, 1652–1838* (Hannover and London: University Press of New England, 1994).

8. Examples of these dialogues include Russel Viljoen, "Indentured Labour and Khoikhoi 'Equality' Before the Law in Cape Colonial Society, South Africa: The Case of Jan Paerl, c. 1796," *Itinerario* 29:3 (2005), 54–72; Patricia van der Spuy, "'Making Himself Master': Galant's Rebellion Revisted," *SAHJ* 34 (1996), 1–28; John Mason, "Hendrik Albertus and His Ex-Slave Mey: A Drama in Three Acts," *JAH* 31:3 (1990), 423–45.

9. Laurel Thatcher Ulrich, *Good Wives: Image and Reality in the Lives of Women in Northern New England, 1650–1750* (New York: Alfred A. Knopf, 1982); Pamela Scully, *Liberating the Family: Gender and British Slave Emancipation in the Rural Western Cape, South Africa, 1823–1853* (Portsmouth: Heinemann, 1997) provides a solid analysis of gendered household labor in the nineteenth century. In *Children of Bondage*, Shell explores the gendered and sexualized nature of master-slave relationships, but without specific evidence from frontier regions, I hesitate to apply his conclusions rooted in the more settled areas of the Cape directly to the Cedarberg, where there was a significant Khoisan labor pool.

10. Achille Mbembe, "Necropolitics," *Public Culture* 15, no. 1 (2003), 11–40; Mbembe, "The Power of the Archives and its Limits," in *Refiguring the Archive*, ed. Carolyn Hamilton, et al., (Cape Town: David Philip, 2002), 19–26.

11. Carl Peter Thunberg, *Travels at the Cape of Good Hope, 1772–1775*, trans. J.& I. Rudner, ed. V.S. Forbes (Cape Town: Van Riebeeck Society, 1986), 51, 191.

12. Guelke, "The Making of Two Frontier Communities: Cape Colony in the Eighteenth Century," *Historical Reflections/Reflexions Historiques* 12: 3 (1985), 419–48. Hermann Giliomee articulates an open and closed frontier model in "Processes in Development of the Southern African Frontier," in *The Frontier in History: North American and South Africa Compared,* eds. Howard Lamar and Leonard Thompson, (New Haven: Yale University Press, 1981), 19–26. For a more detailed historiography of the frontier in South African scholarship, see Chapter 2.

13. On frontier violence, see Penn, *The Forgotten Frontier,* esp. Chapter 4. On desertion, see Penn, *Rogues, Rebels and Runaways.*

14. For South Africa, see Ross on "co-resident groups," *Beyond the Pale,* 146–47. Relevant comparisons of early modern European social, political, and economic households include Jan de Vries and Ad van der Woude, *The First Modern Economy: Success, Failure and Perseverance of the Dutch Economy, 1500–1815* (Cambridge: Cambridge University Press, 1997), 160–64; Ulrike Strasser, *State of Virginity: Gender, Religion and Politics in an Early Modern Catholic State* (Ann Arbor: University of Michigan

Press, 2004), 8; Sarah Hanley, "Engendering the State: Family Formation and State Building in Early Modern Europe," *French Historical Studies* 16:1 (1989), 4–27.

15. Ross, *Beyond the Pale*, 146, n34.

16. In frontier areas, I use "neighboring" to describe the closest farms, which in some cases were adjacent land claims (along a river, for example) or in other cases might have been as much as a half-day's ride away on horseback.

17. Wayne Dooling also recently argued for the importance of women in facilitating the transfer of landed estates in "The Making of a Colonial Elite: Property, Family and Landed Stability in the Cape Colony, c. 1750–1834," *JSAS* 31:1 (2005), 159.

18. Given the limited specific attention paid to households in recent colonial Cape scholarship, however, future research on families, domestic production, and master-servant relationships will undoubtedly challenge, modify, or confirm my assessments made based on evidence from the Cedarberg.

Penn's "domestic group" is frustratingly vague, *The Forgotten Frontier,* 109. Newton-King's use of Wall's definition that a "co-resident domestic group" is a household if the residents ate at least one meal a day together provides some structure, but she does not attempt specific reconstructions, *Masters and Servants,* 154, n25. R. Wall, ed. *Family Forms in Historic Europe* (Cambridge: Cambridge University Press, 1983). More importantly, this definition is not completely satisfactory for pastoralists, some of whose shared assets, servants/slaves, or family members might be away with flocks and herds during transhumant seasons, but still were materially and emotionally connected to people "back home" sharing a daily meal. For example, see Emmanuel Le Roy Ladurie, *Montaillou: The Promised Land of Error,* trans. Barbara Bray (New York: Vintage, 1979). Robert C.-H. Shell clearly situates slaves in colonial households, but does not consider the extent of settler coresidence, or the presence of Khoisan servants in *Children of Bondage,* 303–304. Pamela Scully clearly articulates the tensions between slaves' and masters' family formations in *Liberating the Family?*

19. For example, O.F. Mentzel, *A Geographical and Topographical Description of the Cape of Good Hope (1787),* trans. G. V. Marais and J. Hoge, ed. H. J. Mandelbrote, (Cape Town: Van Riebeeck Society, 1944). For a modern-day assessment, see Guelke, "The Anatomy of a Colonial Settler Population: Cape Colony, 1657–1750," *IJAHS* 21:3 (1988), 453–73.

20. To my knowledge, a widow never appears in the opgaaf as having weapons, even if her husband had them the previous year. Given the regularity with which weapons appear in the opgaaf, they are correspondingly missing from most frontier family inventories and auction records. The appearance of weapons in the opgaaf may have served as a check against the muster rolls (*monster rollen*) of the burgher militia, a way for the Company to gauge potential military resources. Further inquiry into the recording, representation, and actual deployment of weapons along with further analysis of men's coming-of-age and economic independence will likely add to the burgeoning literature on colonial masculinities. For example, see Sandra Swart, "A Boer, His Gun and His Wife are Three Things Always Together," *JSAS* 24:4 (Dec. 1998), 737–51.

21. Ross, *Beyond the Pale* 145–47, esp. n34, which points out that Newton-King disagrees with the opgaaf's utility for household analyses.

22. Ranajit Guha, *Dominance Without Hegemony: History and Power in Colonial India* (Cambridge: Harvard University Press, 1997); James C. Scott, *Domination and the Arts of Resistance: Hidden Transcripts* (New Haven: Yale University Press, 1990).

23. Robert Ross, *Cape of Torments: Slavery and Resistance in South Africa* (London: Routledge & Keegan Paul, 1983); Nigel Worden, *Slavery in Dutch South Africa* (Cambridge: Cambridge University Press, 1985). For a broader discussion of desertion, see Nigel Penn, "Fugitives on the Cape Frontier" and "Droster Gangs of the Bokkeveld and Roggeveld, 1770–1800," both in *Rogues, Rebels and Runaways*, 73–100, 147–66. Desertion by slaves typically was punished by flogging, branding, and work in chains for varying numbers of years; for example ARA: VOC 10934, *OBP*, 57, the case against Titus van Madagascar and others, 27 Oct. 1735; ARA: VOC 10934, *OBP*, 32 the case against Valentijn van de Caab and others, 12 May 1735. In the first half of the eighteenth century it appears only deserters who were involved in the murder or death of a nondeserter were broken; for example ARA: VOC 10925, *OBP*, 14, the case against Cupido van Bengal and others, 18 Dec. 1727. Deserters charged with theft typically were hanged, for example ARA: VOC 4158: 764 the case against Alij van Madagascar and others, 19 Sept. 1743. European deserters were let off more easily than slaves, often only paying court costs, for example, ARA: VOC 10935, *OBP*,: 23, Jan Baptist Pierre, 14 Apr., 1735; ARA: VOC 10935, *OBP*, 4 Johan van Spanghoek; 10935:81 Pieter de Pape van Jugrien, 11 Aug. 1736.

24. Nigel Worden, et al., *Cape Town: The Making of a City* (Cape Town: David Philip, 1998); Simon Schama, *The Embarrassment of Riches: An Interpretation of Dutch Culture in the Golden Age* (London: Fontana Press, 1991).

25. dV&P, 1981: 119, 557 & 569.

26. Susan Newton-King, "In Search of Notability: The Antecedents of David van der Merwe of the Koue Bokkeveld," *Collected Seminar Papers* (University of London, Institute for Commonwealth Studies), No. 48, The Societies of Southern Africa in the Nineteenth and Twentieth Centuries, vol. 20, p. 32; Newton-King, personal communication, 2 Nov. 2006; Heese, *Groep Sonder Grense* (Robertson trans.), 54

27. CA: MOOC 8/2.3, Estate Inventory of Barent Burger, 1 Oct. 1705.

28. For six years he held the lease on Twee Jonge Gezellen: CA: RLR 6:19, 6 Feb. 1725. CA: RLR 8:218, 19 Feb. 1729 (to 1731 per L. Guelke data). After his death, his widow Margaretha Pasman kept the farm for another ten years CA: RLR 9:145, 17 Feb. 1731 (to 1741 per L. Guelke data). Their son Willem appears next to her in the 1740 opgaaf, so presumably she ran the farm with his assistance and the labor of her only slave, ARA: VOC 4143 *OBP*, 1740 opgaaf, Drakenstein p. 12.

29. dv&P 1981: 119–123. Olivier claims: CA: RLR 38:1666, Zevenfonteinen, 21 Mar. 1736 (to 1751 per L. Guelke data); and RLR 10:159, Klipfontein, 28 July 1742 (to 1777 per L. Guelke data). Jacobus Burger claims: CA: RLR 12:36, Aan de Klein Bergje, 16 Aug. 1748 (to 1753 per L. Guelke data).

30. On the early history of Tulbagh, see A.J. Böeseken and Margaret Cairns, *The Secluded Valley—Tulbagh: 't Land van Waveren 1700–1894* (Cape Town and Johannesburg: Perskor, 1989).

31. CA: RLR 4:24, 15 Nov. 1717 (to 1719 per L. Guelke data). RLR 4:174, 20 Nov. 1719 (to 1720 per L. Guelke data). RLR 5:18, Willem Valleij, 20 Nov. 1720 (to 1730 per

L. Guelke data). RLR 6:123, Leeuwenklip, 16 Apr. 1727 (to 1731 per L. Guelke data). Previous owner Samuel Elsevier, RLR 3:128, 1715 per L. Guelke data.

32. dv&P 1981: 119–123, 557, 568; dv&P,1966: 684.

33. Dooling, "The Making of a Colonial Elite."

34. The estate inventory at Willem's death does not mention his shared property interests with Andries, nor does it list any debts or credits. CA: MOOC 8/5.35, Estate Inventory of Willem Burger, 12 July 1731. The undated inventory of Andries's household made at the death of his first wife Maria similarly does not mention debts, credits, or shared interest in loan farm improvements. CA: MOOC 8/4.92 Estate Inventory of Maria van der Merwe, n.d. [1725–27]. Perhaps Willem and Andries disentangled their finances before Willem moved to Houd Constant. Or perhaps the Twenty-four Rivers farms had no buildings in which Willem had a claim, since only the improvements, and not the loan farm itself, were technically transmissible.

35. Willem Burger Andriesz. married Maria Magdalena Burger in 1744. dV&P, 1981: 119–23.

36. On marriage strategies and partible inheritance see Dooling, "The Making of a Colonial Elite," 157–62.

37. Ross also points to evidence that adult sons did not immediately strike out on their own, *Beyond the Pale*, 145.

38. Ross, *Beyond the Pale*, 145.

39. Dooling, "The Making of a Colonial Elite." J. Hoge, "Personalia of Germans at the Cape, 1652–1808," *AYB* 9 (1946) 442. dV&P, 1966: 1082. ARA: VOC 4096 *OBP*, 1725 opgaaf; VOC 4100 *OBP*, 1726 opgaaf; VOC 4103 *OBP*, 1727 opgaaf; VOC 4152 *OBP*, 1742 opgaaf.

40. I have not found the Widow Burger in the opgaaf after 1750. ARA VOC 4180 *OBP*, opgaaf 1750.

41. Newton-King, *Masters and Servants*, 196–201; Guelke, "Frontier Farmers," 94.

42. CA: MOOC 8/13.46, Estate Inventory of Barend Burger, 22 Sept. 1770.

43. CA: MOOC 8/4.92, Estate Inventory of Maria van der Merwe, n.d. [1725–27]

44. It is interesting to note that Willem's and Maria's inventories do not list weapons, even though a musket, a pistol, and a sword are ascribed to Willem and Andries in every opgaaf. When Elsje van der Merwe and Margaretha Pasman appear in the opgaaf as Burger widows, they do not have weapons.

45. ARA: VOC 4143 *OBP*, 1740 opgaaf; VOC 4166 *OBP*, 1746 opgaaf.

46. Anders Sparrman, *A Voyage to the Cape of Good Hope Towards the Antarctic Polar Circle Round the World and to the Country of the Hottentots and the Caffres from the Year 1772–1776,* trans. J. &. I. Rudner, ed. V. S. Forbes (Cape Town: Van Riebeeck Society, 1975), Vol. II, 132.

47. Ross, *Status and Respectability*, 39; Pierre Bourdieu, "Structures, Habitus, Power: Basis for a Theory of Symbolic Power," in *Culture/Power/History*, ed. N. B. Dirks, et al. (Princeton, NJ: Princeton University Press, 1983), 155–99.

48. Newton-King, *Masters and Servants*, 205.

49. None of the settlers' financial reporting to the VOC should be taken as absolute, empirical numbers. People had solid motivation to underreport to both the opgaaf and the Orphan Chamber since both the census and death inventories were the

basis of taxation. Van Duin and Ross make a convincing argument that although the opgaaf numbers are certainly underreported, it is reasonable to assume a consistent enough deviation from actual agricultural production to make comparative assessments across time, region, and households at the Cape. Pieter van Duin and Robert Ross, *The Economy of the Cape Colony in the Eighteenth Century* (Leiden: Centre for the History of European Expansion, 1987).

50. CA: MOOC 8/49.25, Estate Inventory of Schalk Willem Burger, 24 Sept. 1782.

51. ARA: VOC 4180 *OBP*, 1750 opgaaf, Drakenstein pp. 7–8.

52. Willem Burger's claims to Afgaan van de Kartouw: CA: RLR 14:199, 22 Nov. 1756 to 16 Feb. 1788; Schalk Willem Burger's claims to Halve Dorschvloer CA: RLR 11:7, 31 Mar. 1744 to 13 Apr. 1763; Halve Dorschvloer in freehold, DO: OSF II: 296, 15 Dec. 1763.

53. Women's legal status in community property makes some of the logical assumptions about household purchasing postulated by Ulrich for colonial New England in *Good Wives* impossible for South Africa. For examples of Dutch housewives directly engaging in trade on their own accounts (not as capable surrogates for their husbands, as Ulrich argues for New England) see Susannah Shaw, "Building New Netherland: Gender and Family Ties in a Frontier Society (New York)" (PhD diss., Cornell, 2000).

54. Newton-King, *Masters and Servants*, 205.

55. Leibbrandt, *Précis*, 99. DO: OSF II: 296, 15 Dec. 1763, land grant for Halve Dorschvloer. Tweefontein *in de Koude Bokkeveld*, Tygershoek *over de Doorn rivier*, and Breede Rivier, *aan de Olifants Berg*, CA: MOOC 8/49.25, Estate Inventory of Schalk Willem Burger, 24 Sept. 1782.

56. Halve Dorschvloer and adjacent Misgunt, RxD 1,500; outstanding debt RxD 1,930. CA: MOOC 8/49.25, Estate Inventory of Schalk Willem Burger, 24 Sept. 1782. Willem Burger's total estate value 5,131 Cape guilders (equal to RxD 1,710). CA: MOOC 8/5.35, Estate Inventory of Willem Burger, 12 July 1731.

57. Ad Biewinga, *De Kaap de Goede Hoop: Een Nederlandse vestigingskolonie, 1680–1730* (Amsterdam: Uitgeverij Prometheus and Bert Bakker, 1999); Gerrit Schutte, "Between Amsterdam and Batavia: Cape Society and the Calvinist Church Under the Dutch East India Company," *Kronos: Journal of Cape History* 25 (1998–1999), 17–49. Nineteenth-century criminal trial testimony has repeated references to Christian religious practice, including the slaves, led by the male head of the household, "The Trial of Galant and Others" in George McCall Theal, *RCC*, Vol. 20, 188–341.

58. ARA: VOC 4158 *OBP*, 1743–1744, Vol. 2. Testimony in the case against Willem van Wyk. Testimony in Galant's trial similarly places slaves intimately in settler homes, Theal, *RCC*, 188–341. See also Shell, *Children of Bondage*.

59. Sparrman, *Voyage*, I:137.

60. Some of those beds may have been at the couple's other farms, since the Schalk Willem's inventory records houses on them.

61. Rooibos is the "African bush tea" now also widely marketed in North America.

62. H.W. Classens, *Die geskiedenis van boerekos, 1652–1806* (Pretoria: Protea Boekhuis, 2006); Lannice Snyman, *Rainbow Cuisine* (Hout Bay: S&S Publishers, 1998).

63. Peter Linebaugh and Marcus Rediker, "Hewers of Wood and Drawers of Water," in *The Many Headed Hydra: Sailors, Slaves, Commoners, and the Hidden History of the Revolutionary Atlantic* (Boston: Beacon Press, 2000), 36–70; Ulrich, *The Age of*

Homespun: Objects and Stories in the Creation of an American Myth (New York: Alfred A. Knopf, 2001).

64. As points of comparison see Michael Craton, *A Jamaican Plantation: The History of Worthy Park, 1670–1970* (Toronto: University of Toronto Press, 1970); Elizabeth Fox-Genovese, *Within the Plantation Household: Black and White Women of the Old South* (Chapel Hill: University of North Carolina Press, 1988); Leonard Blussé, *Bitter Bonds: A Colonial Divorce Drama of the Seventeenth Century*, trans. D. Webb (Princeton: Markus Weiner, 2002).

65. Ross notes the VOC's complaints about *smousen* as early as 1774, "The Cape of Good Hope and the World Economy, 1652–1835," in Elphick and Giliomee, *Shaping*, 267.

66. Penn, *The Forgotten Frontier*.

67. Gayatri Chatravorty Spivak, "Can the Subaltern Speak?" in *Marxism and the Interpretation of Culture*, 271–313 (Cary Nelson and Lawrence Grossberg, eds. Urbana: University of Illinois Press, 1988); Carlo Ginzburg, "The Inquisitor as Anthropologist," in *Clues, Myths and the Historical Method*, trans. John and Anne Tedeshi (Baltimore: Johns Hopkins University Press, 1989).

68. dV&P, 1981: 557.

69. These moments are death—a complicating twist to Mbembe's "Necropolitics."

70. Guelke, "An Early Colonial Landed Gentry: Land and Wealth in the Cape Colony 1682–1731," *Journal of Historical Geography* 9: 3 (1983), 265–86. Ross, "The Rise of the Cape Gentry," *JSAS* 9: 2 (Apr. 1983), 193–217; Dooling, "The Decline of the Cape Gentry, c. 1838–1900," *JAH* 40:2 (1999), 215–42; Dooling, "Making a Colonial Elite."

71. Values based on Willem's inventory, which accords with Barend the Elder, Barend the Younger, Schalk Willem and Maria van der Merwe's inventories.

72. The case against Willem van Wyk suggests the reach of criminal prosecution extended far into frontier regions. ARA: VOC 4158 *OBP*, 1743–1744, Vol. 2. For other examples see Penn, *Rogues, Rebels, Runaways*. The household inventories of the MOOC series and the land tenure records filed with the Stellenbosch Magistrate's district (cataloged as 1/STB 11/19) frequently show farmers behind in their loan farm payments, delinquencies ranging from several months to decades.

73. Ross, "Belonging and Belongings: On the Material Superstructure of Identity," paper presented at the Historical Association of South Africa Jubilee Meeting, 26–28 June 2006. Ross's argument is not about frontier regions, but the general premise is applicable.

74. Jean and John Comaroff, *Of Revelation and Revolution*, Vol. 1 (Chicago: University of Chicago Press, 1991); Anne McClintock, *Imperial Leather: Race, Gender and Sexuality in the Colonial Conquest* (New York: Routledge, 1995).

75. The VOC intervened to mandate a recording of a married couple's wealth and to oversee the orderly, appropriate transfer of the estate, but unlike nineteenth- and early twentieth-century Java described by Ann Stoler, the eighteenth-century state was not attempting to mandate household composition or material circumstances; *Carnal Knowledge*, particularly chapter 2.

76. Mary Louse Pratt, *Imperial Eyes: Travel Writing and Transculturation* (New York: Routledge, 1995).

77. Guelke, "Freehold Farmers," 93

78. Newton-King presents the range of frontier household wealth from absolute penury to genuine prosperity, *Masters and Servants*, 157–62.

79. Newton-King, *Masters and Servants*, 196–203.

80. "We do not live like beasts," said Landdrost H.C.D. Maynier on the eastern frontier in 1795, a quotation aptly used by Newton-King as a chapter title in *Masters and Servants*, 209 n248.

81. These "rough drafts" immediately follow the indexed formal inventories in the bound MOOC volumes.

82. Eviatar Zerubavel, *Time Maps: Collective Memory and the Social Shape of the Past*. (Chicago: University of Chicago Press, 2003); Sylvie-Anne Goldberg, *La Clepsydre* (Paris: Albin Michel, 2000).

83. Michelle Ruiters, "Re-Imagining and Re-Claiming Identity: Coloured Identities in a Post-Apartheid South Africa," paper presented at the New England Workshop on Southern Africa, 22–25 Apr. 2005, Burlington, VT.

84. Newton-King makes a similar argument in *Master and Servants*.

85. Farming implements made from iron and wood were likely crafted at the Cape; a few farms had smiths (Shell, *Children of Bondage*, 165). General references to luxury goods, such as porcelain, appear in ships cargos, but not with enough detail to source specific types of goods, J.R. Bruijn, et al., *Dutch-Asiatic Shipping in the Seventeenth and Eighteenth Centuries*, 3 vols. (The Hague: Martinus Nijhoff, 1987).

86. Where Burton argues the importance using of personal, domestic documents as sources for colonial history, I, like Stoler, explore the ways in which state documents reveal aspects of the personal, domestic, contours of colonial life.

7. PROPERTY AND COMMUNITY ON DISPLAY

A Lubbe Family Auction

Spring is benevolent in the Cedarberg, a good time to travel. The peak blaze of wildflowers is over by November, but some asters and lilies would still have been in bloom, and seasonal streams were likely to be full, making the journey to the farm at Groote Valleij on the Olifants River pleasant for both man and beast. At least 44 people traveled for more than a day to reach Barend Lubbe's farm late in the spring of 1785; a few made the long journey from Cape Town. Certainly some of those who came to bid on items at Lubbe's estate auction traveled with family members—the list of buyers represented just a portion of those who actually attended the two-day community event.

Whether in town, in a farming district, or on the frontier, an auction was a social and symbolic gathering, as well as an occasion for economic transactions.[1] Immediate family members, other kin, neighbors, and Company officials all attended this public display and redistribution of a family's possessions. Auctions were a regular part of the colonists' social landscape, organized to settle insolvent estates, to liquidate assets for equitable distribution of inheritance, or at the request of a household repatriating or otherwise divesting itself of worldly goods. Occasionally, a criminal or civil judgment forced an auction, but more typically the proceeds from the sale went directly to some of its participants— the heirs of the deceased.

Despite the death that usually prompted an auction, the event was festive, with food, plenty of drink, and socializing. In town, the event created social proximity, physically bringing people together across lines of race, class, gender, and generation as buyers and bystanders.[2] Frontier communities, however, were more circumscribed than in Cape Town or Stellenbosch. Free people of color claimed land in the Cedarberg, but they did not appear in the few eighteenth-century auction records for the region, whether because of limited cash or credit, active exclusion, or disinclination to participate. Although vexing, the absence of independent Khoisan or mixed-race buyers in Cedarberg auctions is understandable, given their liminal status in colonial society. Indentured Khoisan servants and slaves, on the other hand, must have been at work on Groote Valleij at the time of the auction, but the only record of their presence is the sale of Lubbe's slaves.

Labor and race are equally elusive in a narrative account of a late eighteenth-century country auction. Johanna Duminy's description of a 1797 *vendu* in the Overberg, east of the Hottentots-Holland mountains, conveys a party atmosphere, with families arriving by ox wagon prepared to spend the night. Each day of the sale started with a breakfast that included warm meat and butter. Even those close enough to travel home and return the next day chose to stay and enjoy the revelry. Duminy recounts her purposeful decision to remain at the vendu, saying to her husband, "No, I want to stay here and see the fun. I have got our bedding and they have given me a big *katel* to sleep on in the room here." François Duminy replied that he would then sleep in the wagon for the night. The "fun" Johanna referred to included a communal meal and dancing by candlelight to the music of violins.

The silences and assumptions in the Duminys' conversation are telling: "I'll have my bed made up in the wagon," said François, when his wife wanted to stay the night at the auction site. Johanna reports on hours of domestic work, without ever actively seeing or doing any herself:

At nine o'clock our table was laid . . .

After the meal, I ordered our bedding to be brought in, and I had my katel made
   up . . .

At eight o'clock [the next morning] the table was laid . . . the violins were still going
   strong . . .

I ordered my lame ox to be slaughtered . . .

We had our things packed on cousin van Riet's wagon.[3]

Who made up beds, laid tables, cooked meat, slaughtered animals, packed the wagon, and played the violins? A large social gathering intensified the need for domestic labor as it disrupted some household rhythms. Johanna and her husband slept apart; she shared a bed with a female cousin in a room filled with 24 sleepers. No wonder François preferred the wagon in these unusual circumstances. Despite such departures from routine, this event, like daily settler life, depended on labor so commonplace that Johanna Duminy only remarked upon the results, not on the process or the workers themselves.

Not all of the work presumed in Duminy's account was necessarily that of slaves or Khoisan servants, however. The violin players might have been neighbors. The butcher who slaughtered her oxen could have been a burgher or a bondsman. Kin and neighbors of the bereaved family were present; undoubtedly some helped with the many preparations necessary to entertain so large a crowd. In a society and economy predicated on bondage, the division of the labor that produced a good time for Johanna Duminy was unlikely to have been consensual or equitable, however. Its effacement in colonial sources replicates the social hierarchy imposed by dominant settler interests.

Consequently, racial dynamics remain opaque, as ever. *Vendu rolle* like Lubbe's do, however, bring class, gender, and generational dynamics into relief. Barend Lubbe died a rich old man, a longtime frontier farmer who was well-known in the region. He had served as a *veldkorporal* (burgher militia officer) for the Olifants River district. He assumed that post during the period of intense conflict at the end of the 1730s; his sons were subsequently appointed to serve in the colonial administration of the Cedarberg, indicating the family's stable position in frontier society. Given this local prominence, Lubbe's estate auction attracted a wide range of buyers along with others who came, like Johanna Duminy, mostly for the spectacle.

Kin, neighbors, Company officials, and farmers from a wide swath of territory converged on Groote Valleij on November 7 and 8, 1785. The vendu rol documents 68 individual buyers, about one-third of them relatives. Another third were neighbors—those whose Olifants River farms were within a day's ride of the Lubbe's. Four of the buyers were masters of the Orphan Chamber, come from Cape Town to oversee the auction. Their duty imposed a long trip on them—at least six days by ox wagon if they proceeded directly to Groote Valleij. The trip would have taken longer if they had other stops to make—or they could have moved more quickly if they traveled on horseback, counting on shelter and hospitality at farms along the route. Whatever their itinerary, they were not mere referees at the event; the Orphan masters' position gave them preferential access to auctions, a privilege that extended from Cape Town to the frontier.[4] Lubbe's estate was large enough that prestige, family connections, and evident capital from Cape Town still left plenty of room for other bidders. A third of the buyers were farmers from surrounding regions—the Bokkeveld, the Roggeveld, the Swartland, and the Berg River—no relation to the Lubbes, who just came to take a look at a rich man's things and, perhaps, augment their own household's possessions.

HOW THERE CAME TO BE LUBBES IN THESE PARTS

A COMING OF AGE

Barend Lubbe arrived at the Olifants River an orphaned young man with a disabled older brother and limited local connections. A half century later, he headed a large, prosperous family firmly entrenched in the Cedarberg. In addition to whatever means he used to claim land and coerce labor, Barend Lubbe had some lucky breaks come his way, including a government appointment and an advantageous marriage, enabling him to establish the basis of expanding settler claims on the frontier.

The youngest of 12 children, Barend was only 11 years old when his father died. Three of his brothers had died young, before their parents. Barend's two eldest sisters were already married in 1723; their husbands were the family's official witnesses to the inventory and subsequent auction of livestock, farm implements, housewares, and a single slave that marked the dissolution of the Lubbe household at Wolvedans.[5] The inventory stipulated that the four surviving boys and Catharina, the eldest unmarried girl, had livestock of their own among the beasts on the farm; those animals were not sold at auction (with the exception of young Barend's horse, which was sold for him with the proceeds kept separate from the estate). So the Lubbes were not destitute, but even with the livestock set aside and the settlement from the auction proceeds, none of the nine children inherited resources enough to support themselves individually.

Young Barend, it seems, went to live with his sister Aletta and her husband Paul Keyser at their farm, Welgelegen, near Stellenbosch.[6] The couple had four small children by this time; they incorporated care for their growing brood with support for Aletta's siblings, all still living near Stellenbosch (Paul and Aletta would go on to raise 13 children, not counting their contribution to Barend and his sisters). Brothers Jan and Frans both died young and unmarried three years after their parents.[7] Again, Paul Keyser was called to witness the paperwork settling their estates. Brother Hendrik married that year, the daughter of a local farming family. The Lubbe siblings remained in close contact and saw multiple endogamous marriages among their own children, but they chose diverse spouses for themselves. The three younger girls, like their older sisters, went on to marry immigrant men.

Both Johanna and Maria Jacoba married at 17, leaving only Barend as a minor dependent five years after their father's death. Though living with family members, Barend was officially a ward of the Orphan Chamber, meaning he was not legally empowered to make his own financial decisions. As a young man of twenty, ten years after his father's death, Barend Lubbe requested legal

majority.[8] Before Barend applied for *veniam aetatis*, however, his older brother
Hendrik became a ward of the Stellenbosch church. In 1730, the church council approved an annual stipend for Hendrik because he was blind in both eyes.
Brother-in-law Christian Liebenberg also contributed to his maintenance, but
the church saw need great enough that it designated Hendrik for an allowance
normally given only to the elderly.[9] Despite this network of support—or perhaps because the only prospect for real financial independence lay beyond the
embrace of his family—Barend Lubbe left Stellenbosch for the Olifants River.
There he was appointed caretaker of the Company's post at the Warm Baths
(a natural hot springs) near the river, and by the time of the 1739 frontier war,
Lubbe was the veldkorporal for the Olifants River.[10]

Part of Lubbe's acclimatization to the Cedarberg certainly came with his
marriage to Andries Burger's eldest daughter, Martha. Their courtship is buried,
but evidence of Martha and Barend's marriage is clear: 13 children, 12 guided
to adulthood. Martha had the first three children—all boys—between 1737 and
1741, a period that encompassed intense violence. Barend served then as veldkorporal; many of their Olifants River neighbors, as well as farmers near the
Twenty-four Rivers and in the Land van Waveren asked for relief from land-
rent payments in 1739 because the hostilities made their frontier farms uninhabitable. Barend, Martha, and their babies survived the tempest and went on
to flourish.

SECURING THE NEXT GENERATION'S PLACE
IN THE LANDSCAPE

Barend's marriage to Martha Burger incorporated him into the network of
frontier land claims that already existed when they wed in 1736. Their children
subsequently relied upon and reinforced those relationships. Like their parents and their many cousins, the next generation of Lubbe siblings' place in the
community helped to secure their place in the landscape.

With the exception of one daughter, all of Barend and Martha's children
choose partners within a very small social and geographical circle. Four of the
Lubbe siblings married Burgers from neighboring Halve Dorschvloer, children of their mother's first cousin, Schalk Willem. Johanna Catharina and
Elsie married brothers Hendrik and Petrus van der Merwe Hendriksz from
the Sneeuwberg; Willem married another van der Merwe cousin, Elisabeth
Geertruij. Maria Jacoba and Martha married brothers Abraham and Johannes
Paulus Mouton Abrahamsz, whose parents farmed behind the Piketberg; An-
dries married the Mouton's first cousin, Maria Magdalena, whose parents
farmed over the Pakhuis Pass on the east side of the Olifants River. Barend
Fredrik married Johanna Maria Keyser, who as both the Moutons' aunt and

Barend Lubbe's niece epitomized the tight connection established among the Lubbe, Mouton, and Keyser families in two generations of marriages.

Johanna Keyser also symbolized the link between the Lubbes of the Cedarberg and individuals in the more settled areas of the colony. She spent her early years on her parents' farm Welgelegen.[11] She had not yet been born when Barend left Stellenbosch, but her mother, Aletta, must have kept in touch with her faraway brother Barend. The fact that Johanna married her cousin Barend Hendrik—who grew up on the distant Groote Valleij—indicates the families remained in contact at least sporadic enough to facilitate the introduction of the couple. Barend Lubbe may have moved to the Cedarberg to seek his fortune, but he kept up his connections back home.

Elisabeth Lubbe's marriage to Gerhardus Munnik, in contrast, defies presumption. No circumstantial evidence links the families before her marriage, and Gerhardus remained firmly ensconced near Cape Town as a land owner and alcohol *pachter* (licensed monopoly merchant).[12] Yet the frontier-to-town connection that took Johanna Keyser to the Cedarberg as a bride must also have extended to unite Munnik with Elisabeth, and to keep him within the social network even after Elisabeth's death. Six years after Munnik remarried, he journeyed to Groote Valleij for his former father-in-law's auction and made significant purchases there. Whether he was buying for his own account or on behalf of his children, he spent more than double his late wife's share of the estate, which suggests he was not simply taking his children's share home in livestock rather than in cash.

Only one of the Lubbe siblings made a second marriage, also to a partner with local connections. Maria Jacoba's union to Josias Engelbrecht introduced another family to the mix, but did not practically shift frontier alliances. Engelbrecht's own father died in debt when Josias was only one year old.[13] After his mother remarried a year later, Engelbrecht and his three older siblings would undoubtedly have gotten to know their step-father's connections. Jacobus Louw Jacobsz farmed in the Lange Valleij, the same district as Jan Engelbrecht had. In addition, Louw also claimed grazing permits near the Olifants River, and many Louw family members settled in the Cedarberg, thus plausibly situating Engelbrecht within the tightly-knit frontier community.[14] After his marriage to Maria Jacoba, Josias assumed the lease on Berg Valleij, behind the Piketberg, which Maria Jacoba inherited from her first husband, Abraham Mouton, in 1768.[15]

These closely circumscribed social relationships also had a spatial component. Andries, the eldest son, began farming at Modder Valleij, near present-day Citrusdal, the year after his marriage to Maria Magdalena Mouton.[16] The following year, Barend Fredrik and Johanna Maria Keyser established a home at Brakkefontein, also in Olifants River valley. Johanna was widowed young and maintained the farm until she transferred it to her son Paul Willem in 1794.[17] Their sister Martha and her husband Johannes Paulus Mouton joined them on the nearby Modder Rivier farm in 1765. The third brother, Willem, claimed more distant land, but only for three years in the 1770s, suggesting that he farmed in partnership with his brothers or cousins.[18]

By the time the fourth son, Johannes Hendrik, came of age, there was less pressure to leave the family farm, and Barend, then 57 years old, must have welcomed the help. Johannes was also the first of the four Lubbes to marry one of the neighboring Burger children, so he and his wife Elsie had incentive to stay on Groote Valleij near both their families. In 1773, three years after their marriage, Johannes and Elsie appeared in the opgaaf as dependents of Barend and Martha, a position they seem to have accepted until Barend's death.[19]

Frans, the youngest son, complemented the land claims made by his father and brothers, moving out of the river valley, over the Pakhuis Pass and into the Bidouw Valley.[20] The Moutons who raised livestock on farms in that area were his sister-in-law Maria Magdalena's people, so his neighbors—though not situated as close together has his siblings and Burger cousins were who lived near the river—were nevertheless kin.

Sisters Johanna Catharina and Elsie moved south and east of the Olifants River center of the Lubbe family. Hendrik van der Merwe and Johanna Catharina settled in the high Witsenberg valley, the source of the Olifants. Elsie and Petrus van der Merwe traversed another set of mountains to the Koue Bokkeveld.[21] Jacoba and Barend Jacobus Burger moved even farther east, to the Roggeveld.[22] After claiming loan farms in the Cedarberg, Aletta Sophia and Alewijn Jacobus Burger eventually opted for Graaff-Reinet and the Eastern frontier, an unusual move since both partners had large extended family networks in the Cedarberg.[23] Elisabeth, the only Lubbe sibling to marry outside an obvious family or frontier connection, retraced her father's trajectory and returned to Stellenbosch, where her husband served as heemraad of both Stellenbosch and Drakenstein, as well as on the Drakenstein Church council.[24]

Starting from Barend Lubbe's original land claim near the Olifants River, the family's property radiated through the Cedarberg and beyond. Frans and Johanna Adriana extended settler farming into higher elevations while Johannes Hendrik and Elsie Burger maintained the Lubbes' original homestead. Meanwhile Andries, Barend Fredrik, and Martha made additional claims in the Olifants River Valley and Maria Jacoba moved back behind the Piketberg. Johanna Catharina and Elsie gravitated toward a region heavily settled by the van der Merwe family, and other siblings moved further afield, emphasizing the great degree of mobility in frontier communities and the extent to which the frontier regions were deeply connected to the rest of the colony. Within the Cedarberg itself, a proliferation of family farms gradually seeped out across

Fig. 7.6. Continuity of Land Tenure in Lubbe Family Loan Farms
For more on the long-term stability of land claims, see chapter 3.

Source: CA: Receiver of Land Revenue series and L. Guelke RLR data

Fig. 3.6. Cedarberg Loan Farm Tenure Patterns

Continuity of Tenure in Lubbe Family Loan Farms

Farm name	Claimant	Dates of tenure	Sources
Dassen Klip	Paul Keyser (& Aletta Lubbe)	–1756	CA: MOOC 9/9.5
Groote Valleij	Barend Lubbe	1736–1785	CA: RLR 38:178 CA: MOOC 10/15.6
	Johannes Hendrik Lubbe	1785–	CA: MOOC 10/15.6
Modder Rivier	Hendrik Lubbe	1748–1758	CA: RLR 12.42
	Johannes Paulus Mouton (& Martha Lubbe)	1765–1792	CA: RLR 18:282 CA: MOOC8/17.2a
Wedouw	Barend Lubbe	1749–1785	CA: RLR 12:82
	Frans Lubbe	1786–1791	CA: RLR 35.45

Fig. 7.6. (*continued*)

Onrust	Barend Lubbe	1750–1785	CA: RLR 12:143
	Frans Lubbe	1786–1791	CA: RLR 35:44.4
Brakkefontein	Barend Lubbe	1752–1762	CA: RLR 13:58
	Barend Frederik Lubbe	1758–1791	CA: RLR 15:62
	Paul Willem Lubbe	–1810	CA: MOOC 8/58.36a
Modder Valleij	Andries Lubbe	1757–1786	CA: RLR 15:5 CA: MOOC 8/45.123
Wagenbooms Rivier	Jacoba Elisabeth Lubba	1762–1779	CA: RLR 17:23
Berg Valleij	Maria Jacoba Lubbe as Widow of Abraham Mouton	1766–1777	CA: RLR 19:149
	Josias Englebrecht & Maria Jacoba Lubbe	1777–1791	CA: RLR 25:24 CA: MOOC 8/12.41b
Bloemfontein	Jan Hendrik Lubbe	1770–1773	CA: RLR 21:83
	Barend Lubbe d'oud	1776–1785	CA: RLR 24:190
	Frans Lubbe	1787–1791	CA: RLR 36:116.1 CA: MOOC 10/15.6

Brandewijns Rivier	Hendrik Lubbe	1777–1778	CA: RLR 25:102
Hendrik van der Wat's Gat	Johannes Liebenberg	1779–	CA: RLR 26:140
Zanddrift	Frans Lubbe	1780–1793	CA: RLR 27:130
Bosch Kloof	Johannes Lubbe Barendsz	1781–	CA: RLR 28:28
Duijkerfontein	Hendrik Lubbe d'jonge	1788–	CA: RLR 36:12
Marcus Kraal	Paul Willem Lubbe	–1810	CA: MOOC 8/58.36a

the landscape; the Lubbes used the same strategies of marriage and land acquisition as their frontier neighbors and kin.

APPORTIONING A FAMILY'S BELONGINGS

Barend Lubbe outlived his wife and three of his children. His daughter Aletta Sophia and her husband Alewijn Jacobus Burger had moved to Graaff-Reinet, a distance that precluded their return for the auction. The rest of the children, along with many other family members, returned in November of 1785 to the farm where they grew up. The occasion was an infrequent reunion for some, and a sociable visit for others—a time to catch up on family news and to settle debts with kin and neighbors.

The estate was undoubtedly auctioned in order to facilitate an equitable division of inheritance among the many claimants—12 children's portions, two to be directly subdivided to grandchildren, since Elisabeth and Barend Fredrik had already passed on. The principal heirs—Lubbe's sons, sons-in-law (as the public faces of their wives' portions), and a grandson—together bought over half the estate. Eleven family members acquired this significant portion through a limited number of purchases, buying what mattered most to rural agricultural production: land and slaves. They also bought the other high-value equipment indispensable for frontier farm life: ox wagons and a horse-drawn cart. The auction took two days to complete, but the bulk of the estate's value went in just 19 transactions: 13 slave sales—four of which involved an adult with a child or children—four wagons, and the two farms. Family members made 14 of those crucial purchases, a clear indication of the close circulation of wealth, despite widespread community participation.

Although people came from neighboring farms and from distant reaches, at its heart this auction was a family affair, unlike the one Barend experienced as a newly orphaned boy 62 years before. The Groote Valleij vendu raised 23,192:3 rixdollars, nearly ten times the value of Old Barend Lubbe's sale.[25] Then, most of the deceased's children were minors with limited resources of their own. Barend's two brothers-in-law bought livestock, grain, and small tools amounting to about 16 percent of Old Barend's estate, but other buyers clearly outpaced them. Philip Morkel alone bought 450 of the 700 sheep for sale. The rest of the sheep and the cattle were parceled out to a range of buyers, none of them related to the Lubbes. The family's only slave, Pieter van Ceylon, was the single most expensive item at the sale; he went to a neighbor. The 150 sheep Paul Keyser took home that day amounted to just a little more than his wife's share of the estate; her inheritance walked itself from Wolvedans to Welgelegen.

Fig. 7.7. Buyers at Barend Lubbe's Auction Ranked by the Value of Their Purchases

Source: CA: MOOC 10/3,47, Vendu rol, Barend Lubbe, 10 Dec. 1723.

Buyers at Barend Lubbe's Auction Ranked by the Value of their Purchase

Name	Relationship to Barend	Value in Rixdollars
Johannes Hendrik Lubbe	son	8059.6
Mons. Gerhardus Munnik	son-in-law	2873.4
Barend Jacobus Burger	son-in-law	1417.7
Johannes Joosten		1153.2
d'E. Christoffel Brand	Orphan Chamber official	1103.2
Josias Engelbrecht	son-in-law	985.7
Hendrik van der Merwe Hendriksz	son-in-law	733.2
Frans Lubbe	son	517.2
Willem Lubbe d'oude	son	502.6
Isaack Visage Isaaksz.		423
Frans Joosten		417
Barend Voster d'oude	nephew	352.7

Fig. 7.7. (*continued*)

Andries Lubbe	grandson	352.5
Johannes Petrus Smit d'oude	neighbor	316.5
Willem Janse van Rensburg Wmz	neighbor	301
Arnoldus Botman	extended family	257.7
Mons. Micheil Casper Mouton		244
Hendrik Lubbe Hendriksz.	nephew	203
Schalk Willem Burger Schalksz	neighbor	190.6
Jacob Stengel		187
Jacobus van Renen de Jonge	neighbor	157.7
Wynand Louw Jacobusz.		154.2
Johannes Liebenberg d'oude	nephew	151.5
Andries Petrus Dipner		144
Mons' Hend'k O. Eksteen Ptz.		129.4
Ferdin. Nel d'oude		104.4
Jan Gab. du Plessies	neighbor	100

Name	Relationship	Value
Willem Hurter		90.5
Mons. Hendrik Coetse d'oude	neighbor	90
Sebasian van Reenen	neighbor	89
Mons. Piet v.d. Byl de jonge		83.1
Schalk Voster Barendsz	neighbor	82.8
Andries Lubbe d'oude	son	82
Johannes Paulus Mouton	son-in-law	81.4
Petrus van der Merwe Hendriks.	son-in-law	81
David Straus	neighbor	77.2
Johannes Christoffel Gryling d'oude	nephew	73
Andries Gous Pietersz		61
Andries Bester		60.6
Isaak de Villiers Abrahamsz		60.3
Gerrit Coetsee Dirksz		41.1
Mons. Carel van der Merwe Roelofsz		38.4
d'E. Horak	Orphan Chamber official	37.3

Fig. 7.7. (*continued*)

Johannes Petrus Smit de jonge	neighbor	33.8
Johannes Hendrik Beukins	neighbor	33
Jacobus Burman		30.4
Dirk Coetse Dirksz		30
Gerrit Roos Gysbertsz		22.5
Gideon van Zigel Pietersz		17.1
Barend Voster	neighbor	16
Hendrik Lubbe	extended family	14
Pieter Burger		13.7
the widow of Schalk Willem Burger (Hester Smit)	neighbor and extended family	12.7
Floris Visser d'oude		11.3
Christ's Godl'b Baarts		10.6
d'E. Ronnekamp	Orphan Chamber official	9.6
Jacobus Stephanus Burger Schalksz	neighbor	9.1
Isaak Visage		9

Pieter Joosten		8.8
Jan Jacob Meyer		8.1
d'E. Brink	Orphan Chamber official	4.3
Johannes Petrus Gous Pietersz	neighbor	4
Mons Hendrik Cloete junior	neighbor	3.6
Petrus Lok. Terron		3.1
Christian Liebenberg	nephew	3
Abraham Mouton Jacobsz	neighbor	2
Jacobus Smit Alewynsz	neighbor	1.6
Johannes de Clercq Jacobsz		1.3
Coenraad Waldpot		0.8

The Lubbe family, and the family's fortunes, increased dramatically by the time of the Groote Valleij vendu. Lubbe's sons and sons-in-law spent over 15,600 rixdollars; other relatives spent another 1,000 rixdollars, unrelated neighbors from the Olifants River Valley brought over 1,500 rixdollars, and the general public generated an additional 3,500 rixdollars. Considering that trek oxen fetched about the same price at the two sales, but sheep were nearly four times cheaper at the frontier auction, the increase in quality and quantity of goods for sale in 1785 was staggering.

Son Johannes Hendrik made the largest purchase, the opstal at Groote Valleij. Johannes and Elsie clearly wanted to stay on the farm at the heart of their extended network of Lubbe and Burger relations, and in the place they had invested their labor. The sale of the farmhouse and other improvements stipulated that Johannes should received one-third of the coming harvest of wheat, rye, barley, peas, and beans, suggesting that he had a stake in the planting. The couple's willingness to pay 8,050 rixdollars for the farm, over four times Johannes's likely share of his parents' estate, suggests they wanted very much to remain anchored in the Olifants River valley. The high purchase price for the opstal is also a clear indication of extensive built improvements and natural resources on the farm.

In comparison, Johannes' younger brother Frans paid only 224 rixdollars for the opstal on Bloemfontein, a more distant farm, undoubtedly with fewer improvements and not likely to have been as well situated for arable agriculture as Groote Valleij. For Frans, though, the addition of Bloemfontein, beyond the confluence of the Olifants and Doorn Rivers, was a useful complement to his farming enterprise established in the mountainous regions to the east of the Olifants River valley.

Slaves, too, tended to stay in the family, though that did not mean that any families or other relationships among the slaves themselves were kept together. In fact, the 18 slaves sold on the second day of the auction dispersed widely. Andries brought Flora van de Caab and Fortuyn van Sambowa up the river to Modder Valleij. He alone bought two slaves in separate transactions, whether because the slaves wanted to be together, or simply because Andries wanted the labor, is impossible to know. Frans took Frans van Mallabar—a coincidence of naming, or the result of shared experiences in the Lubbe household?

The three slave women sold with their children each went to a son-in-law—who may have been acting explicitly as proxies for their wives.[26] Lea van de Caab and her daughters Sara and Leonora (sold "as is") had only to cross the Piekeniers Kloof Pass to their new home with Maria Jacoba and Josias Engelbrecht. Victoria van de Caab and her daughter Rachel also remained within plausible visiting distance of their old home, moving to the

Witsenberg valley with Johanna Catharina and Hendrik van der Merwe. In contrast, Anna van de Caab and her child Arend presumably went to the Roggeveld with Jacoba and Barend Jacobus Burger, making the chance of reunion with those they liked or loved from Groote Valleij slim indeed. Lubbe's nephews Hendrik Lubbe Hendriksz and Johannes Liebenberg each bought a slave, meaning that Corridon van Mallabar and Goliath van Madagascar might have stayed in the Olifants River valley, as both men had loan farms there.[27] Jephta van Mallabar, however, likely returned with Gerhardus Munnik to Wynberg.

Thus the three men from Malabar were split up after the sale, Frans going over the Pakhuis Pass with Frans Lubbe, Jephta going with Munnik, and Corridon moving to Hendrik Lubbe's farm further down the Olifants River. In the absence of other records, it is impossible to know their response to this separation, though one presumes that life in the company of countrymen who shared a language and religion was easier than life completely among foreigners. Barend Lubbe had multiple farms, however, so this relocation might not have been a separation after all. Whatever their preferences, the slaves had no more choice about their new homes than the sheep. If a slave did run away in protest of the change, he or she would not be left simply to contend with the heat and the jackals. Slaves were too valuable a capital investment to let go. If the Lubbes had a sentimental attachment to any of their slaves, or sense of belonging to a shared (though admittedly hierarchical) household, financial concerns outweighed these emotions.[28] Three slave men and a child were sold out of the family and out of the district.

Johannes Joosten, a Stellenbosch burgher with a farm in the Bokkeveld, made the second largest purchase of the auction, spending 1,151 rixdollars for Joseph van Mozambique. His brother Frans, also a Bokkeveld farmer, acquired Januarij van Sambowa. The Joostens were not kin to the Lubbes, though they were cousins of the Moutons.[29] Roggeveld farmer Isaak Visagie, no connection at all to the Lubbes, purchased Sabandar van Bougies with his son, Abraham van de Caab. Presumably, this locally born boy had a mother, but she was not a factor in this sale.

After land and slaves, Lubbe's wagons commanded the highest prices for a single item. The utility of heavy transportation is clear, but Barend Lubbe's wagons had some additional cachet. First of all, four wagons—three yoked for oxen and one for horses—was an abundance. Every farming household needed one wagon, and many inventories for Lubbe's neighbors and family members list two wagons, but not three. Barend's father's wagon fetched only 50 rixdollars at auction.[30] Other farm wagons in the 1720s and 1730s had similar or lesser values.[31] Among Barend Lubbe's contemporaries, only Joseph de Clercq had wagons valued as highly.[32] The Burgers' transportation, for instance, did not appreciate as Lubbe's did.[33] Lubbe's son Willem bought one ox wagon with a cover for 271 rixdollars; his son-in-law Barend Jacobus Burger bought the second for 258 rixdollars; nephew Barend Vorster snagged the third for only 162 rixdollars, and nephew Arnoldus Botman paid 180 rixdollars for the horse wagon. These four close kin paid handsomely for equipment that could have been gotten cheaper elsewhere. Either there was something special about Lubbe's wagons, or transportation rarely came on the market in the Cedarberg. De Clercq's 300 rixdollar wagons were near Tulbagh, not on the frontier.

Numerically, livestock formed the largest portion of the sale. The auctioning off of sheep in lots of one hundred, trek oxen by twos, cows in twos and tens must have occupied a lot of time. Price variation shows that the auction was not pro forma; buyers gauged prices—offering more here and holding back there. They were not simply buying undifferentiated livestock. Son-in-law Munnik, the wine pachter from the Cape, took home most of the sheep, over 1,400 including the ewes with lambs. One of the Orphan masters, Christoffel Brand, took an additional three hundred sheep and a large portion of the cattle: 24 trek oxen plus an additional 30 young animals. Brand had a farm on the Berg River, so he did not have to drive his herd all the way back to Cape Town, but Munnik did not register any grazing land near the Cedarberg, so either he planned to resell the animals in Stellenbosch or deliver many of them directly for slaughter, since his land was unlikely to support so large a flock.

Selling the livestock and most of the farming implements consumed the first day of the auction, which revealed the working side of an industrious agricultural enterprise. Plows, a harrow, harnesses for draft horses and oxen, empty grain sacks, scythes, and sickles all attest to active cultivation at Groote Valleij, although Barend Lubbe did not report a grain harvest to the opgaaf. Large axes, crow bars, picks, and shovels transferred from one set of working hands to another. An anvil, a bench vice, adzes, hand axes, and wrenches needed specialized skills. Loose barrel hoops suggest someone on Groote Valleij was a cooper. Josias Engelbrecht bought the hoops, along with a few empty barrels. Did he have the skills, or would he hire the hands when he needed them?

Empty barrels and two brandy stills show that like most established Western Cape farms, Groote Valleij made its own liquor. Cow hides, uncut canvas for making wagon covers or grain sacks, even a piece of tanned Russia leather all testify to handiwork on the farm. They also sold thatching reeds and broom straw, another sign of specialized skills. Auctioned individually or in small lots, this wide array of tools and farming supplies went to a range of buyers without following any discernable pattern. Kin, neighbors, and strangers made purchases large and small. Son-in-law Petrus van der Merwe spent just three stuivers on "some tools," but 12:2 rixdollars on an empty barrel.

Neighbor Christiaan Baarts parted with 1:3 rixdollars in exchange for an ax and a scale, while nephew Barend Vorster laid out 60 rixdollars for one of the brandy stills.

On the second day, the auctioneer turned to housewares, including beds with bedding, cookware, and a range of serving pieces. In addition to the expensive wagons, valuable slaves, and specialized tools that speak to hard-nosed agricultural production, the Lubbe household, like their Burger neighbors, had silver spoons, porcelain plates, and copper serving kettles for coffee and tea. The Lubbes had a baffling forty forks (a complement, perhaps, to Schalk Willem and Hester Burger's sixty plates?). If they had an equal number of plates, they did not sell them at the auction. As with the tools, the housewares went individually or in small lots to a wide range of buyers. The most expensive domestic purchase was son Willem Lubbe's bid of 57:1 rixdollars for a bedstead with a mattress, a bolster, four cushions, and both chintz and woolen coverlets. Son-in-law Josias Engelbrecht took home the two other complete beds, though they had only two cushions and no woolen coverlet, and sold for less than half the price.

Son-in-law Petrus van der Merwe—likely advised by his wife Elsie—purchased the other two most costly domestic items: a desk that sold for 25:7 rixdollars and the family Bible—in folio with a copper clasp—at 28:1 rixdollars. They also bought 19 pewter spoons, an iron meat fork and cleaver, two unidentified books, a shelf, and two guns. This eclectic assortment is characteristic of all the household purchasers, with the exception of Hester Smit from the neighboring Halve Dorschvloer.

As the Widow Burger, she was the only woman to buy in her own name. It had been just three years since her husband passed away and her own household inventory recorded modest markers of settler respectability. She made the short trip to the auction at Groote Valleij—now her daughter and son-in-law's farm—and completed just three purchases, all status-conscious housewares. She bought an expensive copper water kettle and brazier meant for table-side tea service. At 7:4 rixdollars, it was the most costly household serving or display item of the sale. The set duplicated the function of the two pewter kettles and iron chaffing dish she already possessed. The Widow Burger also bought a pewter soup tureen with a matching ladle, something she did not have in 1782, and another pair of copper candlesticks. Though Barend Lubbe's greater wealth did not accrue to Halve Dorschvloer, a little bit of status did.

RECKONING A FAMILY'S PLACE ON THE FRONTIER

A public auction was a mechanism of circulation in both broad and narrow orbits. For the Lubbes, this sale served to liquidate assets in order to pay out each heir, so wealth dispersed, following the diaspora of Barend and Martha's children: along the Olifants River, over the Cedarberg mountains, across to the Roggeveld, down to the Bokkeveld, back toward the Piketberg and all the way to Cape Town. But the auction was more than a financial convention. People, goods, and status traveled, too.

Narrowly, resources were redistributed within the family and within the confines of the Olifants River valley. Basic elements of agricultural production formally changed hands, though in a case like Groote Valleij, Johannes Hendrik and Elsie simply became the heads of a household and a farming enterprise in which they were already deeply invested. Most of the slaves, too, as both labor and as members of a household, stayed within the family. In a scattered generation of siblings, however, close kin connections could mean moving a great distance, as Anna and Arend van de Caab found when they followed Jacoba and Barend Jacobus Burger to the Roggeveld. Slaves bought by other households left the immediate family but remained in the area, potentially able to maintain some of their own social network.

Other valuable or valued items also stayed in the family: wagons, furniture, bedding, and the Bible went to children or nephews. General tools, housewares, and livestock were sold widely, but close kin or close neighbors bought the most. The Joosten brothers' expensive slave purchases, and Orphan Master Christoffel Brand's major cattle purchase serve to underscore the public, market-oriented nature of the event. Those in the narrow orbit arrived inclined to buy, undoubtedly hoping to keep some belongings in the family or in the area, but not at any cost.

Thus the auction also created a wider circulation, though on the frontier, the market was limited to those claiming a settler identity. The free people of color and mixed-race individuals present at urban sales were not buyers on the frontier.

NOTES

1. Tracey Randle, "Patterns of Consumption at Auctions: A Case Study of Three Estates" in *Contingent Lives: Social Identity and Material Culture in the VOC World*, ed. Nigel Worden, 54 (Cape Town: University of Cape Town Press, 2007); Martin Hall, "The Secret Lives of Houses: Women and Gables in the Eighteenth-Century Cape," *Social Dynamics* 20 (1994), 1.

2. Randle, "Patterns of Consumption;" Robert C.-H. Shell, "Auctions—their Good and Evil Tendency (Part 1)," *Quarterly Bulletin of the South African Library* 3:4 (June 1985), 147–51.

3. Edmund H. Burrows, *Overberg Odyssey: People, Roads and Early Days* (Swellendam: Swellendam Trust, 1994), 56–58.

4. Randle, "Patterns of Consumption," 56.

5. CA: MOOC 8/4.88, Estate Inventory of Barend Lubbe, 4 Dec. 1723. CA: MOOC 10/3.47, Vendu rol, Barend Lubbe, 10 Dec. 1723.

6. 1731 opgaaf, Hans Heese transcription.

7. CA: MOOC 8/4.114, Estate Inventory of Jan Lubbe, 22 May 1726; CA: MOOC 8/4.113, Estate Inventory of Frans Lubbe, 8 Aug. 1726.

8. Leibbrandt, *Précis*: 670f.

9. Ad Biewenga, *De Kaap de Goede Hoop: Een Nederlandse vestigingskolonie, 1680–1730* (Amsterdam: Uitgeverij Prometheus and Bert Bakker, 1999), 150–52.

10. Nigel Penn, *Forgotten Frontier*, 70. Dan Sleigh, personal communication, 10 Feb. 1998.

11. CA: MOOC 8/7.25, Estate Inventory of Paul Keyser, 26 Apr. 1752.

12. Leibbrandt, *Précis*, 775c. On the alcohol pacht system, see Gerald Groenewald, "From Tappers to *Pachters*: The Evolution of the Alcohol *Pacht* system at the Cape, c.1656–1680," paper presented to the 'Company, Castle and Control' research group meeting, 8 Sept. 2004, University of Cape Town.

13. CA: MOOC 8/6.33a, Estate Inventory of Jan Engelbrecht, 23 Apr. 1740.

14. CA: RLR 14:66, Truto, *over de Olifants rivier*, to Jacobus Louw Jacobsz, 1755–57; CA; RLR 14:96, Bidouw, *over de Olifants rivier*, to Jacobus Louw Jacobsz, 1755–57 (per L. Guelke data).

15. CA: MOOC 8/12.41b, Estate Inventory of Abraham Mouton, 15 Oct. 1768. CA: RLR 25:24, Berg Valleij, *agter Piquetberg*, to Josias Engelbrecht, 24 Jan. 1777–8 Oct. 1791 (per L. Guelke data)

16. CA: RLR 15:5, de Modder Valleij, *over de Olifants rivier* to Andries Lubbe, 12 Jan. 1757–10 Feb. 1786 (per L. Guelke data).

17. CA: 1/STB 11/19, folio 7, LFL, Widow Barend Frederik Lubbe payments on Brakkefontein through 1794; CA: 1/STB 11/19, folio 14, LFL, Paul Willem Lubbe Barendsz, payment for Brakkefontein, 11 Sept. 1794.

18. CA: RLR 23:202, *Kleijn. Fonteijnt. op de S.B.* to Willem Lubbe Barendz, 19 Apr. 1775–20 Jan. 1778 (per L. Guelke data). ARA: VOC 4214, 1764 opgaaf, Drakenstein pp. 26 & 34, (Robert Ross transcription).

19. ARA: VOC 4276, 1773 opgaaf, Drakenstein p. 25 (Robert Ross transcription).

20. CA: RLR 34:44.4, Onrust, *over de Olifants Rivier*, to Frans Lubbe 6 Oct. 1786–18 May, 1791; CA: RLR 35:45, Wedouw, *over de Olifants River*, to Frans Lubbe, 6 Oct. 1786–18 May 1791; CA: RLR 35:116.1, Bloemfontein, *over de Olifants River*, to Frans Lubbe, 11 Apr. 1773–18 May 1791 (per L. Guelke data). CA: 1/STB 11/19 folio 8 p. 37, LFL, Frans Lubbe Payments on Zandrift, in the Biedouw Valley, 1791–1803. CA: 1/STB 11/19 folio 5, LFL, Frans Lubbe, payments on Onrust, Wedouw and Bloemfontein, 1791–1803.

21. CA: RLR 15: 212, *Kaaken Valleij, in het Bokkeveld*, to Petrus van der Merwe, 22 Jan. 1760–25 Oct. 1792 (per L. Guelke data).

22. CA: RLR 28:175, *Renoster Fonteijn, op het Roggeveld*, to Barend Jacobus Burger, 23 April 1782–30 Sept. 1789 (per L Guelke data).

23. dV&P, 1981, 121.

24. Leibbrandt, *Précis*: 391c, Munnik elected to Drakenstein church council 1773; 556h, Munnik appointed heemraad for Stellenbosch in 1775; 1465i, Munnik appointed heemraad for Drakenstein, 1777.

25. Total value was RxD 2,811:0: 1/2. CA: MOOC 10/3.47, Vendu Rol: Barend Lubbe, 10 Dec. 1723.

26. Randle, "Patterns of Consumption;" 58–60.

27. CA: RLR 36:12, *Duijker Fonteijn, aan de Olifants Rivier,* to Hendrik Lubbe Hendriksz, from 28 Feb. 1788 (per L. Guelke data); CA: RLR 26;140, Hendrik van der Wat's *Gat, aan de Olifants Rivier,* to Johannes Liebenberg, from 19 Nov. 1779 (per L.Guelke data).

28. Shell, *Children of Bondage,* 308–309.

29. dV&P, 1981, 367. The Joosten brothers' grandmother, Maria Mouton, was executed in 1714 for conspiring with her slave lover to kill her husband, Frans Joosten. See Nigel Penn, "The Wife, the Farmer, and the Farmer's Slaves: Adultery and Murder on a Frontier Farm in the Early Eighteenth-Century Cape," *Kronos* 28 (2002): 1–20.

30. CA: MOOC 10/3.47, Vendu Rol, Barend Lubbe, 10 Dec. 1723.

31. Two wagons for RxD 100, CA: MOOC 8/4.92, Estate Inventory of Maria van der Merwe, n.d. [1720–27]. One wagon, 50 Cape guilders, CA: MOOC 8/5.11, Estate Inventory of Barend Burger, 12 Sept. 1729. One wagon, 100 Cape guilders, CA: MOOC 8/5.35, Estate Inventory of Willem Burger, 12 July 1731.

32. One horsewagon with traces for 8 horses and 1 ox wagon with canvas cover and yokes, each valued at RxD 300. CA: MOOC 8/20.29, Estate Inventory of Joseph de Clercq, 29 July 1791.

33. One wagon at RxD 50, CA: MOOC 8/13.46, Estate Inventory of Barend Burger, 22 Sept. 1770. One used wagon at RxD 100 and one old wagon at RxD 30, CA: MOOC 8/49.25, Estate Inventory of Schalk Willem Burger, 24 Sept. 1782.

8. *CAABWAARDS*

A Tale of Camphers and Van wyks

Like many settler women, Antoinetta Campher understood strategic marriage. Although she never found affluence, Antoinetta crafted kinship alliances and skillfully navigated serial widowhood to secure a place in the landscape for her family. Two Campher–van Wyk marriages followed her own, connecting households from Cape Town to the Olifants River, but the relationship that makes this association notable was illicit, not matrimonial. The mechanics of this family network emerge in an inadvertent traveler's tale, the day-by-day recollection of a journey from the Klawer Valley to Table Bay.

In Antoinetta's time, long-distance travel in difficult terrain was common-place for Cape residents, a necessity of colonial life and a longstanding feature of the area. Khoikhoi and San moved frequently and regularly throughout the region; they participated in trade that spanned the subcontinent.[1] Colonial settlers—or their forebears—survived a three-month ocean voyage just to reach Table Bay, assuming the Cape was their first port of call. Many of the soldiers, sailors, and officials employed by the VOC who eventually settled at the Cape made at least one return voyage to the Indies, perhaps with a stay in Ceylon or Batavia. In that context, a five-day walk beside an ox wagon or a four-hour jour-ney on horseback to pay a social call—with the return trip made the same day—was not an unreasonable expectation or an uncommon occurrence.[2]

Published narratives illuminate the traveling patterns of visitors to the Cape, but only by inference do they describe the more quotidian movements of ordi-nary residents. Anders Sparrman's account, for example, suggests wagons and oxen were available to those with the means to pay.[3] The existence of a resale market for wagons and spans of oxen implies a common presumption of travel and the necessity of moving heavy loads. The ready availability of existing wagons and full teams of oxen meant that travel with goods or provisions was not limited to farmers with adequate equipment and herds of their own. If few people were going to travel other than established farmers, it would not have been practical for anyone to maintain extra wagons and oxen. If Anders Sparrman could easily procure such materiel at various points in his journey, we can assume that equipment, livestock, and provisions were available to others.

The further Sparrman got from Cape Town, however, the more difficulty he had procuring the services of a driver and guide.[4] He was not hampered by lack of equipment or provisions, but rather by the disinclination of either settlers or Khoisan to undertake a long journey without necessity. The wide dispersion of people across the Cape region, the existence of settler farms at 14 to 20 days' travel from Cape Town,[5] and evidence of intra-African long-distance trade all indicate that people did travel great distances with some regularity. The difficulty experienced by Sparrman and others in obtaining guides and drivers suggests that the locals did not, however, travel for recreation.[6]

Eighteenth-century travelers such as Otto Mentzel, Carl Thunberg, and Anders Sparrman left copious written narratives and extensive scientific catalogs of their expeditions in Southern Africa, but travel as a matter of course is not equally well documented.[7] In order to recover the movements of ordinary inhabitants of the Cape we must turn to archaeological material, oblique documentary references, and circumstantial evidence to piece together the specific movements of individuals and families. Such a reconstruction demonstrates the effectiveness of colonial kin networks and shows that stock-farming households were not isolated entities. Ordinary travels tied frontier areas closely to the settlement at Table Bay. The mechanics of this travel underscore the importance of land tenure and land use in creating effective colonial control across great distances with limited official presence.[8]

All of the available source material on the early Western Cape points to ongoing mobility. Shell middens testify to Khoisan seasonal migrations. Glass beads connect the Cape to the Indian Ocean before the Portuguese did. Post rocks, monumental crosses, and later signal flags tied the southern African littoral to European seafaring empires. After the Dutch East India Company decided to erect a permanent presence in the region, archival practices arrived that enshrined some movements while effacing others. This documentary legacy, including official records as well as travel narratives, foregrounds settlers while Khoisan move like shadows across the landscape.

Although specific evidence of Khoisan movements is sporadic, the ripples it created are in the background of every settler-focused story. The historian and writer Karel Schoeman evokes this certainty in a novel set on the northern frontier: "Of the herdsmen, however, I remember nothing . . . I only know that they were always around somewhere . . . so that one accepted their constant presence without taking any further notice of them."[9] So the documented migration of individuals such as Titus Valentijn, Lijs, and Elsje Abrahamse from the Olifants River to Franschoek was an archival anomaly, an uncharacteristic recording of movements otherwise considered too ordinary to remark upon. This understated presence, like presumed but unnamed labor, permeates the saga linking Camphers and van Wyks.

THE JOURNEY *CAABWAARDS*

Autumn at the Cape was busy; plowing and sowing demanded the full effort of agrarian communities. Slaves, indentured servants, and able-bodied sons worked the land of the farms on which they lived and often gave help to neighbors and relatives as well. Willem van Wyk was a stock farmer, so he had no large fields of grain to tend.[10] His farm in the Klawer Valley undoubtedly had a kitchen garden, but the Kleinfontein household apparently could spare his labor, so during the plowing season in 1742, Willem set off in an ox wagon to take his sister-in-law to Cape Town.[11] Sixteen-year-old Jacoba Alida Campher was going to stay with her Aunt Margaretha. The pair traveled with Hans, a Khoisan drover in van Wyk's service. This trip, like many other journeys between the Cedarberg and Cape Town made by settlers and Khoisan alike, would have gone unrecorded had Alida not given birth the next January.

Aunt Margaretha entreated her niece to disclose the father's identity. When Alida named Willem van Wyk, Margaretha called the *fiscaal* (prosecutor), who investigated the case and charged van Wyk with incest.[12] The case against van Wyk hinged on the sleeping arrangements during the journey *Caabwaards*, so the records of the subsequent investigation inadvertently reveal a great deal about the spatial geography of outlying loan farms and the family relationships that linked those farms to one another.

The testimony also offers brief glimpses of Khoisan life within colonial frontier society. Hans, van Wyk's drover, appears only intermittently in the otherwise detailed account of this trek to Cape Town, foregrounding the issue of Khoisan mobility in the face of an increased settler presence. We can name Hans, noting his presence and his labor, but this superficial appearance only engenders more questions. How many times did he make the trip between the Olifants River and Cape Town? Whom did he know along the way?[13] As a drover or herdsman, did he ever make the trip without his master? As an individual, did he ever take this journey—or others—of his own volition?

Although Hans' appearance is fleeting, the entwined image of the Campher and van Wyk families emerges with clarity from archived sources. Alida's paternal grandmother (and Antoinetta's mother) was a former slave, Ansela van de Caab.[14] Her sister, Johanna, was born two years before her parents married.[15] Cornelis Campher and Dorothea Oelofse went on to have nine children together, Alida being penultimate. She was 19 years younger than Johanna, and only three when Johanna wed Willem van Wyk.

Willem was the third of nine children and part of a large extended family. He and Johanna did their part to help the family grow. They baptized their first child the same day they married, a predicament not unfamiliar to frontier families, for whom long distances often precluded frequent trips to the church. Johanna must have just given birth to their eighth child around the time that Willem and Alida left for Cape Town.[16] The van Wyks lived modestly. In 1742 they had just two horses, 24 cattle, and 150 sheep.[17] Although Johanna bore eight of Willem's children, four of them died young. (Johanna also had an illegitimate daughter, but Dorothea Esterhuijsen does not appear to have been part of the household in 1742.) The couple possessed less livestock than their neighbors and most of their family members, but they did have a loan farm, Kleinfontein, about 15 kilometers north of where the Doorn joins the Olifants, and a wagon.[18]

Willem van Wyk, Alida, and Hans departed these humble circumstances confident of a welcome reception in many households between Klawer Valley and Cape Town. The records from the criminal investigation of Willem van Wyk locate the travelers at specific points in the Western Cape landscape. The party spent the first night of their nine-day trip at Heeren Logement. *Oud Heemraad* Jacob Cloete's farm was on the coastal plain about ten kilometers south of the confluence of the Olifants and Doorn rivers, and a reasonable day's journey from Kleinfontein.[19] The terrain on the east, or Doorn side, of the Olifants River is rugged and hilly south of Klawer Vally, so the most efficient route would have been to cross the Olifants soon and head across the coastal plain. The Olifants River is not deep and would have afforded many crossing points in the autumn, at the end of the dry season. Just north of the Olifants-Doorn confluence there is an obvious pass through the last ridges of the Cape Fold Belt. From that point travel southward toward Heeren Logement and onward to the Cape is over relatively flat and open terrain. In fact, the modern railway line follows a natural path in the contours from Heeren Logement to the Piketberg. That same route was probably the easiest to travel by foot and ox wagon as well.[20]

Jacob Cloete was not at Heeren Logement when Willem and Alida arrived to spend the night there.[21] Although Alida remembered knocking at the door to a house and finding it locked, it seems likely that Cloete used Heeren Logement as a grazing post while he lived on another farm a day's ride to the south. When he was proposed as a heemraad for Stellenbosch in 1739, he lived near Jan Dissels Vlei, suggesting his principal residence was Groote Zeekoe Valleij en Klein Valleij (a farm first claimed by Jan Dissel in 1729).[22] Like many farmers avoiding the violent frontier war, Cloete asked to be excused from paying rent in 1739, because he "had to leave his place on account of the Hottentots."[23] He must have returned to the Olifants River area after the hostilities abated, since he maintained his loan farm claims through 1761.[24]

After camping at the farm at Heeren Logement, the travelers lodged for the next two nights with farmers Alida did not know. Having spent their first night sleeping in the wagon, this hospitality was undoubtedly welcome. The court records give great attention to where Willem and Alida slept on the various nights of their journey, which makes sense in a criminal investigation seeking to establish paternity. The fiscaal did not ask where Hans slept, though. On the nights that the party camped, it is likely that Hans slept nearby. When the group was lucky enough to have shelter at a farm, Hans probably slept with the host family's slaves or other laborers.[25]

Fig. 8.3. List of Stopping Places on the Journey *Caabwaards*

ARA: VOC 4158, OBP, 1743 - 44, vol. 2. Testimony in the case against Willem van Wyk, 1743, ff. 928 - 42, SGO 1:50 000 series.

List of Stopping Places on the Journey *Caabwaards*

	Location	Residents & Distance to the Next Stop
A	Kleinfontein	Willem van Wyk & Johanna Catherina Campher 15-20 km to the next farm
1	Heeren Logement	Jacob Cloete 30 km to the next farm
2	Brandenberg	30 km to the next farm
3	Verloerevlei	20 km to the next farm
4	Kruismansrivier	Gerrit van Wyk & Maria Eykoff 10 km to the next farm
5	Groene Valleij	Jacobus Guildenhuizen & Anna M. Koekemoer 5 km to the next farm
B	Klein Vogelvallej	Widow Joachim Scholtz (Antoinetta Campher) 10 km to the next farm
6	De Hoek	Hendrik Krugel 3–4 km to the next farm
C	Rietfontein	Ernst Christiaan Ehlers 30 km to the next farm
7	De Gunst	Floris Smit & Margaretha Steenkamp 40–50 km to their camping spot
8	Cape Flats	10–20 km to Cape Town
9	Cape Town	

The first farm where the travelers found shelter was near present-day Brandenburg, the second near Verloerevlei. This itinerary broke up the distance between Heeren Logement and the Piketberg into two legs of thirty kilometers and a final leg of twenty kilometers. Assuming a traveling pace of about five kilometers an hour, the approximately eighty kilometers between Heeren Logement and Kruismansrivier would have been feasible in three days.[26] The fourth night of their trip the travelers stayed with Gerrit van Wyk, Willem's brother.

Gerrit van Wyk had recently acquired the permit for Kruismansrivier, which lay on the east side of the Piketberg, along the most likely route from Heeren Logement to Table Bay.[27] When Willem, Alida, and Hans called on him, Gerrit was 38 years old, thrice married, and the father of nine living children.[28] He went on to have 19, 12 with his third wife Maria Eykoff. All of his children lived to adulthood and married, which makes the couple's 1742 opgaaf return a bit perplexing. According to the census, Gerrit and Maria were living in reduced circumstances on Kruismansrivier. It appears that the couple moved to the Piketberg region the previous year, when Gerrit took up the permit on the farm.[29] Prior to 1741, the van Wyks were registered in Stellenbosch. In 1740 they reported eight slaves—six men, a woman, and a boy—eight horses, 25 head of cattle, 150 sheep, and 12 pigs; they grew wheat, rye, and barley.[30] Later in that same year, van Wyk took out a lease on Kruismansrivier in partnership with Jacobus Louw Jacobusz.[31] The next year's opgaaf shows a precipitous decline in the van Wyks' fortunes. By late April 1741 Gerrit, Maria, and their toddler son were living on Kruismansrivier with only one horse and 24 head of cattle. The slaves, sheep, pigs, and agricultural produce of the previous year were gone.[32] Even more curious, van Wyk's seven children from his previous marriages were missing, too.

Gerrit and his second wife, Maria Prevot, appear in the 1731 opgaaf and in Governor de la Fontaine's detailed survey of the colonists, in both cases with six minor children, including four from van Wyk's first marriage.[33] De la Fontaine describes the household as indebted and "living with livestock in the veld," but the couple reported a small grain harvest that year, so they cannot have been itinerant. After Maria Prevot's death, van Wyk predictably remarried, but this wedding dramatically altered his household composition, seemingly separating him from his existing children.

At least van Wyk's offspring were not recorded as part of Gerrit's household after he married Maria Eyckoff. Perhaps these children lived with their mothers' relatives until they married. Perhaps they lodged with other relatives or worked for neighboring families. It appears from the 1743 opgaaf that van Wyk's eldest sons Gerrit Gerritsz and Abraham were living as bachelors in the Cape district.[34] His two teenaged daughters did not marry until 1748, and the next child was only ten in 1743, so she and her younger siblings certainly were not living on their own in the early 1740s. Whatever the case, they remain submerged in the archives from 1731 until Gerrit Gerritsz and Abraham surfaced in 1743 opgaaf, and the rest of the children upon their marriages.

Alida told the fiscaal she slept at Kruismansrivier with her cousin Elisabeth Scholtz, who might have been a lodger, or another guest of the van Wyks. Alida does not explain her cousin's appearance there. Elisabeth's presence on the farm, along with Gerrit's absent children, suggests a certain fluidity among frontier households. Although several elements of the Campher and van Wyk drama imply that Alida, Johanna, Willem, and Gerrit may have lived at the margins of settler conformity, the circulation of labor and family members among Burger, Botma, and Lubbe households indicates Elisabeth's presence was unremarkable in a kin network.

FAMILY OBLIGATIONS: VISITS AND RESOURCES

After four long days of travel, Willem and Alida took advantage of family connections and neighborly obligations to slow their pace. They left Kruismansrivier in Gerrit's company and journeyed an easy ten kilometers to the Groene Valleij farm, where Jacobus Gildenhuizen and his wife Anna Maria Koekemoer ran a household of some means.[35] When Alida visited, Groene Valleij's abundant herds and flocks placed the Gildenhuizens well above the middling ranks of stock farmers.[36] Four slaves—three men and one woman—provided labor to help with both livestock and cultivation. Their efforts the previous season yielded a bumper crop of wheat. This year, Gerrit had come to lend a hand with the plowing.[37] Despite the presence of slaves—and the likelihood of undocumented Khoisan laborers—Groene Valleij nevertheless needed to call on the assistance of neighbors to get the fields prepared.

Only proximity connects the van Wyks and the Gildenhuizens; undoubtedly Gerrit was compensated for his efforts. He planted only one *muid* of wheat that year, his first attempt at arable agriculture after moving to Kruismansrivier.[38] With few stock of his own to tend and limited work to do in his own field, Gerrit might have been inclined to help a neighbor, especially if the return on that labor could help him augment the meager productivity of his own farm.

Willem, Alida, and Hans did not stay to help; instead they proceeded southward the next day. En route, they called on Alida's aunt, Antoinetta Campher, probably at Klein Vogelvlei, a scant five kilometers south of Groene Valleij at the edge of the Piketberg. Antoinetta, the widow of Joachim Scholtz, had previously been married to Ary van Wyk, Willem and Gerrit's cousin. Ary claimed Klein Vogelvlei from 1724 to 1730.[39] Joachim Scholtz, then married to Anna

Maria Swart, took over the lease in 1730. Anna Maria, herself twice widowed before she married Scholtz, brought resources to their marriage.[40] Her previous husband, Marten Mecklenburg, held 11 loan farm permits between 1706 and 1715, all of them in the Berg River area to the south of the Piketberg. Scholtz, by contrast, was fairly poor. He had no property until after his 1727 marriage to Anna Maria.[41]

After his wife's death, Scholtz petitioned the Council of Policy to undertake the care and maintenance of Anna Maria's illegitimate daughter, since he could not afford it. "As the petitioner is maimed and poor, he finds it difficult to earn enough for himself and his own child."[42] He managed somehow to maintain the lease on Klein Vogelvlei until his 1733 marriage to Antoinetta Campher, Ary van Wyk's widow and the previous mistress of the farm. Despite being "maimed and poor," Joachim successfully courted Antoinetta. She was clearly richer, but Joachim had the permit for Klein Vogelvlei. As the mother of ten children and a stock owner, Antoinetta obviously needed land, and Ary van Wyk did not leave them a farm.

In her first year of widowhood, Antoinetta lived with eight of her ten children and one slave. She reported three horses, 48 head of cattle, 63 sheep, and an exceptional crop of 45 *muid* of wheat produced from three *muid* sown.[43] Widower Scholtz lived with his only surviving son and kept two horses, 6 head of cattle, and 50 sheep.[44] In combining their resources, Antoinetta and Joachim had a large household and reasonable, but not exceptional, resources.

By 1740 Antoinetta found herself widowed again, but in straitened circumstances. According to the opgaaf, she lived with five of her ten children still at home but no livestock or agricultural produce.[45] She was unlikely to have been as destitute as she appears on paper. We can surmise from Alida's testimony that Antoinetta continued to live on Klein Vogelvlei after Hendrik Krugel acquired the permit in 1738.[46] Antoinetta's son Willem van Wyk lived close by. Her widowed daughter-in-law was also in the neighborhood and had large flocks and herds.[47] Undoubtedly Antoinetta had access to resources beyond what she reported in the opgaaf.

Although the permit for Klein Vogelvlei belonged to Hendrik Krugel in 1742, he appears to have lived on De Hoek, about ten kilometers to the south. De Hoek was the first farm he claimed; his widow subsequently assumed the title, strongly suggesting it was their principal, residential farm.[48] Krugel held short-term leases on 13 other farms from the Piketberg to the Doorn River, including farms in the Roggeveld, and extending into the Karoo.[49] Krugel and Maria van der Swann were prosperous and productive farmers who could afford to sublet Klein Vogelvlei or to allow the twice-widowed Antoinetta Campher to live in the *hofsteede* (farm house) in exchange for labor or grazing rights. In 1743 the Krugels managed abundant livestock and exceptional grain production with the labor of 12 slaves—seven men, two women, and two boys.[50]

Alida's testimony hints at a labor exchange between the Krugels and the van Wyks. After visiting for an hour with Antoinetta Campher on Klein Vogel-vlei, Willem and Alida traveled only as far as the farm at De Hoek that evening, logging their second consecutive short day. Alida slept that night with her sister Sophia, who was married to Christoffel van Wyk, Antoinetta's fourth child.[51] Surely more than coincidence put Antoinetta's son and daughter-in-law at the Krugel's during the plowing season.[52] Christoffel and Sophia had two sons and a horse, according to the 1742 opgaaf.[53] They had no landed property of their own.[54] The 1743 opgaaf records Christoffel and Sophia immediately after Hendrik Krugel and his wife Maria, which further supports the contention that the younger, poor couple lived in the more prosperous Krugel household.[55]

Following two days of light travel leavened by visits to friends and relatives, the travelers put in another long day. Setting off southward from De Hoek, they first called at the farm of Ernst Christiaan Ehlers, only three to four kilometers from the Krugel house.[56] Somewhere thereabouts they encountered Hans Jacob Brits, who traveled with them to the outskirts of the settlement at Table Bay.[57] Alida does not mention Brits's company, nor does she say why they stopped at a farm at Rietfontein before proceeding onward. Late that evening the party arrived at Floris Smit's farm near Riebeeck's Casteel.[58] Alida did not know Smit and his wife, Margaretha Steenkamp, nor did she recall them by name. Brits identified the couple in his statement to the fiscaal.[59] Although they remembered different details, Hans Jacob's testimony was consistent with Alida's. After spending the night with the Smits at De Gunst, the van Wyk party continued southward, putting in another long day to reach the Cape Flats. They covered between forty and fifty kilometers, a journey that would have taken eight to ten hours of steady progress. According to Brits, they made camp after midnight, while Alida recalled stopping after the moon had set.[60] The group would have had to rest the oxen at some point during the day, allowing them to drink and graze. If the day were warm, they would have sought shade during the hottest part of the afternoon, so a late-night arrival is plausible.

From the Cape Flats it would have been a comfortable journey into Cape Town, perhaps less than four hours, since there were wagon roads in the vicinity. Brits parted company with Willem, Alida, and Hans at the Salt River, leaving Willem to deliver his sister-in-law to her aunt, Margaretha Oelofse.[61] It took this small colonial traveling party nine days to journey from the confluence of the Olifants and Doorn rivers to the settlement at Table Bay. Their steady voyage demonstrates connections between the Cedarberg and Cape Town. The group's relationships to the people they saw along the way reveal the fibers that bound settler society: interconnected land claims, family relationships, and a sense of shared identity that included Alida, despite her slave grandmother, but erased the drover Hans from the landscape.

AN ALMOST TYPICAL TRIP

Other than the allegations of incestuous sexual encounters when Willem van Wyk and Jacoba Alida Campher slept unchaperoned, the trip itself appears to have been unremarkable. There is no room in the format of legal proceedings for the fiscaal or the Council of Justice to interject opinion, except in the transcript of the interrogation of Willem van Wyk. In this moment where they might have made moral judgments, the colonial authorities did not question the premise behind the trip, the trip's length, or its feasibility. Long, slow travel by ox wagon was not just a necessity, it was commonplace. Such travel was important link between Cape Town and the outlying areas, especially frontier regions like the Olifants River. There was no regular postal system—as there was to the Overberg and Swellendam—so the travel of settlers themselves took on an increasing importance. The method of travel by ox wagon, the pace, the practice of lodging with farmers where possible and camping when not, are all consistent with published travel accounts of the eighteenth century.

In a region without roads or inns, travelers would have to know the way to their destination. The course plotted by Willem van Wyk was the most logical and practical route to get from north to south. The stops as recounted by Alida, Hans Jacob Brits (for two nights), and van Wyk make sense. They are all a reasonable day's travel from one another, except for two nights the party spent near the Piketberg. There family and neighborly connections slowed the pace of travel. Alida could have arrived at her aunt a day sooner, had speed or her arrival date been the top priority.

In a society that reckoned time by agricultural cycles rather than calendrical dates, one day more or less en route would not have been as important a consideration as making family visits and maintaining connections across great distances.[62] Those links also must have provided purposeful communication, since Willem van Wyk appeared in Cape Town and was interrogated by members of the Council of Justice in March 1743, ten or eleven months after his trip with Alida.[63] It is unlikely he stayed in Cape Town during that time.

Willem and Johanna van Wyk had livestock and held permits for two outlying loan farms.[64] Consequently Willem had duties which, though they may have afforded him an absence of three weeks or so during the autumn, would have required his presence in the spring for calving and lambing. Surely at least once in those intervening months, he had to move the beasts from one grazing area to another. The van Wyks had no slaves, though Willem may have been able to rely on Khoisan labor, like the drover Hans. The van Wyk sons were too young to manage on their own, the eldest surviving boy being only 3 at the time.[65] Willem and Johanna Catharina were not poor but they did not have an abundance of livestock or other agricultural resources. Their own children were small and neither of their respective families was wealthy. The most reasonable assumption is that Willem returned to the Olifants River area in May or June of 1742, then made another trip to the Cape when he was questioned in March 1743.

THE SPATIAL EXERCISE OF COLONIAL AUTHORITY

Whether he was summoned to the Council of Justice and the message reached him on Kleinfontein, or whether he happened to be in Cape Town and his presence was made known to the Council, Willem van Wyk's story reveals aspects of colonial governance. Knowledge of individuals and their whereabouts, though not necessarily precise and instantaneous, was adequate for the exercise of justice. In a more celebrated case, the insurgent Estienne Barbier remained at large for 17 months in an area only about sixty kilometers from the Castle, a day's ride on horseback.[66] Van Wyk, by contrast, was summoned for questioning from his farm over three hundred kilometers from the Castle, meaning he made the round trip journey at least twice in two years. The cases are admittedly different, since Barbier was harbored on farms as a fugitive. In contrast there is no evidence to suggest that van Wyk did not present himself willingly before the law. Nevertheless, both cases demonstrate the extent to which communication was more effective in the VOC colony than long, thinly populated distances and limited technology might suggest.

In the more densely settled Drakenstein, an area with freehold grants dating to 1691, a popular bandit could find refuge for months.[67] Officials searched the area and posted a notice on the church door to no avail.[68] Although Barbier was a wanted criminal, people understood their own version of events. The populace kept its own counsel and kept Barbier safe from the brutal consequences of VOC justice—at least for a time.[69] Four years later, in a sparsely populated and recently settled area of the frontier stretching from the Piketberg to the Olifants River, settlers maintained communication with colonial authority and with family members near Table Bay. Although the closest church door on which the government could post a notice was the Drakenstein church at Paarl—250 kilometers away—van Wyk nevertheless got the message that he was accused in a criminal case and wanted for questioning.

Willem van Wyk's 1743 appearance in Cape Town should not be used to exaggerate the depth or effectiveness of either official or informal communication at midcentury. This example merely serves to point out that communication over long distances with limited technology and without a formal system of relays did take place. The frontier was not out of touch or beyond the reach of VOC authority centered at the Castle of Good Hope. Although the frontier was attractive to fugitives of all sorts, a notion of authority emanating from

Cape Town nevertheless existed.[70] This authority communicated with individuals such as van Wyk, despite his physical distance from the Castle.

How that message arrived and why van Wyk responded remain historical uncertainties. As Ginzburg points out, historical knowledge is ". . . indirect, presumptive, and conjectural."[71] The documents do not always tell us everything we want to know.

NOTES

1. Richard G. Klein, "The Prehistory of Stone Age Herders in the Cape Province, South Africa," *Prehistoric Pastoralism in South Africa* (South African Archaeological Society Goodwin Series 5, June 1986): 5–12; John Parkington, "Time and Place: Some Observations on Spatial and Temporal Patterning in the Later Stone Age Sequence in South Africa," *South Africa Archaeological Bulletin* 35 (1980), 73–83.

Edwin N. Wilmsen, "For Trinkets Such as Beads: A Revalorization of Khoisan Labor in Colonial Southern Africa," in *Sources and Methods in African History: Spoken, Written, Unearthed*, 80–101, eds. Toyin Falola and Christian Jennings (Rochester: University of Rochester Press, 2003).

2. O.F. Mentzel, *A Geographical and Topographical Description of the Cape of Good Hope* (1787), ed. H. J. Mandelbrote, trans. G.V. Marais and J. Hoge, (Cape Town: Van Riebeeck Society, 1944).

3. Anders Sparrman, *A Voyage to the Cape of Good Hope Toward the Antarctic Polar Circle Round the World and to the Country of the Hottentots and the Caffres from the Year 1772–1776*, 2 vols., ed. V.S. Forbes, trans. J. & I. Rudner (Cape Town: Van Riebeeck Society, 1975), I:135, 175.

4. Sparrman I:176.

5. Sparrman I:146.

6. ARA: VOC 10817, *Kopie-dagregister van vaandrig August Fredrik Beutler van zijn reis in het binnenland van Kaap de Goede Hoop*, 1752, also describes the difficulty procuring guides.

7. Mentzel, *Description of the Cape of Good Hope*; Carl Peter Thunberg, *Travels at the Cape of Good Hope 1772–1775*, ed. V.S. Forbes (Cape Town: Van Riebeeck Society, 1986).

8. For a discussion of how kin networks functioned in nineteenth-century capital accumulation and transfer, see Wayne Dooling, "Agrarian Transformation in the Western Districts of the Cape Colony, 1883–c. 1900" (PhD diss., University of Cambridge, 1996). Both Leonard Guelke and P.J. van der Merwe argue convincingly that frontier households were not economically or socially isolated from the rest of the colony: Guelke, "The Early European Settlement of South Africa" (PhD diss., University of Toronto, 1974), 213–35, 258–90; van der Merwe, *Trek: Studies oor die Mobiliteit van de Pioniersbevolking aan die Kaap* (Bloomfontein: Nasionale Pers Beperk, 1945). For studies of the economic incorporation of the colonial frontier see S.D. Neumark, *Economic*

Influences on the South African Frontier, 1652–1836 (Stanford: Stanford University Press, 1957) and Pieter van Duin and Robert Ross, *The Economy of the Cape Colony in the Eighteenth Century, Intercontinenta* No. 7 (Leiden: Centre for the History of European Expansion, 1987).

9. Karel Schoeman, *This Life*, trans. Elsa Silke (Cape Town: Human and Rousseau, 2005), 30.

10. ARA: VOC 4152, *OBP*, 1742 opgaaf. Van Wyk did not report any grain sowed or harvested.

11. Plowing and sowing season was in April and May. Mentzel, 158; Thunberg, 136.

12. ARA: VOC 4158, *OBP*, 1743–44, vol. 2. Testimony in the case against Willem van Wyk, 1743, ff. 928–43. I explore the ways this case illuminates sexuality and colonial morality in "Sex, Religion, and Other Cultural Exigencies in the Early-Modern Atlantic," paper presented at the Berkshire Conference on the History of Women, Scripps College, Claremont, 2–5 June 2005.

13. Given the numerous examples of connections among slaves and servants provided in court testimony regarding fugitives, it is highly likely that Hans had connections of his own at the various farms where Willem and Jacoba Alida called on their trip.

14. Heese, *Groepe sonder Grense* (Robertson trans), 34; dv&P, 1981, 132.

15. The arrival of an *onegte voorkind*, or an illegitimate child, was not an irredeemable social stigma for either parent. See Gerald Groenewald, "Parents, Children and Illegitimacy in Dutch Colonial Cape Town, c. 1652–1795," paper presented to the 'Company, Castle and Control' research group meeting, 2006, University of Cape Town, 4, 21.

16. Cornelis van Wyk was baptized on 21 Apr. 1742, dV&P, 1966, 1149.

17. ARA: VOC 4152, *OBP*, 1742 opgaaf, Drakenstein p. 16.

18. CA: RLR 38:156, 14 Nov. 1735, Willem van Wyk Willemsz permit for *Kleinfontein, aan de Olifants Rivier,* 1735–56.

19. CA: RLR 38:100, *Heeren Logement, aan de Olifants Rivier,* to Jacob Cloete, 4 July 1732–22 Oct. 1761 (per L Guelke data).

20. The Heeren Logement cave sheltered Governor Simon van der Stel and his traveling party in 1685. The cave was a frequent traveler's waypoint; subsequent visitors carved their names onto the rock wall, creating a tourist site visited since the early 1700s. For more on the site as a tourist attraction, see van Rooyen and Steyn, 23.

21. Jacob was Elsie Cloete's nephew, so he was kin to the van der Merwes (first cousin to Schalk, Marietjie, and their siblings), though not related to the Camphers and van Wyks.

22. Leibbrandt, *Précis*, I: 244i. In addition to Heeren Logement, Cloete claimed another parcel in the region: CA: RLR 9:318, *Groote Zeekoe Valleij, over de Olifants Rivier,* to Jacob Cloete 5 July 1731–1 Dec. 1744. Dissel claimed two farms in the area, Groote Zeekoe Valleij and Renoster Hoek. *Renoster Hoek aan de Piquetberg:* CA: RLR 6:85, 15 July 1726–16 Aug. 1728. CA: RLR 8:30, 19 Aug. 1729–21 Feb. 1731. CA: RLR 9:25, 18 Sept. 1731–31 Oct. 1732. *Groote Zeekoe Valleij over de Olifants Rivier:* CA: RLR 7:54, 14 Apr. 1728–14 Apr. 1729. CA: RLR 8:264, 6 May 1729–6 May, 1731. CA: RLR 9:205, 2 June 1731–5 July 1732. (All per L. Guelke data.)

23. Leibbrandt, *Précis*, I: 244l.

24. CA: RLR 38:100, *Groote Zeekoe Valleij, over de Olifants Rivier,* to Jacob Cloete 5 July 1731–22 Oct. 1761. This permit duplicates the years 1731–44 covered by RLR 9:318 and extends the permit until 1761.

25. In this case, the inquisitor/fiscal failed in his role as an anthropologist of Khoisan actions, since his attention was focused solely on the activities of Willem and Jacoba Alida. Carlo Ginzburg, "The Inquisitor as Anthropologist," in *Clues, Myths and the Historical Method,* trans. John and Anne C. Tedeschi (Baltimore: Johns Hopkins University Press, 1992), 156–64.

26. Guelke reckons a walking pace of about 6 km per hour when figuring the size of loan farms. "Land Tenure and Settlement at the Cape 1652–1812," *History of Surveying and Land Tenure in South Africa, Collected Papers,* Vol. 1., ed. C.G.C. Martin and K.J. Friedlaender (Rondebosch, University of Cape Town Department of Surveying, 1984), 21. Burchell's calculations work out to be 4.7 km/hour, based on traveling 15.25 miles in 5.25 hours, William J. Burchell, *Selections from Travels in the Interior of Southern Africa,* ed. H. Clement Notcutt (London: Oxford University Press, 1935), 115. The notes to Sparrman's text report the average speed of an ox wagon between 4 and 5.5 km per hour, slowing to 2–3 km per hour in the mountains or crossing rivers, Sparrman 145, n71. Traveling time in a day could be anywhere between 5 and 15 hours, depending on the weather and the terrain. John Barrow, *An Account of Travels into the Interior of Southern Africa,* (London: T. Caldwell Jr. and W. Davies, 1801), 55. See also Sparrman 146, n74.

27. CA: RLR 10:132, 21 Nov. 1741 (through 1756 per L. Guelke's RLR data).

28. dv&P, 1966, 1153–54.

29. ARA: VOC 4147, *OBP,* 1741 opgaaf, Drakenstein p. 10.

30. ARA: VOC 4143, *OBP,* 1740 opgaaf, Stellenbosch p. 4.

31. CA: RLR 10:96, 27 Oct. 1740.

32. ARA: VOC 4147, *OBP,* 1741 opgaaf, Drakenstein p. 10.

33. Leonard Guelke, Robert C.-H. Shell and Anthony Whyte, compilers. "The de la Fontaine Report," (New Haven: Opgaaf Project, 1990).

34. ARA VOC 4156, *OPB,* opgaaf 1741, Cape, p. 1

35. CA: RLR 10:94, Groene Valleij to Jacobus Gildenhuizen, 18 Oct. 1740 (through 1764 per L. Guelke data).

36. ARA: VOC 4152, *OBP,* 1742 opgaaf, Drakenstein p. 14: 20 horses, 70 cattle, 300 sheep; 10 *muid* of wheat planted, 100 *muid* harvested.

37. ARA: VOC 4156, *OBP,* 1743–1744, Vol. 2. Criminal inquiry against farmer Willem van Wyk, 1743. Testimony of Jacoba Alida Campher, f. 938, 16 Mar. 1743.

38. ARA: VOC 4152, *OPB,* 1742 opgaaf, Drakenstein p. 14.

39. CA: RLR 5:130, 18 May 1724 & CA: RLR 8:153, 1 Dec. 1729 (through 1730 per L. Guelke data).

40. dV&P, 1966: 856.

41. CA: RLR 9:90, *Klein Vogel Valleij aan de Piquetberg* to Jochem Scholtz, 20 Nov. 1730–7 Jan. 1738 (per L. Guelke data).

42. Leibbrandt, *Précis:* 1053c, 26 June 1732.

43. ARA: VOC 4118, *OBP,* 1732 opgaaf, Drakenstein p. 9.

44. ARA: VOC 4121, *OBP,* 1733 opgaaf, Drakenstein p. 7.

45. ARA: VOC 4143, *OBP,* 1740 opgaaf, Drakenstein p. 10.

46. CA: RLR 10:8, 31 Dec. 1738 (through 1791 per L. Guelke data).

47. ARA: VOC 4143, *OBP*, 1740 opgaaf, Drakenstein p. 10. Willem possessed a horse and 30 cattle. Widow van Wyk had 12 horses, 30 cattle, and 500 sheep.

48. CA: RLR 9:152, 1 Mar. 1731 (through 1750 per L. Guelke data). CA: RLR 38: 53, 1 Mar. 1731 recapitulates the original lease, then transfers it to Krugel's widow (through 1792 per L. Guelke data).

49. Krugel's farms included CA: RLR 9: 15, [unnamed farm, probably Klein Vogel Valleij] *aan dese hoek aan de Piquetberg*, 1 Mar. 1731 to 21 May 1750. CA: RLR 38: 53, [unnamed farm, probably Klein Vogel Valleij] *aan dese hoek aan de Piquetberg*, to the Widow Hendrik Krugel, 1 Mar. 1731 to 21 Nov. 1792. CA: RLR 11:156, *Elandsdrift, in het Karroo*, 31 Apr. 1747 to 24 Apr. 1748. CA: RLR 15:128, *Blinde Fonteijn, aan de Piquetberg*, 1 Feb. 1759 to 29 Dec. 1759. CA: RLR 16:94, *De Grendel, aan de Roggeveld*, 8 Dec. 1760 to 24 Dec. 1761. CA: RLR 16:181, *De Vondeling, aan de Hantam*, 24 Sept. 1761 to 18 Sept. 1762. CA: RLR 17:72, *Kleijn Riet Rivier, op de Roggeveld*, 10 May 1762 to 9 May 1765. CA: RLR 17:120, *Modder Fonteijn, over de Kleijn Riet Rivier*, 13 Oct. 1762 to 29 Mar. 1769. CA: RLR 18: 65, *Matijes Fonteijn, in 't Romst Veldt*, 3 Dec. 1763 to 29 Sept. 1769. CA: RLR 18: 269, *Ratel Fonteijn, aan 't Roggeveld*, 18 Mar. 1765 to 29 Sept. 1769.

50. ARA: VOC 4156, *OBP* 1743 opgaaf, Drakenstein p. 17: 6 horses, 56 cattle, 350 sheep; 7 *muid* of wheat planted, 140 *muid* harvested, about twice the average grain production.

51. dv&P, 1966: 1149. dV&P, 1981: 132.

52. In addition to being Antoinetta's daughter-in-law, Sophia Campher was also Antoinetta's niece. Consequently her husband Christoffel was also her first cousin.

53. ARA: VOC 4152, *OPB* 1742 opgaaf, Drakenstein p. 3.

54. Christoffel van Wyk first appears in the loan farm records in 1746. CA: RLR 11:105, 28 Mar. 1746, for the farm Bokjesfontein in the Koude Bokkeveld.

55. ARA: VOC 4156, *OPB* 1743 opgaaf, Drakenstein p. 17.

56. CA: RLR 9:160, *Rietfontein, om die hoek van de Piquetberg over de Bergrivier*, 17 Mar. 1731 (through 1763 per L. Guelke data).

57. ARA: VOC 4158, *OBP*, 1743–44, Vol. 2. Criminal inquiry against farmer Willem van Wyk, 1743. Testimony of Hans Jacob Brits, folio 940, 1 Apr. 1743.

58. CA: RLR 10:90, De Gunst, 5 Oct. 1740 (through 1756 per L. Guelke data).

59. ARA: VOC 4158, *OBP*, van Wyk inquiry, Brits statement, f. 940, 1 Apr. 1743.

60. ARA: VOC 4158, *OBP*, van Wyk inquiry, Brits statement, f. 940, 1 Apr. 1743; Campher statement, f. 938, 16 Mar. 1743.

61. ARA: VOC 4158, *OBP*, van Wyk inquiry, Brits statement, f. 940, 1 Apr. 1743.

62. On the social reckoning of time, see Sylvie-Anne Goldberg, *La Clepsydre* (Paris: Albin Michel, 2000).

63. ARA: VOC 4158, *OBP*, van Wyk interrogation, f. 943, 13 Apr. 1743.

64. ARA: VOC 4152, *OBP* 1742 opgaaf, Drakenstein p. 16. ARA: VOC 4146, *OBP* 1743 opgaaf, Drakenstein p. 17. CA: RLR 38:156, *Kleinfontein, aan de Olifants Rivier*, 14 Nov.1735–15 Apr. 1756. CA: RLR 10: 139, 25 Jan. 1742 *Vleermuijs, aan de Bergrivier* (through 1745 per L. Guelke data).

65. dV&P,1966: 1149.

66. Nigel Penn, "Estienne Barbier: An Eighteenth Century Cape Social Bandit," in *Rogues, Rebels and Runaways: Eighteenth-Century Cape Characters* (Cape Town: David Philip, 1999), 101–130.

67. L. Guelke, *The Southwestern Cape Colony 1657–1750, Freehold Land Grants.* Map, no scale (Department of Geography Publication Series, Occasional Paper No. 5. University of Waterloo, 1987).

68. The Drakenstein gemeente of the Dutch Reformed Church was established at Paarl in 1691.

69. Barbier was tortured and executed on 14 Nov. 1739. Penn, "Estienne Barbier," 126.

70. For a detailed discussion of fugitives, see Nigel Penn, *Rogues, Rebels and Runaways: Eighteenth-Century Cape Characters* (Cape Town: David Phillip, 1999).

71. "Clues, Roots of an Evidential Paradigm," 106.

IV

Endings

The Olifants River has fixed starting and ending points. It originates in a mountain spring and ends where it meets the Atlantic Ocean near Papendorp. Crafting a history of the peoples who have lived from its waters requires active intervention to mark the beginning and ending of a narrative, however. The communities acting in this drama lived before 1725 and persisted well beyond 1838—although Khoisan groups lived in dramatically altered circumstances by the end of the eighteenth century. The interactions at the heart of colonial dynamics also had precedent before the first settler land claims in the Cedarberg, while some aspects of domination persisted well into the twentieth century—and indeed exist today.

This final section of the book provides two approaches to summing up. Chapter 9 interrogates the historical practice of periodization. It argues that characterizing a frontier region as orthodox—or not—productively complicates temporal as well as geographic and social frameworks of frontier studies. Emphasizing the ebbs and flows of conquest reminds us that settler success was not the result of steady progress, but rather an ongoing battle waged in fits and starts. Consequently, no single end point clearly marks the triumph of colonial households, which were so crucial to settler survival throughout the eighteenth century. The Appendix provides chronological details of the process I discuss in Chapter 9. Chapter 10 considers the Cedarberg's place in the broad sweep of South African history.

9. IMPOSING ORTHODOXY ON THE FRONTIER,

OR WHY ENDINGS MATTER

The eighteenth-century Cedarberg was a time and place of intersections. The fluidity of social and geographic boundaries allowed space for people to negotiate the terms of belonging: to families, to households, to communities. But whether on the frontier or in Cape Town, colonial society was far from infinitely flexible. As the social norms of the ruling class—rooted in Christian, European customs—became increasingly dominant, the material benefits of membership in that society were evident. Although not all settlers had access to land and labor, very few who were not settlers could make a claim to those resources on the northern frontier by the end of the century.

The preceding chapters demonstrate how settlers construed, imposed, and maintained colonial orthodoxy in the Cedarberg—which remained a frontier region for a century precisely because those norms remained contested. While many inhabitants conformed to orthodox expectations, some pointedly did not. When the van der Merwes, Burgers, and Lubbes moved north in search of land, they brought ideas about family and property ownership along with them. They also increasingly acquired material goods that demonstrated their inclusion in the dominant culture and that served as symbols of their status within it. The Camphers and van Wyks were less economically secure, yet these individuals still clearly belonged to the orthodox social order—despite illegitimate births, the Camphers' mixed-race heritage, and a sexual transgression significant enough to warrant criminal proceedings against Willem van Wyk. These deviations from normative expectations suggest that everyone did not need to adhere completely in order for orthodoxy to prevail in the settler community. In fact, the persistence of some exceptions to the prevailing order demonstrates how powerful social norms became over three generations of frontier families. The status quo was entrenched enough to tolerate some nonconformity without being challenged fundamentally.

Household by household, colonial society fashioned this hegemony on an apron string, relying on domestic relationships to nurture a shared sense of community that permitted some variations. Maintaining claims to a frontier nevertheless required ongoing force. Two generations of Lubbe militia appointments highlight the active resistance that needed quelling. In 1739 Veldkorporal Barend Lubbe was directed not to "antagonize the 'Hottentot Pokkebaas Claas,' or any other peaceful Khoikhoi."[1] The colony was, however, at war with several hostile indigenous groups, and for months during 1739 the settler occupation of the Cedarberg was precarious. Five decades later, colonists still defended their property with arms. In October 1793, *Veldwagmeesters* (militia officers) Frans Lubbe (Biedouw) and Johannes Hendrik Lubbe (Olifants River) sent Donderbosch Pokkebaas and four companions *Caabwaards* as prisoners accused of fomenting rebellion on the frontier.[2] In light of Khoikhoi naming practices, it is likely that the men called Pokkebaas were related—possibly grandfather and grandson, though perhaps they simply shared a clan name.[3] In any event, Pokkebaas is an unusual enough moniker that a connection between them seems likely, making specific the Khoisan challenge to the Lubbe family's claims to the farms at Groote Valleij and Bloemfontein. Clearly, the Cedarberg was still actively contested in the 1790s and the dispossession of Khoisan clans was not forgotten easily.

Such frontier intersections in the archives were often unexpected, providing the kernels of good stories. Coaxing a larger meaning from these tales involves imposing order on messy, many-headed human experience, and shaping the events of the past into a coherent narrative that ". . . is essential to individual and social identity."[4] Narrative structure, however, requires a beginning, a middle, and an end, demarcations that neither lived history nor its traces— whether in the landscape or the archives—provide in tidy packages.

The starting and stopping points of a story extracted from the longer flow of human events are hardly arbitrary.[5] Periodization is integral to interpretation.[6] The history of the Cedarberg is as old as the hills themselves, but the history of the frontier opens exactly in 1725, when settlers began making land claims that brought the region into sustained colonial engagements between two groups of peoples with different cultural concepts of what claiming the land meant. Trekboere changed the physical and legal landscape of the Olifants River Valley indelibly by asserting permanent, alienable, and bounded claims to land, and by appropriating commonly used territory from Khoikhoi and San, eliciting violent retribution.

This shift in land tenure regimes was a monumental change with a precise date, but the subsequent imposition of dominant colonial norms was uneven, gradual, and long incomplete. The analytical tension between the characterization of frontier regions as either serially opened and closed or as orthodox and heterodox is particularly acute around questions of periodization. Working from Guelke's articulation of frontier orthodoxy as a model, instead of working with the organizing principle of opening followed eventually by closure, makes specifying exact endings more difficult. But this approach provides other intellectual rewards—including the small comfort that a troubling periodization reflects the region's troubled history.[7]

ORTHODOXY AND CLOSURE

If one conceptualizes a frontier as opening and closing—in many ways a visually and analytically useful metaphor of contested expansion—then bringing the region's story to a close comes naturally.[8] Part of the appeal of "closure" for historians is the comfortable parallel to periodization—demarcating beginning and ending points for processes, events, and lives subjected to scrutiny. The disciplinary form of history obliges scholars to frame such scrutiny with dates. For Susan Newton-King, the frontier era in Graaff-Reinet ended with the quelling of a two-pronged rebellion against VOC authority from 1799 to 1801.[9] In Nigel Penn's view, the northern frontier closed a decade later, marked by the formal subjugation of Khoisan labor with the Caledon Code and the careful administrative scrutiny recorded in the Collins Report, both in 1809.[10]

Closing a frontier conceptually seems, however, to shut off other analytical possibilities. How, for example, can we account for the visible eruption of resistance in a closed frontier zone? Penn himself chronicles the "Onder Bokkeveld Ear Atrocity" of 1812, when a newly assertive British state appeared to surprise settlers by its strict punishment of vigilante violence against Khoisan suspected of livestock depredations and the murder of a Khoisan herdsman.[11] Consider also the Hou den Bek slave rebellion in 1825. Thirteen people, including slaves, Khoisan servants, and one white tenant farmer, were accused variously of murder, desertion, and rebellion when they acted in concert to kill their masters, terrify neighbors, and violently demand their liberty.[12] Both events can be read as direct affronts to colonial order. Of course, even long-established and well-policed cities confront pockets of shifting lawlessness and resistance.[13] A newly closed rural frontier zone would hardly be exempt from these challenges to state control. Government authorities responded decisively to both of these northern frontier crimes, so one could argue that these acts of insurgency, suppressed, demonstrate the reach of legal sovereignty to the fringes of the Cedarberg and beyond. I, however, am particularly intrigued by the persistence of specific frontier characteristics evident in these events.

In the retelling of an extrajudicial murder and mutilation and a slave rebellion, shared features of frontier zones stand out: the distance between homesteads, the importance of kin relationships linking those farms, the physical distance of legal authorities from the site where individuals violently contested the terms of colonial power relationships, and a sense of possibility that provocateurs might escape detection and get away with their challenge to prevailing norms.

Here settler orthodoxy, with the implied foil of heterodoxy—present among settlers, Khoisan and slaves—describes the terrain more aptly than the model of a closed frontier. Over the course of a century, colonists established prevailing social norms tied to an identity rooted in belonging to the community of the ruling class. Even though many inhabitants of the Cedarberg remained poor and minimally literate, their shared identity was based on kinship, material culture, household structures, community ritual (including Christianity), and participation within the rule of law.

An orthodox frontier thus allows for the prevalence of a dominant ideology without presuming hegemony or complete closure, leaving space—however small—for negotiations both historical and intellectual. The limited possibilities for Khoisan and mixed-race individuals to own land at the end of the eighteenth century that I document in Chapter 3; the "breathing space" achieved by Khoisan on the eastern frontier at the turn of the nineteenth century so poignantly evoked by Susan Newton-King;[14] the individual settler reprisals against Khoisan; and the ongoing squabbles among settlers that punctuate Penn's work all point to a heterodox undercurrent in frontier regions, one that persists past logical dates of frontier closure.

Analytically highlighting the heterodox, putting an intellectual wedge into the frontier's liminal spaces as though planting an explorer's flag, adds to the critical mass of scholarship that productively troubles presumptions of uniform, monolithic colonial power.[15] But it complicates efforts to demarcate the end of the frontier period in the Cedarberg.

ORTHODOXY AND PERIODIZATION

Along the Olifants River, intermittent colonial penetration became sustained and permanent with a group of five land claims first asserted in 1725. Territory initially exploited by Johannes Ras, François Smit, Jürgen Hanekom, and

Arnoldus Basson—extended quickly by Willem Burger, Pieter van Heerden, Daniel Pfeil, and Jan Steenkamp—was tenuously colonial in the 1730s. The frontier war of 1739 significantly curtailed violent opposition to settler presence, and from the 1740s the region was increasingly stabilized (from the perspective of the settlers, at least) by a steady increase in the number and extent of settler households living there permanently.

Thus the Cedarberg was arguably incorporated into colonial geography as early as 1739, with the end of widespread, armed Khoisan resistance. The terms of daily life were hardly secure at that point, though, and the penetration of settler homesteads was thin. Nevertheless, from that point on settlers dominated access to land; individual, alienable, demarcated, and permanent land tenure predominated—but was not yet exclusively white. Throughout the eighteenth century there was space—albeit limited—for people of color to claim land. Meanwhile communities of settlers and communities of people descended from slaves, Khoisan, and mixed-race unions created separate identities, and also had identities with legal, hierarchical consequences imposed upon them. Yet together they forged households as masters and servants. As colonial land tenure practices prevailed, so gradually did elements of orthodox settler identity; until by the end of the 1830s, the area was indisputably within the fold of settler norms.

This dominance emerged gradually, marked by a series of changes evident between the 1780s and the 1830s. Since colonial conquest was multifaceted, there were many markers of ultimate settler success: economic ascendance, the spread of settler kin networks, the prevalence of colonial material culture, the imposition of labor regimes, the exercise of effective legal control, the establishment of a local political presence (a magistrate's office in Clanwilliam), the creation of a Christian religious infrastructure for the settlers (in the form of an NGK gemeente in Clanwilliam), and the increased subordination of the Coloured population (formally recognized and ministered to by a Rhenish mission at Wupperthal).[16]

None of these markers alone signals a moment when orthodoxy at last prevailed. Instead they are macrolevel indications of consolidation created at the local level of the household. Inhabitants of the Cedarberg were either settlers—construed as European-descended, Christian, and Dutch-speaking—or not.[17] Even the Irish settlers of 1820 were integrated into the community in a generation.[18] These settler households were increasingly orthodox in character, traits already evident along the Olifants River by the 1780s. The end of the frontier period in the Cedarberg was a culmination rather than a climax, a conjunction of processes whose cumulative effects were entrenched by the end of the 1830s—the point at which settler orthodoxy was unassailable.

ORTHODOXY EXPERIENCED

Undoubtedly Khoisan, slaves, freed slaves, and settlers experienced this nineteenth-century transition differently from one another. For some Khoisan individuals, the opportunity for an independent existence diminished dramatically from the arrival of the first settler land claimants. Their descendents were subordinated into colonial labor structures before the frontier itself was secured. For other individuals of Khoisan heritage, the contested frontier offered possibilities for formal land tenure in the last quarter of the eighteenth century that nineteenth-century changes subsequently precluded.[19] For this small group of people, the triumph of settler orthodoxy would have been particularly harsh. Slaves, meanwhile, found emancipation just as frontier orthodoxy was consolidated, constraining the possibilities of independent existence for individuals described outside the parameters of settler identity. Limited access to land kept most former slaves in service to a master.[20]

For farmers seeking land and stability on the outer limits of colonial settlement, orthodoxy proved ambivalent. The increasing presence of state and church structures stabilized community life, but land tenure regulations after 1813 limited possibilities for undercapitalized individuals and families. The rise and fall of family fortunes seems more important for individual opportunity than any administrative fiat, as the case of Gerrit van Wyk suggests. Head of a household with moderate resources one year, he was a hired laborer the next.[21] Such a dramatic reversal of fortune in an agrarian household would not likely change with the status of the frontier. For farmers making a living from the land, settler ascendancy ensured their physical security and societal stability, but did not change the elements of water, sunshine, and pests that ultimately determined their economic success or failure.

Despite the vagaries of individual fortune, we can see real continuities among settler households in the Cedarberg from the 1780s to the 1830s. Land claims passed down trough generations. When Paul Willem Lubbe died in 1810, his wife Jacoba Mouton assumed ownership of Brakkefontein, the farm he had inherited from his mother, Johanna Maria Keyser.[22] She had taken over the farm at the death of her husband, Barend Fredrik Lubbe Barendsz, who in turn bought it from the original claimant, Daniel Pfeil, underscoring the firm connection of a community to places in the landscape. The couple's household inventory also suggests continuity in material culture. Paul and Jacoba had a variety of household goods, though only one porcelain bowl, and nothing described as copper or silver. They also had basic farm equipment, hand tools, and ample livestock—a typical inventory for middling farmers in the 1760s, the 1780s, and the early nineteenth century.[23]

Although Paul and Jacoba's household was far from grandiose, not all of Oud Barend's grandchildren achieved even this limited level of economic success.

Elsje Sophia Lubbe, like many of her kinsmen (including Paul and Jacoba), married a first cousin—Schalk Willem Petrus Burger. The couple's four minor children had many fewer assets to divide than were evident in Oud Barend's auction or in Schalk Willem Petrus's grandparents' estate inventory, an indication that partible inheritance forced each generation to coax new wealth from the land—and to expand settler land claims in the process.[24] Schalk Willem Petrus and Elsje Sophia were not wealthy when Elsje died; their household inventory does not mention a farm, but they must have lived at least in "rough comfort."[25] They had a wagon, trek oxen, and two saddle horses, suggesting mobility. They also had livestock enough to suggest the beginnings of prosperity: six breeding horses, 27 cows, 321 sheep, and 56 goats. Their housewares were not elaborate; they possessed only three pewter plates, five pewter spoons, and five steel forks for a family of six. Apparently they all snuggled into two beds; the youngest child was nearly 7 years old, too big for a cradle. The inventory does not mention any farming implements, but does list 18 feet of cedar planks and various carpenter's tools. Schalk Willem Petrus must have earned at least some of their keep by woodworking. Even with this limited material comfort, they fared better than their cousin Jacobus Lubbe Andriesz, who died in 1829, a 73-year-old bachelor with only 11 old silver buttons and two silver shoe buckles to his name.[26]

Another significant continuity in nineteenth-century households was the continued subordination of labor, including Khoisan servants and slaves.[27] Although Emancipation dramatically changed the terms of subjugation for enslaved individuals, in most cases, it did not significantly improve their material circumstances. The earlier abolition of the slave trade, mandated by the British Parliament in 1807, was a more abrupt challenge to the labor supply at the Cape. For example, Paul Lubbe and Johanna Mouton's household included two slaves from Mozambique. The presence of Moses and Damon in the Olifants River Valley points to the ongoing connections between this frontier region and the wider world.

FRONTIER ORTHODOXY IN A GLOBAL CONTEXT

This broader context is important for understanding the gradual consolidation of settler identity and colonial dominance in the Cedarberg. Continuities in land tenure, marriage patterns, material culture, and labor subordination crystallized against a backdrop of global changes.[28] The collapse of the Dutch East India Company brought major shifts in imperial oversight at the turn of the nineteenth century.[29] Britain claimed the Cape during a period of dramatic changes in the world economy; the accelerated, capitalist incorporation of colonial territories and the ongoing extraction of resources fueled the industrial revolution.[30] Meanwhile, a revitalized evangelical, European Christianity began sponsoring increased missionary activity worldwide. This religious outreach had direct consequences for the end of slavery and a greater focus on southern Africa as a multidenominational mission field.[31] By 1800, concerted armed reprisals on the part of Khoisan had petered out, though individual assaults and livestock depredations continued.[32] These ongoing challenges posed limited, specific threats, so the grandchildren of the first colonial settlers found themselves firmly entrenched in the Cedarberg. This increased local stability combined with global changes to draw the frontier into the colony's embrace, securing the region for settler farmers at the expense of independent Khoisan and agricultural laborers. By the end of the 1830s, the Cedarberg was firmly in the administrative, judicial, and religious orbit of the Cape Colony. Although still relatively thinly populated, the region was no longer a frontier zone.

The most significant large-scale change for the Cedarberg was the Cape's transition to British rule, officially instituted by 1806. The Cedarberg became part of a global empire trying to trying to regularize its rule, promote local economic growth, and make itself profitable. Though still remote from seats of power in Cape Town and London, the Cedarberg increasingly was connected to imperial administration and incorporated into a modern, bureaucratizing state.[33]

The continuities evident on the frontier by the end of the eighteenth century were compatible with markers of formal inclusion into the colonial order that came later. The Cedarberg became a place that both needed and could sustain a magistrate's office and an NGK gemeente. These outposts of civilization did not arrive to subdue a wilderness—settler households had already done that work over the previous century. The magistrate and the pastor were not colonial vanguards, they were the signs of colonial success. This ascendance of settler orthodoxy in the Cedarberg did not, however, end intense frontier interactions across the nineteenth century. Hostilities continued along the eastern frontier,[34] bubbled up elsewhere in South Africa,[35] and emerged with renewed ferocity along with the mineral revolution.[36]

The inescapable dominance of colonial land tenure, the restructuring of land claims in outlying districts, the penetration of settler kin networks, the prevalence of settler material culture, the formal imposition of Khoisan labor bondage, and the arrival of local church and government administration all mark significant turning points in the Cedarberg, moments when orthodoxy vanquished alternatives.

ORTHODOXY AND IDENTITY

Frans and Johannes Hendrik Lubbe surely did not think of themselves as "orthodox land owners" when they arrested Donderbosch Pokkebaas and other troublemakers, casting them as rebels and sending them to the Castle to be questioned. Yet in this event, the brothers demonstrated conformity with the colonial government, acted to secure their own property interests, and operated within the rule of law—unlike some of their neighbors who were frequently reprimanded by the landdrost and other authorities for inappropriate violence against Khoisan.[37] Even for families like the Lubbes and the Burgers, who clearly cast their lot with colonial conformity, life in the Cedarberg at the end of the eighteenth century was a struggle—against the elements to make a living and against Khoisan who still fought to evict them. In spite of these challenges, the settlers stayed put. In retrospect, their saga is one of incremental conquest finally achieved—over and over again. Colonists did not win a single or decisive victory in their struggle to claim the Cedarberg. Instead, there were many moments that consolidated the settler community and worked to impose social orthodoxy in much the same way as colonial farmers sought to cultivate fields from the wilderness.

NOTES

1. Nigel Penn, *The Forgotten Frontier: Colonist and Khoisan on the Cape's Northern Frontier in the Eighteenth Century* (Cape Town: Double Storey Books and Athens: Ohio University Press, 2005), 70

2. CA: C 219, *Resolutions of the Council of Policy*, 14 Oct. 1793, pp. 76–131.

3. J.A Englebrecht, *The Korana* (Cape Town: Maskew Miller, 1936), 151–53. Thanks to Robert Ross for sending me this reference.

4. Joyce Appleby, Lynn Hunt, and Margaret Jacob, *Telling the Truth About History* (New York: W.W. Norton, 1994), 235.

5. Peter N. Stearns, "Periodization in World History Teaching: Identifying the Big Changes," *The History Teacher* 20:4 (Aug. 1987), 561.

6. See, for example the *American History Review* forum on periodization, *AHR* 101 (June 1996), 749–82.

7. Leonard Guelke, "The Making of Two Frontier Communities: Cape Colony in the Eighteenth Century." *Historical Reflections/Reflexions Historiques* 12:3 (1985): 419–48. I discuss my appropriation of Guelke's frontier insights in Chapter 2.

8. Hermann Giliomee, "Processes in Development of the Southern African Frontier." In *The Frontier in History: North American and South Africa Compared*, Howard Lamar and Leonard Thompson, eds. (New Haven: Yale University Press, 1981), 76–119.

9. Susan Newton-King, *Masters and Servants on the Eastern Cape Frontier, 1760–1803* (Cambridge: Cambridge University Press, 1999), 210–31. Having a firm end point for her narrative, Newton-King opens her book with a meditation on colonial beginnings (pp. 1–10), a point I did not consciously seek to mirror. As coincidence, it suggests to me that colonial periodization is still very much open to fruitful debate.

10. Penn, *Forgotten Frontier*, 274.

11. Nigel Penn, "The Onder Bokkeveld Ear Atrocity," *Kronos* 31 (2005): 62–106.

12. George McCall Theal, "Trial of Galant and Others," *RCC*, Vol. 20 (London: Printed for the Government of the Cape Colony, 1904), 188–341; Patricia van der Spuy, "'Making Himself Master': Galant's Rebellion Revisted," *SAHJ* 34 (1996): 1–28; Robert Ross *Cape of Torments: Slavery and Resistance in South Africa* (London: Routledge & Kegan Paul. 1983), 105–16; Mary Rayner, "Wine and Slaves: The Failure of an Export Economy and the Ending of Slavery in the Cape Colony, South Africa, 1806–1835. (PhD diss., Duke University, 1986), 174–89; R.L. Watson, *The Slave Question: Liberty and Property in South Africa* (Hanover: University Press of New England, 1990), 50–59.

13. Peter Linebaugh, *The London Hanged: Crime and Civil Society in the Eighteenth Century*, 2nd ed. (London: Verso, 2006).

14. Newton-King, *Masters and Servants*, 230–31.

15. Fredrick Cooper, *Colonialism in Question: Theory, Knowledge, History* (Berkeley: University of California Press, 2005).

16. Readers unfamiliar with nineteenth-century Cape history may refer to the Appendix for an elaboration of these events as they relate to the Cedarberg.

17. Hermann Giliomee, *The Afrikaners: Biography of a People* (Charlottesville: University of Virginia Press, 2003), 21.

18. Graham Brian Dickason, *Irish Settlers to the Cape: History of the Clanwilliam 1820 Settlers from Cork Harbour* (Cape Town: A.A. Balkema, 1973).

19. Dawn Nell, "Land, Land Ownership and Occupancy in the Cape Colony During the Nineteenth Century With Special Reference to the Clanwilliam District." (BA Honours thesis, University of Cape Town, 1997).

20. Pamela Scully, *Liberating the Family? Gender and British Slave Emancipation in the Rural Western Cape, South Africa, 1823–1853* (Portsmouth, NH: Heinemann, 1997); Clifton Crais and Nigel Worden, eds., *Breaking the Chains: Slavery and its Legacy in the Nineteenth-Century Cape Colony* (Johannesburg: Witwatersrand University Press, 1994).

21. The decline in Gerrit van Wyk's fortunes is recorded in the opgaaf records of 1740 and 1741. ARA: VOC 4143 *OBP* 1740 opgaaf, Stellenbosch p. 4. ARA: VOC 4147 *OBP* 1741 opgaaf, Drakenstein p. 10.

22. CA: MOOC 8/58.36a, Estate Inventory of Paul Willem Lubbe, 7 Mar. 1810.

23. CA: MOOC 9/58.36a, Estate Inventory of Paul Willem Lubbe, 7 Mar. 1810.

24. CA: MOOC 8/70.26b, Estate Inventory of Elsie Sofia Lubbe, 24 Oct. 1826; CA: MOOC 8/49.25, Estate Inventory of Schalk Willem Burger, 24 Sept. 1782; CA: MOOC 10/15.6, Vendu rol, Barend Lubbe, 7–8 Nov. 1785.

25. Guelke, "Freehold Farmers and Frontier Settlers, 1657–1780," in *The Shaping of South African Society, 1652–1840*, eds. Richard Elphick and Hermann Giliomee, 2nd ed. (Johannesburg: Maskew Miller Longman, 1989), 93.

26. CA: MOOC 8/45.123, Estate Inventory of Jacobus Lubbe, 16 July 1829.

27. Fred Morton and Elizabeth Eldredge, eds., *Slavery in South Africa: Captive Labor on the Dutch Frontier* (Boulder: Westview Press, 1994).

28. In her keynote address at the 2007 World History Association Annual Meeting, Marnie Hughes-Warrington provided an imaginative look at the insights possible from shifting between local and global perspectives.

29. C.L.R. Boxer, *The Dutch Seaborne Empire 1600–1800* (London: Hutchinson, 1965; reprint Penguin Books, 1973); William M. Freund, "The Cape Under the Transitional

Governments, 1795–1814" in *The Shaping of South African Society, 1652–1840*, eds. Richard Elphick and Hermann Giliomee, 2nd ed. (Johannesburg: Maskew Miller Longman, 1989); C.A. Bayly, *Imperial Meridian: The British Empire and the World 1780–1830* (London: Longman, 1989).

30. Immanuel Wallerstein, *World-Systems Analysis: An Introduction* (Durham: Duke University Press, 2004); Kenneth L. Pomeranz, *The Great Divergence: China, Europe, and the Making of the Modern World Economy* (Princeton: Princeton University Press, 2001).

31. Elizabeth Elbourne, *Blood Ground: Colonialism, Missions and the Contest for Christianity in the Cape Colony and Britain, 1799–1853* (Montreal: McGill-Queen's University Press, 2002).

32. For example, Penn, "Ear Atrocity."

33. Clifton Crais, *The Politics of Evil: Magic, State Power and the Political Imagination in South Africa* (Cambridge: Cambridge University Press, 2002).

34. Noel Mostert, *Frontiers: The Epic of South Africa's Creation and the Tragedy of the Xhosa People* (New York: Knopf, 1992); Clifton Crais, *The Politics of Evil*.

35. Norman Etherington, *Great Treks: The Transformation of Southern Africa, 1815–1854* (London: Longman, 2001).

36. William H. Worger, *South Africa's City of Diamonds: Mine Workers and Monopoly Capitalism in Kimberley, 1867–1895* (New Haven: Yale University Press, 1987).

37. Penn, *Forgotten Frontier*, 187–97.

10. CELEBRATING THE CEDARBERG'S STORIES

The longing for human stories is pervasive and powerful, in tension with the VOC's propensity to list objects, a merchant company's interest in ledgers and balance sheets.[1] To make a list mean something more than the sum of its contents, imagination intervenes: seeing connections, discovering relationships, invoking human concerns, telling tales.[2] Although postmodern and postcolonial critics have mounted formidable intellectual challenges to its primacy, the structuring of narrative nevertheless can make sense of complicated events and processes, as this collection of stories about the Cedarberg attests.[3]

This book demonstrates possibilities of using statistical data to write narrative history, excavating the stories in lists, tallies, enumerations, and ledgers, recovering individual human experience from data that was created as a picture of aggregation, not individuation. In going beyond the written record to incorporate archaeological sources, I describe colonial society more broadly than the VOC did, actively including Khoisan who were not subordinated laborers. Structuring their stories around relationships of inclusion and exclusion brings slaves, Khoisan, women, and poor settlers into relief, in spite of their limited presence in the archives of the Dutch East India Company.

The long eighteenth century in Southern Africa was a remarkable moment. Colonial relationships unfolded in all their messy complexity, as they did in the Americas and Asia. Understanding these events in the Western Cape shakes up some received wisdom of African history: colonization on an imperial model took place before the industrial revolution and the rise of social Darwinism; people with stone tool technology, no fixed abode, and no governmental structure succeeded in limiting European colonial presence for a century.

Without a doubt, this is a history of brutal domination and violent resistance; it is impossible not to see colonial hegemony, land alienation, and labor oppression—a familiar saga of European conquest accompanied by the creation of a hierarchical, racialized society. The lines in this society were not drawn neatly or evenly, however. The boundaries were permeable; categories were elastic, leaving space—particularly in frontier areas like the Cedarberg—for individuals to negotiate the terms of interaction. Land claims, family formation, and identity creation ultimately privileged Christian, Dutch-speaking farmers. Evidence of the interactions that eventually asserted this hierarchy may have been painted on rocks,[4] but contours of colonial society were not etched in stone.

Settler kin networks sustained this dynamic society, spanning multiple generations and long distances, connecting people across the frontier region and linking the frontier to the established areas of the colony. These relationships were closely linked to patterns of land tenure and land use based on the concept of private property. It was these intertwined notions of family and property that enabled the spread of a cohesive colonial entity across the landscape. Understanding these frontier patterns is crucial to understanding how a far-flung and sparsely populated area could remain a contested frontier for over a hundred years and nevertheless maintain its colonial nature.

Recovering the contested history of the Cedarberg is a version of Norman Etherington's "heartland" shift.[5] Adjusting our field of vision lets us appreciate a different historical perspective. A lens trained on the Olifants River shows that the history of the Western Cape was not all about the Mother City. The frontier, however, could not have existed without the growing cosmopolitan hub on the shores of Table Bay that nourished the elements of social, political, and economic dominance evident in colonial society.

The success of settler society depended fundamentally on land claims, whether it was the ground under the Castle of Good Hope or unfenced terrain for grazing sheep in the Cedarberg. The land equally sustains this book's overarching arguments:

- Agrarian history offers a particularly insightful window into South Africa's past. The nexus of land and labor at the heart of agricultural production mirrors a critical intersection between frontier studies and slave histories.
- Colonial conquest, more domestic than martial, was rooted in frontier homesteads.
- Malleable elements of social identity—particularly those which came to constitute race—were gradually reified over the course of the eighteenth

century, bound up in family connections and the related ability to make and sustain land claims.

The picture I have painted of a gradually domesticated, orthodox settler community that emerged over the course of the eighteenth century presents a sharp contrast to Lance van Sittert's analysis of the Cedarberg as a bastion of wilderness and a cradle of alpinism in the twentieth century.[6] Of course the Cape Town Mountain Club members were not idealizing the farmyards and citrus groves along the Olifants, but rather the rugged peaks on the farmers' horizon. Middle-class Capetonians began to celebrate this mountainscape from the early years of the twentieth century. The national government subsequently declared 71,000 hectares as a conservation area in 1973, a result of an environmentalist campaign.

This terrain, now construed as wilderness, had been part of the resource landscape for hunters and herders since long before colonial settlement. These same mountains remained in the orbit of seasonal transhumance for colonial farmers. Their laborers must have regularly walked routes over ridges and around peaks, both herding flocks of sheep and moving without livestock between farms, or back and forth to the mission station at Wupperthal.

Colonial farmers succeeded in wresting control of this land and its resources from hunting and herding Khoisan. In the process, the settlers increasingly identified not with the contested frontier but with values emanating from Cape Town. A century later, Capetonians looked back at the Cedarberg and recast it as a frontier region, in spite of evidence to the contrary.

The higher elevations and remote areas of the Cedarberg certainly escaped the domestication of fenced kraals, plowed fields, and porcelain table settings, but along the Olifants and Doorn Rivers and in the mountain valleys where settlers established homesteads, land use and material culture connected farming households to colonial society. Those very sites of domestication would later provide staging areas for twentieth-century alpinist excursions into the Cedarberg wilderness.

Had the modern mountaineers not been seeking to create a climate of exploration and discovery, they might have hired local shepherds as guides and saved themselves considerable effort.[7] As it was, encounters with livestock and "out-of-the-way" farms occasionally spoiled the sense of untamed adventure.[8] Twentieth-century outdoor enthusiasts willfully ignored extant maps and physical evidence in the landscape in order to see the Cedarberg as a wilderness, using the language of alpinism to distort historical memory. Settlers struggled to control this region in the eighteenth century; by the end of the nineteenth century the Cedarberg was considered so securely positioned within the dominant geography of the state that subsequent generations could consider it to be a frontier worth claiming all over again. Although the focus of the dominant society's exploitation of the Cedarberg shifted from economic survival to an urban, bourgeois glorification of an untrammeled natural world, an undercurrent of colonial conquest persists. In both the eighteenth and the twentieth centuries, one group sought to exercise power over a landscape, its resources, and its inhabitants. The Cape Town alpinists could ignore the previous history of conquest in the Cedarberg because, it seems, they did not look at the tidy fields along the river or notice the evidence of permanent occupation even in the higher elevations.

The centrality of the Olifants River to human endeavors in the Cedarberg is evident in long-term patterns of land use, the geography of colonial land claims, and the history of human interactions in the region. Various societies have, over time, imparted very different social meanings to the landscape. Khoikhoi, San, colonial settlers, and modern outdoorsmen used resources differently. Equally important, they had very different understandings of their place in the environment and their relationships to nature. Ideologies of nature, however, lie beyond the scope of this book, which documents the material conditions of colonial contest and the social implications of settler conquest. Evidence of possession and elements of identity emerge in the ledgers of colonial administration.

Belongings and belonging have a particular documentary presence that firmly situates the Cedarberg in the mainstream of South African history, despite its contested status throughout the eighteenth century, and efforts to categorize the region as a wilderness throughout the twentieth. Throughout this turmoil, the Olifants has flowed unabated. Dammed, drained, and redirected in recent decades, the river nevertheless continues to connect the Witsenberg Valley with the Atlantic Ocean, to link related biomes, and to serve as a conduit between people and their history.

NOTES

1. Paul Ricoeur, *Time and Narrative*, trans. Kathleen McLaughlin and David Pellaur (Chicago: University of Chicago Press, 1983); Hayden White, *Tropics of Discourse: Essays in Cultural Criticism* (Baltimore: Johns Hopkins University Press, 1985).

2. Carmel Schrire, *Digging Through Darkness: Chronicles of an Archaeologist* (Charlottesville: University Press of Virginia, 1995).

3. As recent defenders of narrative argue, "In our emphasis of the need for narrative coherence, causal analysis, and social contextualization, . . . we are attempting to go beyond the current negative or ironic judgments about history's role. We as historians are nonetheless making our own aesthetic choices." Joyce Appleby, Lynn Hunt, and Margaret Jacob, *Telling the Truth About History* (New York: W.W. Norton, 1994), 228.

4. Simon Hall and Aron Mazel, "The Private Performance of Events: Colonial Period Rock Art from the Swartruggens," *Kronos* 31 (2005): 124–51.

5. Norman Etherington, *Great Treks: The Transformation of Southern Africa, 1815–1854* (London: Longman, 2001).

6. Lance van Sittert, "Seeing the Cedarberg: Alpinism and Inventions of the Agterberg in the White Urban Middle Class Imagination, c. 1890–c. 1950," *Kronos* 31 (Nov 2005), 152–83.

7. Many chronicles of colonial exploration in Africa gloss over the active contributions of local guides and interpreters, thus effacing the role of local knowledge and consequently aggrandizing the accomplishment of white adventurers. For example, see Adam Hochschild's description of Henry Morton Stanley's reportage in *King Leopold's Ghost: A Story of Greed, Terror, and Heroism in Colonial Africa* (Boston: Houghton Mifflin, 1998).

8. van Sittert, "Seeing the Cedarberg," 164–65.

APPENDIX

A NINETEENTH-CENTURY CHRONOLOGY
IN THE CEDARBERG

For readers who are unfamiliar with the broad strokes of South African history in the nineteenth century, I have included a brief description of the events that I mention in Chapter 9: "Imposing Orthodoxy on the Frontier, or Why Endings Matter." In each case I consider the relative merits of taking one of these events as single marker of frontier orthodoxy's success. Each event fails to stand on its own, hence my argument in Chapter 9 that the frontier period ended not in a single moment, but in a constellation of processes that culminated by the end of the 1830s.

THE END OF VOC RULE

It makes sense to end a discussion of the Cedarberg frontier with the end of VOC rule at the Cape. The Company's collapse in 1795 ended 143 years of commercial steward-ship at the Cape of Good Hope. Then, for both economic and geopolitical goals, British imperial interests claimed the Cape in order to enhance trading opportunities in the Indian Ocean. Britain saw both necessity and opportunity at the Cape in 1795. First, British traders wanted to safeguard the sea route to India, ensuring that neither bel-licose, revolutionary France nor tenacious Portugal would lay claim to the harbor at

Table Bay and prevent British passage. Second, Britain saw a claim to the Cape as a way to preempt rival France both overseas and in the context of European politics, making sure France had no additional claims either to resources or to status greater than Britain's.

The end of Company rule at the Cape shifted the seat of colonial authority from Amsterdam to London, but it did not immediately transform the day-to-day operations of the colony or the daily life of frontier settlers. This administrative change did not alter the status of slaves or inboekselinge, nor did it affect labor demand in the colony. Neither the legal basis of land tenure nor the process of claiming land changed in 1795. From the perspective of imperial and regional histories, 1795 is an important turning point, but on the Cedarberg frontier, little change took place.

To close a study of the Cedarberg in the eighteenth century with the demise of the Dutch East India Company implies two false assumptions. First, such an ending privileges the top levels of society at the expense of local developments. The frontier magnifies local actors and events, so the conclusion should not shift attention abruptly to the top of the social hierarchy and the center of political authority. Second, ending this study in 1795 implies that that the legal and administrative structures of empire are the most salient features for understanding the colonial frontier, which was not true for the Cedarberg. These broader structures were important, but not paramount. The collapse of the VOC did not change interactions between settlers and Khoisan, it did not change labor relationships, and it did not directly alter frontier identities.

THE ERA OF TRANSITIONAL GOVERNMENTS

The demise of the VOC ushered in nearly two decades of uncertain political control at the Cape. The British were not committed unanimously to claiming either power or territory in southern Africa at the turn of the nineteenth century.[1] Moreover, the British did not find their new acquisition particularly easy to govern. Bill Freund points out that "The development of the colony was only in part a direct result of the policies and wishes of the Heren XVII; the successor regimes would find, often to their disgust or to their cost, that the Cape social structure was sufficiently resilient and deeply rooted to defy administrative attempts at change."[2]

The Cape during the first British occupation was particularly chaotic.[3] The Khoikhoi, Xhosa, and frontier settlers all rebelled against British rule (although not in a co-ordinated or concerted revolt, which might have changed the course of both South African and British imperial history). Given the initial British ambivalence toward claiming the Cape and the subsequent difficulties with day-to-day administration, there was little discontent among British policy makers when Cape was returned to Dutch control in 1803.

The subsequent Batavian period, especially under Commissioner-General J.A. de Mist, has been seen since Theal's era as a period of attempted progressive reform.[4] Freund argues that the period was, in fact, not a huge departure from previous policies and that many of de Mist's proposed changes were not carried out, since de Mist was constrained both by a lack of resources and by the unstable social order at the Cape.[5]

The British reclaimed the Cape in 1806 but had neither the inclination nor the power to initiate significant local changes for several years. Although British possession resulted in new faces leading the Cape government, the underlying administrative structures remained constant during the era of transitional governments. The official working language of the colony did not switch from Dutch to English until several years into the second British occupation, and even after that time official correspondence frequently appeared in Dutch.

Thus the figureheads of government changed in rapid succession between 1795 and 1806, but the functional administration remained stable and the daily life of most inhabitants unchanged. This quotidian continuity was particularly true on the Cedarberg frontier, where interaction with state power took place through the mediation of veldkornets and, occasionally, the landdrost himself. This process was not altered by shifts in colonial power at the turn of the nineteenth century. Consequently, it is difficult to argue that this period, though important for the development of state structures in South Africa, was crucial to consolidating orthodoxy in the Cedarberg.

ABOLITION OF THE SLAVE TRADE

The one edict of the transitional era that did have far-reaching implications for the Cedarberg frontier was the abolition of the slave trade throughout the British Empire in 1808. This steep change in the availability of labor at the Cape gradually transformed the composition of the labor force.[6] The percentage of slaves in Cape Town's urban population fell by half between 1806 and 1834.[7] Robert C.-H. Shell demonstrates that this decline was accompanied by an increase in the number of slaves in outlying districts, including the Cedarberg region.[8] It is plausible that abolition of the trade served to further entrench the use of slave labor on the frontier, and that this led to a firm, final preeminence of settler command of agricultural labor, thus cementing settler orthodoxy.

Although there were undoubtedly more slaves in the frontier districts in the early decades of the nineteenth century than there had been in the eighteenth century, the shift of slaves away from Cape Town after 1808 should not be seen as a displacement or replacement of Khoisan laborers. On the frontier, most labor was impressed Khoisan, so it was not directly affected by a change in the slave trade regulations.[9]

An increase in the number of slaves in the frontier districts accompanied a gradual increase in the settler population and a concomitant demand for more labor on the frontier. Although there were more slaves in the frontier districts after 1808, this addition to the available labor pool did not serve to diminish points of conflict between settlers and Khoisan.[10] Nor, it seems, did it diminish conflict between slaves and indentured servants. The labor relations fraught with racial implications and struggles over independence that characterized the Cedarberg in the eighteenth century continued into the nineteenth century beyond the moment that the slave trade was abolished in British possessions.

Finally, ending a study of frontier struggles with abolition places more emphasis on the importance of labor relative to the importance of land in an agricultural nexus. The interconnectedness of land and labor underpinned the agricultural society of the

Cedarberg, so an ending date that directly affects only one piece of that equation leaves the story unbalanced.

CLANWILLIAM BECOMES A SUBDROSTDY

There are, however, other valid reasons for ending a study of the Cedarberg frontier in 1808. The administrative units of the Cape were occasionally reapportioned during both the VOC and the British periods of rule. One of those redistricting efforts affected the Cedarberg in 1808, when a subdrostdy was established in the village of Jan Dissels Vlei. This change represents the first time that government officials resident at the Cape recognized the need for local administration in the Cedarberg.

When colonists first began claiming land near the Olifants River in 1725, the Cedarberg region fell under the jurisdiction of the Stellenbosch landdrost. Despite the more than two hundred kilometers separating present-day Clanwilliam from Stellenbosch, the Cedarberg's initial incorporation into the Stellenbosch district was not anomalous. In 1725 the VOC recognized only three spatial and administrative divisions in the European settlement. The Cape district included Table Bay, Table Valley, the Cape Peninsula, part of the Cape Flats, and the west coast from the Peninsula north to the mouth of the Berg River.[11] The Stellenbosch district included all other territory claimed and administered by the VOC. The third division was land outside the purview of the Company, as yet unseen or unclaimed by colonial forces. Thus the Cedarberg region, not falling within the narrow confines of the Cape District, was by default part of Stellenbosch, distance notwithstanding.

After 1700 most new colonial settlement moved eastward from the village of Stellenbosch. The pass through the Hottentots-Holland Mountains leading to the Overberg district was well traveled throughout the eighteenth century.[12] This easterly direction of travel and colonial expansion was more popular than northerly expansion and thus has received much more attention from subsequent historians.

The Hottentots-Holland Kloof, although hardly the most dramatic vista to be seen from the coastal plain between the mountains and False Bay, was a focal point for anyone traveling eastward from Cape Town.[13] The passage on both sides was treacherous for draft animals and wagons alike. A graded road was not built until 1830, leaving travelers to manage the steep and rocky terrain as best they could. The lower reaches of the pass were of soft red clay, which added to the difficulty of approaching the pass. The naturalist Anders Sparrman described his crossing of the Kloof in 1776:

"The next day . . . we got up at day-break, in order to take our journey over Hottentots Holland's Mountain, in the cool of the morning. The way up it was very steep, stony, winding, and, in other respects, very inconvenient. Directly to the right of the road there was a perpendicular precipice, down which, it is said, that wagons and cattle together have sometimes the misfortune of falling headlong, and are dashed to pieces."[14]

Despite its limitations as a thoroughfare, the Kloof was the only means of traversing the imposing mountain range that divided the more developed districts of the Cape and Stellenbosch from the eastern frontier regions known generally as the "Overberg," or "over the mountain." Wild game, hunters, and pastoralist Khoikhoi used the pass—called Gantouw or "Elands Path" by the Khoikhoi—prior to the arrival of European settlers.[15]

Although the passage there was difficult, the Overberg district on the far side of the Hottentots-Holland offered rich pasture and fertile soil for farming. The region was more attractive to settlers than the more easily accessible northern frontier area of the Cedarberg and the Olifants River Valley.

The VOC formally recognized the eastern frontier's increasing appeal for colonial settlement and its increasing importance as a locus of agricultural production in 1745 when it created a third magisterial district with its seat in Swellendam. Colonial settlement in the Overberg increased from that time onward, and the Hottentots-Holland Kloof saw increasing traffic in farmers, frontiersmen, livestock, and communication between the Overberg on one side and the Cape and Stellenbosch districts on the other.

The more thinly populated and more arid Cedarberg region remained a part of the Stellenbosch drostdy. As the areas between Stellenbosch and the Cedarberg became more densely settled, the colonial government created more new magisterial districts to which the administration of Clanwilliam was assigned. In 1804 the region was incorporated into the newly created Tulbagh district. In 1822 the administrative locus shifted to the Worcester district.

In the mean time, the region centered on the lower Olifants River Valley was constituted as a subdrostdy. A localized increase in cattle raiding and reprisals proved difficult for the Cape government to manage. In response, the government purchased the opstal on the farm Zeekoevlei—originally claimed by Jan Andries Dissel—from its current owner, Sebastian van Reenen. The subdrostdy and nascent village took its name from the farm's first claimant. This official recognition of the population settled near Jan Dissel's Vlei suggests that the colonial administration for the first time recognized the settlement as large enough and significant enough to need local governance.

Areas further from Cape Town than Jan Dissels Vlei were drawn more quickly and directly into the administrative structure of the colony that the Cedarberg was.[16] Until the early nineteenth century the Cedarberg received scant official attention from Cape Town. The establishment of a subdrostdy in 1808 was certainly a turning point in the colonial history of the Olifants River Valley and the Cedarberg region, giving settlers easier access to land registration and an arbitrator for labor disputes. This change also meant that settlers, slaves, and Khoisan could be subject to a more strict application of colonial law.

The importance of administrative recognition marking the closer incorporation of the Cedarberg into larger colonial power structures is undeniable. However, to pick the 1808 founding of the subdrostdy as the ending date for the frontier era implies that centrally determined administrative function was the salient point for establishing uncontested settler control of the region, rather than such control being determined by the relationships between settlers and Khoisan. Ongoing attempts after 1808 to restrict further the Khoisan population, maintain control of slave and bonded labor, and exercise increased colonial control over land use suggests that although settler efforts were bolstered by the new subdrostdy, important aspects of land and labor control remained contested. Thus the frontier cannot be construed as conquered by 1808.

THE CALEDON CODE

Farmers in the established regions of the colony as well as on the frontier continually clamored for a larger and more stable labor supply. The need to secure adequate farm labor intensified after the abolition of the slave trade, whereupon increased attention was directed toward Khoisan laborers. The first official response came in 1809 from Governor Caledon. His Hottentot Proclamation of November 1 simultaneously restricted the free movement of Khoikhoi and attempted to regulate their conditions of service to colonists.

The Caledon Code was the first legal change to local labor customs after the British assumed control of the Cape.[17] The new regulations required labor contracts between each worker and employer. The contracts had to be completed in triplicate: one copy going to the employer, another copy to the laborer, and a third copy to be filed with the landdrost. The proclamation further required that every Khoikhoi individual within the boundaries of the Colony have a fixed place of residence registered with either the fiscaal or the landdrost; Khoikhoi were required to procure passes for moving out of their district of registration. Landdrosts were charged with issuing passes to Khoisan laborers, a regulation that affected individual work seekers in particular. Landdrosts thus had enormous power over individual Khoisan, and increased power relative to colonial settlers, since the landdrost in effect distributed labor among farmers in his district. "These requirements placed the Khoikhoi (they applied only to 'Hottentots') at the mercy of those most interested in tying them down."[18]

These detailed changes did not, however, provide explicit provisions for the servitude of youths. In 1812 Governor Cradock responded to pleas from landdrosts and settlers alike. His Apprenticeship of Servants Law, promulgated 23 April 1812, authorized a ten-year period of apprenticeship for young Khoikhoi who were maintained on a settler farm during their early childhood. Thus a child raised on a settler farm until she turned 8 would then be obligated to serve that homestead until she was 18. This provision constrained Khoisan of all ages, since parents—even if they had served out their contractual obligations—could not leave a farm if they wanted to keep their family intact.

These increasing restrictions on the mobility of labor first established by the Caledon Code were extended gradually. In 1817 "apprenticeship" was expanded to include some "Bushmen" children. Two years later, youth "apprenticeship" was extended to orphaned Khoikhoi, a provision that was easily abused by labor-hungry settlers and colonial officials. The proclaimed goal of protecting Khoisan and their children from abuse by requiring registration and fixed periods of time for "apprenticeship" served in actuality to limit the mobility of individual Khoisan, depress wages for farm servants, and increase the labor supply available to settler farmers.

In the same period that the colonial economy was firmly entrenching Khoisan labor in a subordinate position, settler farms were also increasingly absorbing previously independent San individuals and their labor power. Between 1806 and 1808, there was a marked improvement in relations between San and settlers in the northeast regions of the colony, including Sneeuwberg, Tarka, and Nieuwveld. An increased number of San in these regions went to work on settler farms.[19] Increasing Khoikhoi subordination worked in conjunction with a greater incorporation of San and Bastaard laborers, leading to a further blurring of the distinctions among individuals of indigenous origins. Legassick argues, "From this time, it would seem, the colonial mind steadily assimilated the Bastaards into the category of a homogenous 'Hottentot' (Coloured) labouring class. Commissioner Bigge referred to '. . . the Hottentots . . . in which class is generally included the mixed race of Hottentots and the white and free coloured inhabitants denominated 'Bastaards.' "[20]

Freund's assertion that after 1809, "The new British authorities stood for a policy of rigidly subordinating servants while also protecting them against contractual abuses," is an apt summation of labor regulation in the early nineteenth century.[21] Ultimately the "reforms" of 1809 and 1812 entrenched the landless status of Khoisan laborers. Thus the change in labor regulations initiated by the Caledon Code provides a plausible closing point for a discussion of labor relations on the Cedarberg frontier. These regulations also effectively limited independent Khoisan access to land, thereby further assuring the dominance of settler culture and agricultural practices on the frontier. Subsequent events, however, indicate that settler hegemony on the frontier was not yet assured, despite the significant restrictions on Khoisan mobility initiated in 1809.

INTRODUCTION OF QUITRENT LAND TENURE

Gradual changes in labor policy were accompanied by adjustments to the system of land tenure both for settlers and indigenous claimants to land. A two-tiered system of land tenure prevailed at the Cape under the VOC. The Company granted a limited number of farms in freehold, most of them in the Cape District and the area immediately surrounding the village of Stellenbosch.[22] The overwhelming majority of land claimed by settlers were loan farms. Although legally limited to a series of renewable one-year leases, in practice loan farms were long-term, stable, alienable property claims.[23]

After 1806 the new British government at the Cape began to take a more active interest in both agricultural production and land tenure policies. Officials drew a direct correlation between formal land tenure legislation and what they perceived to be inadequate levels of agricultural production among the colony's settlers.[24] Convinced that more permanent and secure land tenure would encourage farmers to make the necessary capital improvements in order to increase productivity, British planners set about modifying the land tenure system to provide for longer terms of occupation and higher, more consistent collection of rents.[25]

Discussion of possible changes culminated in Governor Cradock's Proclamation of August 6, 1813, that introduced the quitrent system that prohibited the further granting of loan farms, including the approximately 2,000 pending applications for new claims.[26] The Proclamation further stipulated that existing loan farms should be reregistered as quitrent farms with 99-year leases. The measure was intended to provide farmers with a greater degree of security about their property, to give the state with greater control over the distribution of settlers in the landscape, and to promote greater efficiency in recording and collecting fees. In actuality, farmers felt secure enough with loan farm tenure to make significant capital improvements to the land, as the auction price for Barend Lubbe's farm at Groote Valleij attests.[27]

The burden of reregistering their existing claims and the higher barriers to new claims imposed by the Proclamation in fact made frontier settlers less secure on the land, not more. Cradock's proclamation also limited the amount of frontier land available to settlers, a squeeze on frontier farmers that Freund argues led directly to the Slachtersnek Rebellion in 1815 and the Great Trek that began in 1834.[28]

For Cedarberg farmers who held land through loan farm claims in 1814, Cradock's Proclamation was a short-term, bureaucratic inconvenience that was not likely to change their long-term view of their stability on the land. For farmers—or aspiring farmers—who did not yet have their own land claims in 1814, the change in tenure system only made it more difficult to make an independent bid for a farm.

Although the quitrent system did not have an immediate effect in the Cedarberg area, in the long term, Cradock's Proclamation served notice that the relative land free-for-all enjoyed by any settler (and the few Khoisan) who cared to make a land claim was at an end. In this sense an administrative fiat closed options on the Cedarberg frontier that had been available for 88 years, limiting both settler and Khoisan claims to land.

IRISH SETTLERS ARRIVE IN CLANWILLIAM

Existing colonial settlers may have seen the quitrent system in a negative light, but that same form of land tenure was billed as a great advantage in the general British recruitment of new colonists for the 1820 settlement scheme. The plan to export working people from an overcrowded Britain to help shore up the Cape Colony's beleaguered eastern frontier was conceived in Britain, not in South Africa, and thus was designed to serve domestic and imperial aims rather than to meet the needs of the Cape.[29]

Overall, 4,000 British settlers went out to South Africa as part of the 1820 program. Of 32 total ships, 27 sailed between 19 December 1819 and August 1820.[30] Officials at the Cape were poorly prepared for the early waves of immigrants. Administration was sloppy and three parties of migrants originally from County Cork were directed up the west coast instead of along the Indian Ocean coastline to Albany. The ships from Ireland arrived at Saldanha Bay in May and June of 1820. From there the parties made their way overland to the subdrostdy at the recently renamed Clanwilliam.[31]

The efforts to bolster colonial settlement in the Cedarberg with the Irish settlers at Clanwilliam did not succeed for a variety of reasons. First, like their counterparts in Albany, too few of the immigrants had practical farming experience, though it appears there were more farmers among the Clanwilliam settlers than among those who went directly to Albany.[32] Second, the climate and landscape of the Cedarberg were particularly ill suited to agricultural techniques practiced in Ireland. Finally, the parties of Irish immigrants were settled on too little productive land. A survey completed in April 1820 concluded that the four tracts of land allocated to the incoming settlers could support eighty families. The four parties of Irish immigrants comprised 125 families, who were nevertheless settled on the originally allocated land.[33]

The leaders of each of the four parties—Butler, Ingram, Synnot, and Parker—were responsible for allocating land among the families in their respective groups. Squabbling in the groups began from the moment of the first land allocation. By September 1820—only four months after his arrival—Butler had already sold his individual allocation and left the region.[34] When His Majesty's Commissioners Mssrs. Hayward and Marsh arrived to hear grievances in March 1825, they found only two men and their families living in the locations originally allocated to them. Only 12 men and their families plus three unmarried women remained in the area at all.[35]

The majority of the Irish settlers originally sent to Clanwilliam moved to the eastern frontier areas near Albany as soon as they could. Because they did not stay in large numbers, their effect on the economy and social fabric of the region was not pronounced. Synnot gave his name to a peak near the village of Clanwilliam. A few other Irish surnames survive in the district to the present day, though the region remains predominantly Afrikaans speaking. Thus the English-speaking Irish were not a significant enough presence to prompt a change in local language, even though their presence in the area coincided with the beginning of the Cape administration's Anglicization program that began in 1822.

The government's decision to send two shiploads of 1820 settlers to the Cedarberg frontier indicates the region had gained the attention of administrators. It also suggests that they thought the northwestern frontier, like the eastern frontier, could benefit from an infusion of settlers to help bring the frontier firmly into the colonial fold. However, the rugged landscape, arid climate, and poor planning combined to foil colonial efforts a bit longer.

APPARATUS OF CHRISTIAN CHURCHES ARRIVE

From the perspective of the colonial administration, there were a series of concerted attempts to establish state control and settler hegemony during the first third of the nineteenth century. First, a subdrostdy was established in 1808, then there was the purposeful dispatch of new settlers to the region in 1820. These developments were clear signals from the Cape colonial government that the Cedarberg was considered a functional part of the colony.

Further efforts to regularize colonial social structure in the Cedarberg came from Christian churches, first from the predominant Dutch Reformed Church (NGK) and soon after from Rhenish missionaries.[36] The formal, active establishment of religious authority came to the Cedarberg over a century after the first Dutch Reformed settlers arrived, but this delay in establishing churches in outlying areas is in keeping with the circumscribed role played by the NGK during its first 150 years at the Cape.

During the VOC era, the NGK was the official church of the colony, and was both controlled and funded by the Company. The VOC made appointments to the Church Council and until the later eighteenth century prohibited other denominations at the Cape. As a commercial enterprise the VOC was interested primarily in profitability, and secondarily in mechanisms of social control necessary to maintain the order that is prerequisite for smooth economic functions.

In its Indian Ocean possessions, the VOC actively encouraged Dutch Reformed proselytizing, but in places such as Formosa, Ceylon, and Amboina the Company faced direct competition from Islamic and Roman Catholic interests.[37] At the Cape there were no such competing interests, either economically or religiously, and thus the VOC did not expend much money or effort on the Church.[38] In 1790 there were fewer than ten Dutch Reformed ministers. All were employed by the VOC and primarily served the settler population.[39]

At the Cape, initial efforts to convert Khoikhoi were not particularly fruitful.[40] There were vehement discussions throughout the eighteenth century about the issue of converting slaves. The NGK's Synod of Dort in 1618 stated that Christians could not enslave other Christians, thus the conversion of slaves presented real logistical and economic problems for slave owners. As a result there was not much instruction—secular or religious—provided to slaves.[41] Theoretically the NGK was open to converted slaves and free blacks, but in practice the Church primarily served white European and European-descended colonists. Elphick and Shell conclude that,

> [I]n the Company period the spread of Christianity among privately owned slaves was slow, and among Khoikhoi negligible, and that its presence at the Cape did not narrow the social and cultural gulf between settlers and officials on the one hand and Khoikhoi and slaves on the other.[42]

Consequently, when the Dutch Reformed Church began to give attention—and permanent pastors—to the outlying areas of the colony, it was ministering primarily to settlers and not to their slave or Khoisan laborers.

Neither encouraged nor financially supported by the VOC to do more among its settler flock, the Dutch Reformed Church left the religious life of frontier settlers largely to their own ministrations until the nineteenth century. The lack of Christian infrastructure on the frontier did not, however, imply a lack of religious practice or belief among settlers. Household heads led regular worship services. The celebration of *nachtmaal*, or Holy Communion, was a notable rural event worthy of a two- or three-day journey to participate. Traveling NGK preachers, *predikanten*, made their rounds, baptizing children born since their last visit and solemnizing marriages that had not waited for the blessing of an ordained minister to begin.

Thus the formal expansion of the NGK into rural or frontier areas was not a missionary effort to convert new or lapsed souls, but rather a service to practicing Calvinist believers who requested ministration. In some ways, the creation of new NGK gemeente mirrored the creation of new landdrost districts, dividing both congregations and constituencies into manageable sizes in terms of geography and population.

Despite the tight level of state control of the NGK, Church policies and intentions did not always reflect the desires of VOC officials. Administrative structure of the NGK developed very differently from that of secular governance at the Cape.

The first NGK gemeente was established in Cape Town in 1665. The second was created in Stellenbosch in 1686 and the third in Paarl/Drakenstein in 1691. Unlike secular administrative districts that next spread eastward, the Church created two new gemeentes to the north of the village of Stellenbosch, but still in the Stellenbosch district, establishing the Roodezand (modern Tulbagh) congregation in 1743 and the Swartland gemeente in 1745, half a decade before the Church created a ward in Swellendam in 1798.[43]

The Church thus subdivided congregations in the most populous areas of the Southwestern Cape before turning its attention to frontier areas in either the northwest, northern, or eastern districts. This pattern demonstrates that in the VOC period, the NGK did not follow the administrative lead of the Company. The Church did not establish any new gemeente during the period of transitional governments. Soon after the British assumed definite control of the Cape in 1814 the NGK created a series of new wards by subdividing existing gemeentes. This effort was confined to the Western Cape, in direct contradistinction to the British government's efforts on the colony's eastern frontier.

This comparison of church and governmental administrative expansion suggests that the NKG was not an active participant in the colonizing project at the Cape.[44] The church established new gemeente where conditions were relatively stable and where there was a receptive Dutch Reformed population.

In the Cedarberg, increasing attention from centralized Church and state authorities overlapped in the first third of the nineteenth century. The NGK assigned the first missionary, Leopold Marquard, to Clanwilliam in 1816.[45] Ten years later, the NGK established a church in the village.[46] These decisions by the NGK are a strong indication of settler dominance in the region.

A Rhenish mission station was established at Wupperthal four years later, in 1830.[47] The mission—about fifty kilometers from Clanwilliam as the crow flies, but considerably further over the rough mountain passes—was not in competition with the NGK because it was ministering to the Khoisan population, which suggests that the Khoisan were no longer seen as a hostile threat but rather as potential converts, labor to support the mission, and—in the most charitable reading—a population in need of sanctuary from labor-hungry settlers.[48]

The advent of a Rhenish mission at Wupperthal in 1830 and a Dutch Reformed gemeente in Clanwilliam in 1826 are strong indications that settler norms were prevailing in the contest over lifestyle and social structure in the Cedarberg.[49]

ORDINANCE 50

At the same time that churches were asserting their presence among settlers and Khoisan in the Cedarberg, the State enacted new legislation intended to afford Khoisan equality and some measure of protection under the law. Ordinance 50 of 1828 built on Ordinance 49, issued two days earlier, which ended apprenticeship for Khoisan laborers. Ordinance 50 went further, abolishing passes for Khoisan, guaranteeing equality before the law, mandating that all employment agreements over one month had to be put in writing and could not extend beyond one year, ensuring that Khoisan were not subject to compulsory service, stating that children could not be apprenticed without their parents' consent, and clarifying Khoisan right to own land.

In other parts of the colony, particularly the eastern frontier, where missionaries such as John Phillips worked actively on behalf of Khoisan and Bastaard civil rights, Ordinance 50 was welcome and provided tangible results, such as the land ownership that underlay the Kat River Settlement, established in 1829.[50] In the Cedarberg, however, the provisions of Ordinance 50 produced few tangible effects.

Colonial opinion was split regarding Khoisan legal right to hold title to land. Ordinance 50 settled this debate in 1828.[51] But regularizing access to land and land tenure for European-descended settlers and indigenous-descended Khoisan and Bastaards in fact produced little change in the Cedarberg region. Prior to legal clarification of land tenure rights in 1828, Khoisan and Khoisan-descended people held title to farms in the Cedarberg and other areas of the northern frontiers.[52] Dawn Nell's study of land tenure in the Clanwilliam district during the nineteenth century does not indicate a shift in ownership patterns immediately after 1828, but instead suggests continuity through the first half of the nineteenth century, changing only when increasing population put heavier demands on access to land in the final quarter of the century.[53]

In general terms, Ordinance 50 affected the Cedarberg much as it did the rest of the colony. At this point in the nineteenth century, undercapitalized farmers throughout the settled areas of the Cape badly need their laborers at a time when more goods were being offered by traveling traders. Colonial authorities, influenced by the work of John Philips and others, intervened on the side of Khoisan labor to provide protection.

There is little explicit documentation of this issue for the Cedarberg, though we can assume that settlers sought to keep their land and engage labor on terms favorable to themselves. Nell's work demonstrates that a few families of Khoisan or slave origin managed to keep a tenuous hold on land through the first half of the nineteenth century, but for most Khoisan in the region, it is safe to assume that, as Giliomee wrote about the eastern frontier, "Such was the structure of colonial society that even Ordinance 50 of 1828 failed materially to change the position of the Khoikhoi."[54]

Ordinance 50, interpreted as direct state intervention into the relationship between masters and servants, limited the availability of farm labor in the Cedarberg, as settlers claimed it did in other areas of the colony.[55] The legislation shows that frontier farmers were being incorporated more tightly into colonial legal structures, and indicates that labor relations between farmers and Khoisan were increasingly regulated, with stronger distinctions between free and bonded labor, but it was not a step change that definitively ended frontier engagements.

EMANCIPATION OF THE SLAVES

The emancipation of the slaves at the Cape had a much more profound effect on labor relations than did Ordinance 50.[56] As such the event—whether dated to the proclamation in 1834 or the end of the transitional apprentice period in 1838—merits consideration as a closing point for a study of labor relations in the Cedarberg. Moreover, the fact of newly freed workers in search of postslavery alternatives had important implications for land tenure: would freed slaves be able to establish farms of their own? Thus the era of emancipation offers tantalizing prospects for analyzing changes in labor relations and land tenure at precisely the period when both church and state were exercising increasing authority and claiming an increasing presence on the Cedarberg frontier. Unfortunately, too little research has been done on the effects of emancipation in frontier regions to make conclusive statements about the Cedarberg.

By drawing comparisons with other areas of the Cape Colony we can, however, make tentative suggestions that bear further investigation. Following an initial labor shortage immediately after the 1 December 1838 emancipation, a number of former slaves may have returned to their previous masters seeking work in a familiar environment.[57] Other freed slaves probably moved to more densely settled areas of the colony in search of work, as did some Khoisan from the region.[58]

Whatever the individual outcomes of emancipation for freed slaves and their former owners, collectively the act of emancipation served to regulate further labor relations in frontier regions. The combined effects of emancipation and Ordinance 50 ended bonded labor at the Cape. Where Ordinance 50 made clear the distinction between free Khoisan labor and chattel slavery, emancipation ten years later made the Khoikhoi-slave distinction irrelevant, combining slaves of Indian Ocean and Asian descent with descendants of indigenous Khoikhoi and San into a single category of laborers, mostly landless and differentiated from their masters or bosses by skin color.

This change, although not directly related to issues of a contested geographical frontier, was an important turning point for later developments in both race relations and labor relations in South African history.

THE CLANWILLIAM MAGISTERIAL DISTRICT

This series of increasing regulatory intrusions on the part of the state peaked in 1837, when Clanwilliam was proclaimed the seat of a newly created magisterial district. The arrival of the new magistrate marked the culmination of a gradual consolidation of the Cedarberg frontier, rather than a firm, single point of dominance. Starting early in the nineteenth century, a number of changes affected land tenure for both settlers and Khoisan. Competition for land was already in evidence when the Irish settlers arrived in 1820, a point of contention that intensified throughout the nineteenth century and took on increasingly racial overtones over time.[59]

Simultaneously, a series of government decrees increasingly regulated the relationship between masters and servants on rural farms, including those in the Cedarberg. These proclamations, Ordinance 50 in particular, were intended to offer some measure of protection to bonded labor, especially to Khoisan. This level of attention from the colonial government implies a growing sense of responsibility on the government's part for a group of people being incorporated into the colonial realm, albeit at a subordinate level.

Thus the establishment of a new magistrate's office in Clanwilliam was more of a symbolic ending to the process of frontier conquest than it was an active mechanism for resolving conflict or asserting settler hegemony. That hegemony was assured by progressive control of land tenure and conditions of employment in the preceding decades of the nineteenth century.

NOTES

1. Vincent Harlow, "The British Occupations 1795–1800," *Cambridge History of the British Empire*, VIII (Cambridge: Cambridge University Press, 1936); John S. Galbraith, *Reluctant Empire: British Policy on the South African Frontier 1834–1854* (Berkeley: University of California Press, 1963).

2. William M. Freund, "The Cape Under the Transitional Governments, 1795–1814" in *The Shaping of South African Society, 1652–1840*, 2nd edition, eds. Richard Elphick and Hermann Giliomee (Johannesburg: Maskew Miller Longman, 1989), 324.

3. For a general discussion of the period, see Hermann Giliomee, *Die Kaap tydens die eerste Britse bewind, 1795–1803* (Cape Town: Hollandsch Afrikaansch Uitgevers, 1975).

4. For a more recent reassessment that focuses on the available nineteenth-century source material, see Karel Schoeman, "Die Kort Bataafse era aan die Kaap, 1803–1806—'n oorsig van eietydse bronne," *Quarterly Bulletin of the South African Library* 52:4 (1998), 162–81.

5. Freund, "The Cape Under Transitional Governments," 325.

6. Robert C.-H. Shell, *Children of Bondage: A Social History of the Slave Society at the Cape of Good Hope, 1652–1838* (Hannover, NH: Wesleyan University Press, 1994), 143–44.

7. Andrew Bank, "The Erosion of Urban Slavery at the Cape" in Nigel Worden and Clifton Crais, eds., *Breaking the Chains: Slavery and its Legacy in the Nineteenth-Century Cape Colony* (Johannesburg: Witwatersrand University Press, 1994), 80–81.

8. Shell, *Children of Bondage*, 144–47.

9. Nigel Worden, *Slavery in Dutch South Africa* (Cambridge: Cambridge University Press, 1985), 138.

10. Susan Newton-King, *Masters and Servants on the Cape Eastern Frontier* (Cambridge: Cambridge University Press, 1999), 207.

11. J.S. Bergh and J.C. Visagie, *The Eastern Cape Frontier Zone, 1660–1980* (Durban: Butterworths, 1985), 2, 7.

12. For a discussion of colonial settlement east of Stellenbosch in the nascent Swellendam district, see Edmund H. Burrows, *Overberg Outspan: A Chronicle of People and Places in the Southwestern Districts of the Cape* (Cape Town: Maskew Miller Limited, 1952; reprint, Swellendam: Swellendam Trust, 1988).

13. Sparrman, 1: 137–40. Carl Peter Thunberg, *Travels at the Cape of Good Hope 1772–1775*, ed. V.S. Forbes (Cape Town: Van Riebeeck Society, 1986), 111. Lady Anne Barnard, *The Cape Journals of Lady Anne Barnard 1797–1798*, ed. A. M. Lewin Robinson with Margaret Lenta and Dorothy Driver (Cape Town: Van Riebeeck Society 1994), 305–6.

14. Anders Sparrman, *A Voyage to the Cape of Good Hope . . . 1772–1776*, 2 vols., ed. V. S. Forbes, trans. J. & I. Rudner (Cape Town: Van Riebeeck Society, 1975), 1: 137.

15. C. Graham Botha, *Place Names in the Cape Province*, (Cape Town and Johannesburg: Juta, 1926), 33.

16. For example, the Swellendam district was divided in 1785 with the creation of a new district at Graaff-Reinet, nearly six hundred kilometers east of Cape Town. The further division of the eastern frontier into districts including Somerset, Albany, George, and Uitenhage happened earlier than the parallel creation of new magisterial districts in northern frontier areas. For an outline of the creation of eastern frontier districts, see Bergh and Visagie, *The Eastern Cape Frontier Zone*, 24–39.

17. Dooling, "The Origins and the Aftermath," 50.

18. Richard Elphick and V.C. Malherbe, "The Khoisan to 1828," in Elphick and Giliomee, *Shaping*, 41.

19. P.J. van der Merwe, *Die Noordwaarste Beweging van die Boere voor die Groot Trek (1770–1842)* (The Hague: W.P. van Stockum & Zoon, 1937; reprint, Pretoria: Die Staatsbiblioteek, 1988), 153–75.

20. Martin Legassik, "The Northern Frontier to 1840," in Elphick and Giliomee, *Shaping*, 374; citing *RCC*, XI, 252–56; XII, 111–12, 242–48; XXVIII, 37.

21. Freund, "The Cape Under Transitional Governments," 336.

22. For a visual representation of the freehold farms, see Leonard Guelke's map, "The Southwestern Cape Colony, 1667–1750: Freehold Land Grants" scale, 3 inches = 10 km. (Department of Geography Publication Series, Occasional Paper No. 5. University of Waterloo, 1987.)

23. The most recent general overview of loan farm practices is Leonard Guelke, "Land Tenure and Settlement at the Cape, 1652–1812" in C.G.C. Martin and K.J. Friedlaender, eds., *History of Surveying and Land Tenure in South Africa* (Cape Town: UCT Department of Surveying, 1984), 7–34. The standard reference for early Cape land tenure is C. Graham Botha, *Early Cape Land Tenure* (Cape Town: Cape Times Limited, 1919).

24. Botha, *Early Cape Land Tenure*.

25. The standard work on land tenure policy in the nineteenth century remains L.C Duly, *British Land Policy at the Cape, 1795–1844: A Study of Administrative Procedures in the Empire* (Durham: Duke University Press, 1968).

26. *RCC,* IX "Cradock's Proclamation," 6 Aug. 1813, 204–8.

27. Guelke, "Land Tenure and Settlement," 20, 23–24.

28. Freund, "The Cape Under Transitional Governments," 332.

29. J.B. Pieres presents a succinct discussion of the 1820 settlement scheme in "The British and the Cape, 1814–1834," in Elphick and Giliomee, *Shaping,* 472–518.

30. Graham Brian Dickason, *Irish Settlers to The Cape: History of the Clanwilliam 1820 Settlers from Cork Harbour.* (Cape Town: A.A. Balkema, 1973), 16.

31. Governor Cradock renamed the post and the region for his father-in-law, Earl of Clanwilliam, in 1814.

32. According to the only study devoted exclusively to the settlement of Irish immigrants at Clanwilliam, 42 percent of the new arrival were farmers, 32 percent were skilled craftsmen or artisans, and 21 percent were involved in commerce, trade, military, and professions. Dickason, *Irish Settlers to the Cape,* 15–16. As Peires points out, it is probable that the percentage of farmers is overstated, since applicants might have exaggerated their agricultural experience in order to secure passage for themselves. Even so, the proportion of farmers originally settled in Clanwilliam is higher than the 36 percent attributed to the immigrant population in Albany. Peires, "The British and the Cape," 475.

33. Dickason, *Irish Settlers to the Cape,* 15–17.

34. Dickason, *Irish Settlers to the Cape,* 51–52.

35. Dickason, *Irish Settlers to the Cape,* 18–19.

36. I will refer to the Dutch Reformed Church by its Dutch initials, NGK, for *Nederlands Gereformeerde Kerk.*

37. C.R. Boxer, *The Dutch Seaborne Empire 1600–1800,* (London: Hutchinson, 1965, reprint London: Pelican Books, 1973), 138–49

38. Ad Biewinga, "Kerk," Chap. 4 and "Gemeente," Chap. 5 in *De Kaap de Goede Hoop: Een Nederlandse vestigingskolonie, 1680–1730* (Amsterdam: Uitgeverij Prometheus and Bert Bakker, 1999).

39. Richard Elphick and Hermann Giliomee, "The Origins and Entrenchment of European Dominance at the Cape 1652–c.1840) in Elphick and Giliomee, *Shaping,* 535.

40. The story of Eva, or Krotoa, a Khoikhoi woman raised in Jan van Riebeeck's household and a self-proclaimed Christian, ended in her tragic alcoholism and suicide. Other early examples of Khoikhoi Christian converts led similarly troubled lives and as such were not popular models for conversion. For an evaluation of Krotwa's life and position in Dutch colonial society at the Cape, see V.C. Malherbe, *Krotoa, Called Eva: A Woman Between,* Communications No. 19 (Cape Town: UCT Centre for African Studies, 1990) and Mansell Upham, "In a Kind of Custody: For Eva's Sake, Who Speaks for Krotwa?" unpublished paper, 1997.

For an account of the one successful mission in the eighteenth century see Bernhard Krüger, *The Pear Tree Blossoms: A History of the Moravian Church in South Africa, 1737–1869* (Genadendal: Moravian Book Depot, 1966).

41. Shell points out the levels of religious and secular instruction differed between Company slaves and privately owned slaves held by burghers. For a discussion of this distinction see Shell, *Children of Bondage,* xxxi–xxxiii. For his discussion of Christian conversion (or lack thereof) among Cape slaves, see *Children of Bondage,* 330–56.

42. Richard Elphick and Robert Shell, "Intergroup Relations: Khoikhoi, Settlers, Slaves and Free Blacks, 1652–1795," in Elphick and Giliomee, *Shaping*, 191.

43. R.T.J. Lombard, *Handleding vir Genealogiese Navorsing in Suid-Afrika* (Pretoria: Raad vir Geestewetenskaplike Navorsing, 1990), 116–20.

44. This conclusion is preliminary and warrants further investigation. To date the role of the NGK in settler society and in colonizing the Cape has received little attention from historians. Elphick and Giliomee also point out the lack of a good study of the Church at the early Cape, "European Dominance at the Cape," 527.

45. Dickason, *Irish Settlers to the Cape*, 19.

46. D.A. Kotzé, *Van Roodezand tot Gariep: Die 150 jarige bestaan van die NGK gemeente Clanwilliam 1826–1976* (Goodwood: Nasionale Boekdrukkery, 1981).

47. Stephen Granger, "Land Tenure and Environmental Conditions at Wupperthal," (MSc thesis, University of Cape Town, 1982).

48. For a discussion of the role of missions in protecting Khoikhoi labor, see Russell Viljoen, "Khoisan Labor and the Moravian Mission Movement, 1792–1795," Chap. 7 in "Khoisan Labour Relations in the Overberg Districts During the Later half of the Eighteenth Century, c. 1755–1795" (MA thesis, University of the Western Cape, 1993). For a history of early missions in South Africa, see Bernhard Krüger, *The Pear Tree Blossoms*.

49. The Moravian Church took over the administration of the Wupperthal mission in 1965. Berhard Krüger and P.W. Schaberg, *The Pear Tree Bears Fruit: A History of the Moravian Church in South Africa Western Cape Province, 1869–1980* (Genadendal: Moravian Book Depot, 1980), 154.

50. On the Kat River settlement, see Robert Ross, "The Kat River Rebellion and Khoikhoi Nationalism: The Fate of Ethnic Identification," *Kronos: Journal of Cape History* 24 (1997): 91–105 and Jane M. Sales, *Mission Stations and the Coloured Communities of the Eastern Cape, 1800–1852* (Cape Town: A.A. Balkema, 1975). On Griqua settlements, see Robert Ross, *Adam Kok's Griquas: A Study in the Development of Stratification in South Africa* (Cambridge; Cambridge University Press, 1976). For the effects of Ordinance 50 see Clifton Crais, "Gentry and Labour in Three Eastern Districts," *SAHJ* 18 (1986), 125–46; Leslie C. Duly, "A Revisit with the Cape's Hottentot Ordinance of 1828," in M. Kooy, ed., *Studies in Economics and Economic History* (London: Macmillan, 1972).

51. W.H. Macmillan, *Cape Colour Question* (London: Faber & Gwyer Limited, 1927; reprint Cape Town: A.A. Balkema, 1968), 147.

52. Penn, "The Northern Cape Frontier Zone," 37, 287.

53. Dawn D'Arcy Nell, "Land, Landownership and Land Occupancy in the Cape Colony During the Nineteenth Century with Specific Reference to the Clanwilliam District," (BA Honours Thesis, University of Cape Town, 1997), 8–10, 17–21.

54. Hermann Giliomee, "The Eastern Frontier, 1770–1812," in Elphick and Giliomee, *Shaping*, 452.

55. V.C. Malherbe, "Indentured and Unfree Labour in South Africa: Toward an Understanding," *SAHJ* 24 (1991): 8–10.

56. For the effects of emancipation, see John Edwin Mason, *Social Death and Resurrection: Slavery and Emancipation in South Africa* (Charlottesville: University of Virginia Press, 2003); Nigel Worden and Clifton Crais, editors, *Breaking the Chains: Slavery*

and its Legacy in the Nineteenth-Century Cape Colony (Johannesburg: University of Witwatersrand Press, 1994); Pamela Scully, *Liberating the Family? Gender and British Slave Emancipation in the Rural Western Cape, South Africa, 1823–1853* (Portsmouth, NH: Heinemann, 1997).

57. For example, see Elizabeth Anne Host, "Capitalization and Proletarianization on a Western Cape Farm: Klaver Valley 1812–1898," (MA thesis, University of Cape Town, 1992). Klaver Valley is south of the Cedarberg, but not an unlikely point of comparison.

58. CA: 1/STB 18/195; 1/STB 18/196; 1/STB 18/197 *Lists of Indentured Bastaard-Hottentots* 1776, 1829. CA: 1/STB 16/142, *Hottentot Register*, 1818–1819.

59. Nell, "Land, Land Ownership and Land Occupancy," 31–54.

GLOSSARY

TERMS USED AT THE CAPE IN THE EIGHTEENTH CENTURY

BASTAARD person of mixed race

BASTAARD- HOTTENTOT person of mixed race with Khoisan ancestry

BASTERS Christian community of mixed Khoisan, slave, and European ancestry; Basters eventually settled north of the Cedarberg, including areas in present-day Namibia

BOER farmer (see also trekboer and veeboer)

BUITENPOST VOC outpost

BURGHER citizen

BUSHMAN, ALSO BOSJESMAN San, indigenous hunter-gatherers

CAABWARDS towards Cape Town

THE COMPANY the Dutch East India Company (VOC)

DAGBOEK journal, official VOC log for the Cape

D'OUDE the elder

DROSTDY   magisterial seat

DROSTER   runaway

FREE BLACK   a person of neither indigenous nor European origin and not enslaved

FISCAAL   VOC official, second in command at the Cape; responsible for legal prosecution

FYNBOS   shrubs endemic to the Western Cape; part of Cape floral kingdom; fynbos comprises the majority of native plants in the Cedarberg

GEMEENTE   church congregation, parish

GRIQUAS   Christian community of mixed Khoisan, slave, and European ancestry; Griquas eventually settled in the eastern Karoo, near what would become the boundary between the Cape Colony and the Orange Free State

HEEMRAAD   landdrost's advisory council, a member of that council

HEREN XVII   Lords XVII, directors of the VOC

HOFSTEEDE   farmhouse

HOTTENTOT   Khoikhoi, pastoralist

INBOEKSELING/INBOEKSELINGE   Khoisan indentured servant(s)

INBOEKSELSEL   system of indenturing

INGEBOEKT   registered as indentured

KAAPENAAR   resident of the Cape

KAROO   semi-desert region to the east of the Cedarberg

KAMER   chamber, administrative division of the VOC

KHOIKHOI, ALSO KHOI, KHOE   indigenous pastoralists

KHOISAN   encompassing term for hunters and herders when a more accurate description is not possible

KLOOF   ravine

KNECHT   servant, usually a VOC employee working for wages; often employed as an overseer, or as a teacher

KRAAL   Khoisan encampment; livestock corral; homestead

LANDBOUWER   farmer

LANDDROST   magistrate

NAMAQUAS   Khoikhoi community living in Namaqualand, north of the Cedarberg

NGK   *Nederlands Gereformeerde Kerk* Dutch Reformed Church in South Africa

MUID   unit of dry volume, equivalent to 3.1 bushels

OPGAAF   census and taxation rolls

OPSTAL   farm buildings

PACHT   monopoly trading rights in specific commodities, including beer, wine, and meat. The VOC granted the trading rights to approved pachters in return for a rent, the pachtgeld.

PREDIKANT   preacher

TOGT   hunting trip

TREKBOER   pastoralist, migrant farmer

VEEBOER   cattle or livestock farmer

VELD   field, landscape

VELDKORNET   a burgher appointee, subordinate to the landdrost

VELDKORPORAL   officer in the burgher militia; appointed by districts (wyk) in rural areas to fulfill both military duties and some civil administration

VELDWAGMEESTER   burger militia officer, appointed by districts

VENDU ROL/ROLLE   auction roll(s)

VOC   *Verenigde Oostindische Compagnie* Dutch East India Company

WYK   administrative subdivision within a landdrost's district

CURRENCY AND MEASURES

1 rixdollar	3 Cape guilders or 8 skellings
1 Cape guilder	16 stuivers or 2 skellings and 4 stuivers
1 skelling (shilling)	6 stuivers
1 Dutch guilder	20 stuivers
1 morgen	2.12 acres
	0.859 hectares
1 muid	3.1 bushels
1 leaguer	153.7 US gallons

From Leonard Guelke, "The Early European Settlement of South Africa," (PhD diss., University of Toronto, 1974), 409.

BIBLIOGRAPHY

PRIMARY SOURCES

Archives and Other Collections

ALGEMEENE RIJKSARCHIEF, THE HAGUE (ARA)

VOC   Dutch East India Company, *Overgekomen brieven en papieren*

BIBLIOTHEQUE NATIONALE DE FRANCE, PARIS (BNF)

SHM   Service de la Marine

Photo Catalog vol. 170
Photo Catalog vol. 187

DEEDS OFFICE, CAPE TOWN (DO)

OSF   Old Stellenbosch Freeholds

PUBLIC RECORDS OFFICE, LONDON (PRO)

CO   Colonial Office
MPH   Maps
MPI   Maps
MR   Maps
MPG   Maps

RIJKSMUSEUM, AMSTERDAM

Jan Brandes Collection

SOUTH AFRICAN ARCHIVES, CAPE ARCHIVES DEPOT (CA)

CJ   Council of Justice
G2   *Doop Register* (NGK baptismal records)
J   *Opgaaf*
Maps   Map collection
MOOC   Master of the Orphan Chamber
RLR   Receiver of Land Revenue, *Oud Wildschutte Boeke*
                and the computerized database compiled by Leonard Guelke
1/STB   Stellenbosch Magisterial District records

UNIVERSITY OF CAPE TOWN, SPATIAL ARCHAEOLOGY
RESEARCH UNIT (SARU)

Site reports, Cedarberg region.

Published Primary Sources

Barnard, Lady Anne. *The Cape Journals of Lady Anne Barnard 1797–1798*, ed. A.M. Lewin Robinson with Margaret Lenta and Dorothy Driver. Cape Town: Van Riebeeck Society, 1994.
Barrow, J. *An Account of Travels into the Interior of Southern Africa in the Year 1797 and 1798*. London: T. Cadwell, Jr., and W. Davies, 1801.

Bird, William. *State of the Cape of Good Hope in 1822*. Facsimile reprint. Cape Town: Struik, 1966.

Kolb, Peter. *The Present State of the Cape of Good Hope*. New York: Johnson Reprint Corp., 1968.

Mentzel, O.F. *A Geographical and Topographical Description of the Cape of Good Hope (1787)*. Translated by G.V. Marais and J. Hoge, ed. H.J. Mandelbrote. Cape Town: Van Riebeeck Society, 1925.

Opgaven van de veldkornetschappen en derzelver grenzen, als aanbevolen door de onderscheiden Resident Magistraten, te worden bevat in hunne respective districten. Cape Town: S. Solomon & Co., "Gazette" Kantoor, 1850.

Sparrman, Anders. *A Voyage to the Cape of Good Hope Towards the Antarctic Polar Circle Round the World and to the Country of the Hottentots and the Caffres from the Year 1772–1776*. Translated by J. and I. Rudner, ed. V.S. Forbes. Cape Town: Van Riebeeck Society, 1975.

Thunberg, Carl Peter. *Travels at the Cape of Good Hope 1772–1775*. Edited by V.S. Forbes. Cape Town: Van Riebeeck Society, 1986.

Valentyn, François. *Beschryvinge van de Kaap der Goede Hoop met de zaaken daar toe behoorende (1726)*. Ed. P. Serton, R. Raven-Hart, W.J. De Kock, and E.H. Raidt. Cape Town: Van Riebeeck Society, 1971.

Maps Consulted

ALGEMEENE RIJKSARCHIEF

De Tafelbaai met omgeving met afbeeldingen van Kaapstad, 't fort de Gode Hoopa, de Duivelsberg, de Tafelberg, de Leeuwekop en de Leeuwstaart of Leeuwebil. (4.AANW 1420)

Kaart van Afrika door den Heer d'Anville. 47 mm = 200 zeemijlen van de 20 graad. ca. 1:23.000.000. Amsterdam: Isaac Tirion, 1763. (4.AANW 1477)

Kaart van de zuidkust van Zuid Afrika. 1776. (4.AAANW 271)

Kaart van het zuidelijkste gedeelt van Afrika of het land der Hottentotten. 72mm = 60 franse mijl, 45 Dutch miles. Amsterdam: Isaac Tirion, 3rd quarter, eighteenth century. (4.BMF 471)

Nieuwe Kaart van de Kaap der Goede Hoope en der naby gelegen Landen, volgens de Afmeeting van de Abt. de la Caille in 1752. 75 mm = 30.000 fr. toises of halve roeden. ca. 1:7.8000.000. Amsterdam: Isaac Tirion, 1763. (4/AAMW 1478; also 4.BMF 489)

BIBLIOTHEQUE NATIONALE DE FRANCE, PARIS (BNF)

Afrika. 1772. (Port. 179. no. 63)

Afrique divisée en ses Empires, Royaumes et Républiques. 1805. (Port. 202 no. 50 a–d)

Afrique pour la Géographie Comparée, seconde partie. 1778. (Port 179 no. 64)

Carte Encyprotype de l'Afrique. 1814. (Port 202 no. 51 a–d)

*Nieuwe en Naauw Keurige Kaart van Africa naar de beste en meeste beproevde he-
dendaagsche Kaarten ontwerpen, en volgens sterrekundige waarneemingen ingeri-
ent door Eman. Bowen verbeterd door W.A. Bachiene.* 1782. (Port 179 no. 65)

RIJKSMUSEUM, AMSTERDAM

R.J. Gordon Map of Southern Africa

RIJKSUNIVERSITEIT TE LEIDEN

Kaart van het zuidelykste gedelte van Afrika of het land der Hottentotten. in Dutch and
French miles. Amsterdam: Isaak Tirion, eighteenth century. In "Verzameling Zuid
Afrika." (Atlas 1503 504–02, map 1)

Kaart van Zuidelyk gedeelt van Afrika tot Verstand van de Twee Reizen van le Vaillant.
In "Verzameling Zuid Afrika." (Atlas 1503 504–02, map 2)

*Kart vom Süd End Afrika von dem Cap-Colonie lande nach Barrow, Lichtenstein,
Campbell, Burchell, Latrobe, u.a.* 1819. In "Verzameling Zuid Afrika." (Atlas 1503
504–02, map 3)

*Nieuwe Kaart van Caap de Goede Hoop in have rechte jegenwoordinge staat vertoond
door François Valentyn.* Dutch miles. : J. van Braam et G. onder de Linden. In
"Verzameling Zuid Afrika." (Atlas 1503 504–02, map 5)

Zuid Afrika, "Hottentotten Landen". In "Verzameling Zuid Afrika." (Atlas 1503
504–02, map 4)

*Plan of te Afteekening van de Staad en 't Casteel aan Cabo de Goede Hoop mitg's de
langste Strand leggende Batterijen en Redoleten neevens een groot gedeelt der Tafel
Baaij, etc. etc. etc. (second half of 18th c.).* (VI 12/31/38)

SOUTH AFRICAN SURVEYOR GENERAL'S OFFICE (SASG)

1:250,000 Topographical Maps

3118	Calvinia	1989
3218	Clanwilliam	1997
3318	Cape Town	994
3319	Worcester	

1:50,000 Topographical Maps

3118 DD	Bulshoek	1986
3118 CA	Papendorp	1980

3119 CB	Lutzville	1980
3118 DA	Van Rhynsdorp	1989
3118 DB	Uironskraal	1971
3119 CC	Doringbos	1971
3218 CD	Bergrivier	1982
3218 AB	Hopfield	1980
3218 DC	Klawer	1980
3218 BA	Graafwater	1986
3218 BC	Redelinghuis	1986
3218 DA	Goergap	1986
3218 CA	Citrusdal	1986
3218 DD	Piketberg	1975
3218 DB	Eendekuil	1986
3218 BD	Oliewenboskraal	1986
3218 BB	Clanwilliam	1986
3218 AB	Lamberts Bay	1986
3218 AD	Elandsbaai	1986
3218 CB & CA	Aurora	1986
3218 DC	Moravia	1975
3219 CC	Keerom	1986
3219 AC	Wupperthal	1986
3219 AA	Pakhuis	1986
3219 CD	De Meul	1986
3219 CB	Groot Rivier	1986
3219 AD	Grootberg	1986
3219 AB	Uitspankraal	1986

PUBLISHED MAPS

Guelke, Leonard. *The Southwestern Cape Colony 1657–1750, Freehold Land Grants*, Department of Geography Publication Series, Occasional Paper No.5, University of Waterloo, 1987.

Nieuwe Caarte van Kaap de Goede Hoop. Amsterdam: Balthazar Lakeman, 1727.

SECONDARY SOURCES

Published Books, Chapters, and Journal Articles

Adams, Julia. *Ruling Families and Merchant Capitalism in Early Modern Europe.* Ithaca: Cornell University Press, 2005.

Afigbo, A. E. "Colonial Historiography." In *African Historiography: Essays in Honour of Jacob Ade Ajayi,* ed. Toyin Falola, 38–51. London: Longman, 1993.

Appiah, Kwame Anthony. "Is the Post in Post-Modernism the Post in Post-Colonial?" *Critical Inquiry* 17:2 (December 1991): 336–57.

Anderson, Benedict. *Imagined Communities: Reflections on the Origin and Spread of Nationalism.* London: Verso, 1983.

Appleby, Joyce, Lynn Hunt, and Margaret Jacob. *Telling the Truth About History.* New York: W.W. Norton, 1994.

Armstrong, James C. "The Estate of a Chinese Woman in the Mid-Eighteenth Century at the Cape of Good Hope." In *Contingent Lives: Social Identity and Material Culture in the VOC World,* edited by Nigel Worden, 75–90. Cape Town: University of Cape Town Press, 2007.

———. "The Slaves, 1652–1834." In *The Shaping of South African Society, 1652–1840,* edited by Richard Elphick and Hermann Giliomee. 1st ed. London: Maskew Miller Longman, 1979.

Armstrong, James C. and Nigel Anthony Worden. "The Slaves, 1652–1834." In *The Shaping of South African Society, 1652–1840,* edited by Richard Elphick, and Hermann Giliomee, 109–183. 2nd ed. London: Maskew Miller Longman, 1989.

Baesjou, René. "The Historical Evidence in Old Maps and Charts of Africa, with Special Reference to West Africa." *History in Africa* 15 (1988): 1–83.

Bank, Andrew. *The Decline of Urban Slavery in Cape Town, 1806 to 1843,* Cape Town: UCT Centre for African Studies, 1991.

———. "The Erosion of Urban Slavery at the Cape." In *Breaking the Chains: Slavery and its Legacy in the Nineteenth-Century Cape Colony,* eds. Nigel Worden, and Clifton Crais, 79–98. Johannesburg: Witwatersrand University Press, 1994.

Barend van Haeften, M.L. "Travel Literature at the Time of the Dutch East India Company (1602–1795)." *International Conference on Shipping, Factories and Colonization,* eds. J. Everaert, and J. Parmentier, 317–22. Brussels, 24 November 1994. Brussels: Koninklijke Academie voor Overseese Wetenschappen, 1996.

Barnard, Alan. *Hunters and Herders of Southern Africa: A Comparative Ethnography of the Khoisan Peoples.* Cambridge: Cambridge University Press, 1992.

Barry, Sarah. "Hegemony on a Shoestring: Indirect Rule and Access to Agricultural Land." *Africa: Journal of the International African Institute* 62:3 (1992): 327–55.

Bayly, C.A. *Imperial Meridian: The British Empire and the World 1780–1830.* London: Longman, 1989.

Beinart, William, Colin Bundy, and Stanley Trapido, eds. *Putting a Plough to the Ground: Accumulation and Dispossession in Rural South Africa, 1850–1930,* Johannesburg: Ravan Press, 1986.

Bentley, Jerry. "Cross-Cultural Interaction and Periodization in World History." *American Historical Review* 101 (June 1996): 749–70.

Bergh, J.S., and J.C. Visagie. *The Eastern Cape Frontier Zone, 1660–1980: A Cartographic Guide for Historical Research.* Durban: Butterworths, 1985.

Beyers, Coenraad. *Die Kaapse Patriotte gedurende die laaste kwart van die agtiende eeuw in die voortlewing van hul denkbeelde.* Pretoria: J.L., 1967.

Bhabha, Homi. *The Location of Culture.* London and New York: Routledge, 1994.

Biesele, Megan. "Interpretation in Rock Art and Folklore." *New Approaches to Southern African Rock Art,* South African Archaeological Society, Goodwin Series 4 (1983): 54–60.

Biewinga, Ad. *De Kaap de Goede Hoop: Een Nederlandse vestigingskolonie, 1680–1730.* Amsterdam: Uitgeverij Prometheus and Bert Bakker, 1999.

Blussé, Leonard. *Bitter Bonds: A Colonial Divorce Drama of the Seventeenth Century.* Translated by D. Webb. Princeton: Markus Weiner, 2002.

———. *Strange Company: Chinese Settlers, Mestizo Women and the Dutch in VOC Batavia.* Dordrecht: Foris Publications, 1986.

Böeseken, Anna, and Margaret Cairns. *The Secluded Valley—Tulbagh: 't Land van Waveren 1700–1894.* Cape Town and Johannesburg: Perskor, 1989.

Boserup, Ester. *The Conditions of Agricultural Growth: The Economics of Agrarian Change Under Population Pressure.* New York: Aldine Publishing Company, 1965.

Botha, C. Graham. *Early Cape Land Tenure.* Cape Town: Cape Times Limited, 1919.

———. *Place Names in the Cape Province.* Cape Town and Johannesburg: Juta, 1926.

Boucher, M. *French-Speakers at the Cape in the First Hundred Years of Dutch East India Company Rule: The European Background.* Pretoria: University of South Africa, 1981.

Boulle, P.H., Leonard Blussé, and Femma S. Gaastra, eds. *Companies and Trade: Essays on Overseas Trading Companies in the Ancien Regime.* Leiden: Leiden University Press, 1981.

Bourdieu, Pierre. "Structures, Habitus, Power: Basis for a Theory of Symbolic Power." In *Culture/Power/History,* edited by N.B. Dirks, G. Eley and S.B. Ortner, 155–99. Princeton, NJ: Princeton University Press, 1983.

Boxer, C.R. *The Dutch Seaborne Empire 1600–1800.* London: Hutchinson, 1965; reprint Penguin Books, 1973.

Bradlow, Edna. "Mental Illness or a Form of Resistance? The Case of Soera Brotto." *Kleio* 23 (1991): 4–16.

Bradlow, F.R. and Margaret Cairns, *The Early Cape Muslims.* Cape Town: A.A. Balkema, 1978.

Braudel, Fernand. *The Mediterranean and the Mediterranean World in the Age of Philip II.* Translated by Siân Reynolds. New York: Harper Row, 1972.

Bravman, Bill. "Using Old Photographs in Interviews: Some Cautionary Notes About Silences in Fieldwork." *History in Africa* 17 (1990): 327–34.

Brink, André. *A Chain of Voices.* London: Minerva, 1995.

Brooks, James F. *Captives and Cousins: Slavery, Kinship, and Community in the Southwest Borderlands.* Chapel Hill: The University of North Carolina Press, 2001.

Bruijn, J.R., F.S. Gaastra, and I. Schoeffer, eds. *Dutch-Asiatic Shipping in the Seventeenth and Eighteenth Centuries,* with assistance of E.D. van Eyck van Heslinga. The Hague: Nijhoff, 1979.

Burchell, William J. *Selections from Travels in the Interior of Southern Africa*, ed. Clement H. Notcutt. London: Oxford University Press, 1935.

Burke, Peter, ed. *New Perspectives on Historical Writing*. University Park, Pa.: Pennsylvania State University Press, 2001.

Burrows, Edmund H. *Overberg Outspan: A Chronicle of People and Places in the South Western Districts of the Cape*. Swellendam: Swellendam Trust, 1988. First published 1952 by Maskew Miller.

———. *Overberg Odyssey: People, Roads and Early Days*. Swellendam: Swellendam Trust, 1994.

Burton, Antoinette, ed. *Archive Stories: Facts, Fictions and the Writing of History*. Durham: Duke University Press, 2005.

———. *Dwelling in the Archive: Women Writing House, Home and History in Late Colonial India*. Oxford: Oxford University Press, 2003.

Cartwright, Margaret Findlay. *Maps of Africa and Southern Africa in Printed Books, 1550–1750*. Cape Town: UCT School of Librarianship, 1955.

Chakrabarty, Dipesh. *Provincializing Europe: Postcolonial Thought and Historical Difference*. Chicago: University of Chicago Press, 2000.

Classens, H.W. *Die geskiedenis van boerekos, 1652–1806*. Pretoria: Protea Boekhuis, 2006.

Cobbing, Julian. "The Mfecane as Alibi: Thoughts on Dithakong and Mbolompo." *Journal of African History* 28 (1988): 487–519.

Coertzen, Pieter with Charles Fensham. *The Huguenots of South Africa 1688–1988*. Cape Town: Tafelberg, 1988.

Coetzee, J.M. *White Writing: On the Culture of Letters in South Africa*, New Haven and London: Yale University Press, 1988.

Comaroff, John and Jean. *Of Revelation and Revolution: Christianity, Colonialism and Consciousness in South Africa*, vol.1. Chicago: University of Chicago Press, 1991.

———. *Of Revelation and Revolution: The Dialectics of Modernity on a South African Frontier*, vol. 2. Chicago: University of Chicago Press, 1992.

Constantine, Stephen. "Monarchy and Constructing Identity in 'British' Gibraltar, c. 1800 to the Present." *Journal of Imperial and Commonwealth History* 31:1 (2006): 22–44.

Cooper, Frederick. *Colonialism in Question: Theory, Knowledge, History*. Berkeley: University of California Press, 2005.

———. "Peasants, Capitalists, and Historians: A Review Article." *Journal of Southern African Studies* 7:2 (April 1981): 284–314.

Cornell, Carohn and Antonia Malan. *Household Inventories at the Cape, a Guide for Beginner Researchers*. Cape Town: UCT Historical Studies Department, 2005.

Cory, G.E. *The Rise of South Africa*, vol.1. London: Longmans, 1921.

Crais, Clifton. "Gentry and Labour in Three Eastern Districts." *South African Historical Journal* 18 (1986): 125–46.

———. *The Making of the Colonial Order: White Supremacy and Black Resistance in the Eastern Cape, 1770–1865*. Johannesburg: Witwatersrand University Press, 1992.

Crais, Clifton and Nigel Worden, eds. *Breaking the Chains: Slavery and its Legacy in the Nineteenth-Century Cape Colony*. Johannesburg: Witwatersrand University Press, 1994.

Craton, Michael. *A Jamaican Plantation: The History of Worthy Park, 1670–1970*. Toronto: University of Toronto Press, 1970.

Crosby, Alfred W. *Ecological Imperialism: The Biological Expansion of Europe, 900–1900.* Studies in Environment and History. Cambridge: Cambridge University Press, 1986.

Davis, Natalie Zemon. *Fiction in the Archives: Pardon Tales and Their Tellers in Sixteenth-Century France.* Stanford: Stanford University Press, 1987.

De Kock, Victor. *Those in Bondage: An Account of the Life of the Slaves at the Cape in the Days of the Dutch East India Company.* Cape Town: H.B. Timmins, 1950.

de Villiers, Christoffel Coetzee. *Geslagsregisters van die ou Kaapse families* (Genealogies of Old South African Families*).* Completely revised, augmented and rewritten by C. Pama. 1st ed. Cape Town and Rotterdam: A.A. Balkema, 1966.

———. *Geslagsregisters van die ou Kaapse families* (Genealogies of Old South African Families*).* Completely revised, augmented and rewritten by C. Pama. 2nd ed. Cape Town and Rotterdam: A.A. Balkema, 1981.

de Vries, Jan, and Ad van der Woude. *The First Modern Economy: Success, Failure and Perseverance of the Dutch Economy, 1500–1815.* Cambridge: Cambridge University Press, 1997.

Deacon, J. "Later Stone Age People and Their Descendants in Southern Africa." In *Southern African History and Paleoenvironments,* edited by R. Klein, 221–38. Rotterdam: A.A. Balkema, 1984.

Deacon, Janette, and Thomas A. Dowson, eds. *Voices from the Past: /Xam Bushmen and the Bleek and Lloyd Collection.* Johannesburg: Witwatersrand University Press, 1996.

Delius, Peter, and Stanley Trapido. "*Inboekselings* and *Oorlams*: The Creation and Transformation of a Servile Class." *Journal of Southern African Studies* 8:2 (April 1982): 214–42.

Dickason, Graham Brian. *Irish Settlers to the Cape: History of the Clanwilliam 1820 Settlers from Cork Harbour.* Cape Town: A.A. Balkema, 1973.

Dooling, Wayne. "The Origins and the Aftermath of the Cape Colony's 'Hottentot Code' of 1809." *Kronos: Journal of Cape History* 31 (November 2005): 50–61.

———. "The Making of a Colonial Elite: Property, Family and Landed Stability in the Cape Colony, c. 1750–1834." *Journal of Southern African Studies* 31:1 (March 2005): 158–61.

du Plessis, A. J. "Die geskiedenis van die graankultuur in Suid-Afrika, 1652–1752." *Annals of the University of Stellenbosch* 11 Series B1 (September 1933): 2–5.

du Plessis, I.D. *The Cape Malays: History, Religion, Folk Tales.* Cape Town: A.A. Balkema, 1972.

Duly, Leslie Clement. *British Land Policy at the Cape, 1795–1844: A Study of Administrative Procedures in the Empire.* Durham: Duke University Press, 1968.

———. "A Revisit with the Cape's Hottentot Ordinance of 1828." In *Studies in Economics and Economic History: Essays in Honour of Professor H.M. Robertson,* edited by M. Kooy, 26–56. London: Macmillam, 1972.

Edwards, Clive. *Turning Houses into Homes: A History of the Retailing and Consumption of Domestic Furnishings.* Aldershot: Ashgate, 2005.

Edwards, I. *Towards Emancipation: A Study of South African Slavery.* Cardiff: Laandyssul, 1942.

Elbourne, Elizabeth. *Blood Ground: Colonialism, Missions and the Contest for Christianity in the Cape Colony and Britain, 1799–1853.* Montreal: McGill-Queen's University Press, 2002.

Eldredge, Elizabeth, and Fred Morton, eds. *Slavery in South Africa: Captive Labor on the Dutch Frontier.* Boulder: Westview Press, 1994.

Elphick, Richard. *Kraal and Castle: The Khoikhoi and the Founding of White South Africa.* New Haven: Yale University Press, 1977.

Elphick, Richard, and Hermann Giliomee, eds. *The Shaping of South African Society, 1652–1840.* 2nd ed. Johannesburg: Maskew Miller Longman, 1989.

——. "The Origins and Entrenchment of European Dominance at the Cape 1652–c. 1840." In *The Shaping of South African Society, 1652–1840,* edited by Richard Elphick and Hermann Giliomee, 521–66. 2nd ed. Johannesburg: Maskew Miller Longman, 1989.

Elphick, Richard, and Robert Shell. "Intergroup Relations: Khoikhoi, Settlers, Slaves and Free Blacks, 1652–1795." In *The Shaping of South African Society, 1652–1840,* edited by Richard Elphick and Hermann Giliomee, 184–239. 2nd ed. Johannesburg: Maskew Miller Longman, 1989.

Emmer, P.C. *Colonialism and Migration: Indentured Labour Before and After Slavery.* Comparative Studies in Overseas History, vol. 7. Dordrecht: M. Nijhoff, 1986.

Engelbrecht, J.A. *The Korana.* Cape Town: Maskew Miller, 1936.

Etherington, Norman. *Great Treks: The Transformation of Southern Africa, 1815–1854.* London: Longman, 2001.

Feierman, Steven. "African Histories and the Dissolution of World Histories." In *Africa and the Disciplines: The Contributions of Research in Africa to the Social Sciences and Humanities,* edited by Robert Bates, V.Y. Mudimbe, and Jean O'Barr, 167–212. Chicago: University of Chicago Press, 1993.

Feinberg, Harvey M. "South Africa and Land Ownership: What's in a Deed?" *History in Africa* 22 (1995): 439–43.

Foucault, Michel. *Discipline and Punish: The Birth of the Prison.* New York: Vintage Books, 1979.

Fox-Genovese, Elizabeth. *Within the Plantation Household: Black and White Women of the Old South.* Chapel Hill: University of North Carolina Press, 1988.

Fransen, Hans, and Mary Alexander Cook. *The Old Buildings of the Cape.* A.A. Balkema: Cape Town, 1980.

——. *The Old Houses of the Cape: A Survey of the Existing Buildings in the Traditional Style of Architecture of the Dutch Settled Regions of the Cape of Good Hope.* A.A. Balkema: Cape Town, 1965.

Freund, William M. "The Cape Under the Transitional Governments, 1795–1814." In *The Shaping of South African Society, 1652–1840,* edited by Richard Elphick, and Hermann Giliomee, 324–57. 2nd ed. Johannesburg: Maskew Miller Longman, 1989.

Gaastra, Femma S. *Bewind en beleid bij de VOC, 1672–1702.* Zutphen: Walberg Pers, 1989.

——. *De Geschiedenis van de VOC.* 2nd ed. Zutphen: Walberg Pers, 1991.

Galbraith, John S. *Reluctant Empire: British Policy on the South African Frontier 1834–1854.* Berkeley: University of California Press, 1963.

Gengenbach, Heidi. *Where Women Make History: Gendered Tellings of Community and Change in Magude, Mozambique.* New York: Columbia University Press, 2005. http://www.gutenberg-e.org/geho1/guide.html

Giliomee, Hermann. *The Afrikaners: Biography of a People*. London: Hurst, 2003.

———. "The Eastern Frontier, 1770–1812." In *The Shaping of South African Society, 1652–1840*, edited by Richard Elphick and Hermann Giliomee, 421–71. 2nd ed. Johannesburg: Maskew Miller Longman, 1989.

———. "Processes in Development of the Southern African Frontier." In *The Frontier in History: North American and South Africa Compared*, edited by Howard Lamar and Leonard Thompson, 76–119. New Haven: Yale University Press, 1981.

———. *Die Kaap tydens die eerste Britse bewind*. Cape Town: Hollandsche Afrikaansch Uitgevers, 1975.

Ginzburg, Carlo. *The Cheese and the Worms: The Cosmos of a Sixteenth-Century Friulian Miller*. Translated by John and Anne Tedeshi. Baltimore: Johns Hopkins University Press, 1982.

———. *Clues, Myths and the Historical Method*. Translated by John and Anne Tedeshi. Baltimore: Johns Hopkins University Press, 1989.

Goldberg, Sylvie-Anne. *La Clepsydre*. Paris: Albin Michel, 2000.

Goody, Jack. *The European Family: An Historico-Anthropological Essay*. Oxford: Blackwell Publishers, 2000.

Gordon, David. "History on the Luapula Retold: Landscape, Memory and Identity in the Kazembe Kingdom." *Journal of African History* 47 (2006): 21–42.

Greenstein, L.J. "Slave and Citizen: The South African Case." *Race* 15:1 (1973): 25–46.

Guelke, Leonard. "The Anatomy of a Colonial Settler Population: Cape Colony, 1657–1750." *The International Journal of African Historical Studies* 21:3 (1988): 453–73.

———. "An Early Colonial Landed Gentry: Land and Wealth in the Cape Colony 1682–1731." *Journal of Historical Geography* 9:3 (1983): 265–86.

———. "Freehold Farmers and Frontier Settlers, 1657–1780." In *The Shaping of South African Society, 1652–1840*, edited by Richard Elphick and Hermann Giliomee, 66–108. 2nd ed. Johannesburg: Maskew Miller Longman, 1989.

———. "Land Tenure and Settlement at the Cape 1652–1812." In *History of Surveying and Land Tenure in South Africa, Collected Papers*, vol. 1., edited by C.G.C. Martin, and K.J. Friedlaender, 7–34. Rondebosch: UCT Department of Surveying, 1984.

———. "The Making of Two Frontier Communities: Cape Colony in the Eighteenth Century." *Historical Reflections/Reflexions Historiques* 12:3 (1985): 419–48.

Guelke, Leonard and Jeanne Kay Guelke. "Imperial Eyes on South Africa: Reassessing Travel Narratives." *Journal of Historical Geography* 30:1 (2004): 11–31.

Guelke, Leonard and Robert C.-H. Shell. "Landscape of Conquest: Frontier Water Alienation and Khoikhoi Strategies of Survival, 1652–1780." *Journal of Southern African Studies* 18:4 (1992): 803–24.

———, comps. *The Deeds Book: The Cape Cadastral Calendar*. New Haven: Opgaaf Project, 1990.

———. "An Early Colonial Landed Gentry: Land and Wealth in the Cape Colony 1682–1731." *Journal of Historical Geography* 9:3 (1983): 265–86.

Guelke, Leonard, Robert C.-H. Shell and Anthony Whyte, comps. "The de la Fontaine Report." New Haven: Opgaaf Project, 1990.

Guha, Ranajit, ed. *A Subaltern Studies Reader 1986–1995*. Minneapolis: University of Minnesota Press, 1997.

Guha, Ranajit. *Dominance Without Hegemony: History and Power in Colonial India.* Cambridge: Harvard University Press, 1997.

Hall, Martin. "The Secret Lives of Houses: Women and Gables in the Eighteenth-Century Cape." *Social Dynamics* 20 (1994): 1–48.

Hall, Simon and Aron Mazel. "The Private Performance of Events: Colonial Period Rock Art from the Swartruggens." *Kronos: Journal of Cape History* 31 (2005): 124–51.

Hamilton, Carolyn et al., eds. *Refiguring the Archive.* Cape Town: David Phillip, 2002.

——, ed. *Mfecane Aftermath: Reconstructive Debates in Southern African History.* Johannesburg: Witwatersrand University Press, 1995.

Hanley, Sarah . "Engendering the State: Family Formation and State Building in Early Modern Europe." *French Historical Studies* 16:1 (1989): 4–27.

Harlow, Vincent. "The British Occupations 1795–1800." *Cambridge History of the British Empire.* Cambridge: Cambridge University Press, 1936.

Hartman, Mary S. *The Household and the Making of History: A Subversive View of the Western Past.* Cambridge: Cambridge University Press, 2004.

Hay, Douglas, et al., eds. *Albion's Fatal Tree: Crime and Society in Eighteenth-Century England.* New York: Pantheon Press, 1975.

Heap, Peggy. *The Story of Hottentots Holland.* Somerset West: Peggy Heap, 1993.

Heese, H.F. *Reg en onreg: Kaapse regspraak in die agtiende eeu.* Bellville: Instituut vir Historiese Navorsing, 1994.

——. *Groepe sonder grense: Die rol en status van die gemengde bevolking aan de Kaap, 1652–1705.* Bellville: Instituut vir Historiese Navorsing, 1985; translated by Delia Robertson as *Cape Melting Pot: The Role and Status of the Mixed Population at the Cape, 1652–1795.* Johannesburg: self-published, 2006.

Heese, J.A., and R.T.J. Lombard. *South African Genealogies,* 5 vols. Pretoria: Raad vir Geestewetenskaplike Navorsing, 1986–1999.

Hobsbawm, Eric and Terrence Ranger, eds. *The Invention of Tradition.* Cambridge: Cambridge University Press, 1992.

Hochschild, Adam. *King Leopold's Ghost: A Story of Greed, Terror, and Heroism in Colonial Africa,* Boston: Houghton Mifflin, 1998.

Hofmeyr, Isabel. *"We Spend Our Years as a Tale That is Told:" Oral Historical Narrative in a South African Chiefdom.* Portsmouth, NH: Heinemann, 1993.

Hoge, J. "Personalia of Germans at the Cape, 1652–1808." *Archives Yearbooks for South African History* 9 (1946): 1–495.

Huizinga, J.H. *Dutch Civilisation in the Seventeenth Century and Other Essays,* selected by Pieter Geyl, and F.W.N. Hugenholtz. Translated by Arnold J. Pomerans. New York: Frederick Ungar Publishing Co., 1968.

Israel, Jonathan I. *The Dutch Republic: Its Rise, Greatness, and Fall, 1477–1806.* Oxford: Oxford University Press, 1995.

Jacobs, Jaap. *New Netherland: A Dutch Colony in Seventeenth-Century America.* Leiden: Brill, 2005.

Jacobs, Nancy. "The Flowing Eye: Water Management in the Upper Kuruman Valley, South Africa, c. 1800–1962." *Journal of African History* 37:2 (1996): 237–60.

Jeffreys, K.M. et al., eds. *Kaapse plakkaatboek.* Cape Town: Government Printer, 1951.

Jeppson, Patrice L. "Colonial Systems and Indigenous Responses: Black Material Expressions at a British Mission in South Africa." *Society for Historical Archaeology Conference on Historical and Underwater Archaeology,* Richmond, Va., 9 January 1991.

Johnson, Townly, Hyme Rabinowitz, and Percy Sieff. *Rock-Painting of the South-Western Cape.* Cape Town: Nasionale Boekhandel BPK, 1959.

Kinahan, J. "The Archaeological Structure of Pastoral Production in the Central Namib Desert." *Prehistoric Pastoralism in South Africa,* The South African Archaeological Society Goodwin Series 5 (1986): 69–82.

Klein, Richard G. "The Prehistory of Stone Age Herders in The Cape Province, South Africa." *Prehistoric Pastoralism in South Africa,* South African Archaeological Society Goodwin Series 5 (June 1986): 5–12.

Klieman, Kairn. *"The Pygmies Were Our Compass": Bantu and Batwa in the History of West Central Africa, Early Times to c. 1900 C.E.* Portsmouth, N.H.: Heinemann, 2003.

Klooster, Wim. *Dutch in the Americas, 1600–1800.* New Castle, Del.: Oak Knoll Press, 1997.

Kopytoff, Igor, ed. *The African Frontier: The Reproduction of Traditional African Societies.* Bloomington: Indiana University Press, 1987.

Kossmann, I.H. *The Low Countries 1780–1940.* Oxford: Clarendon Press, 1978.

Kotzé, D.A. *Van Roodezand tot Gariep: Die 150 jarige bestaan van die NGK gemeente Clanwilliam 1826–1976.* Goodwood: Nasionale Boekdrukkery, 1981.

Kriger, Colleen E. "Museum Collections as Sources for African History." *History in Africa* 23 (1996): 129–54.

Krüger, Bernhard. *The Pear Tree Blossoms: A History of the Moravian Church in South Africa, 1737–1869.* Genadendal: Moravian Book Depot, 1966.

Krüger, Bernhard and P.W. Schaberg. *The Pear Tree Bears Fruit: A History of the Moravian Church in South Africa Western Cape Province, 1869–1980.* Genadendal: Moravian Book Depot, 1980.

Ladurie, Emmanuel Le Roy. *Montaillou: The Promised Land of Error.* Translated by Barbara Bray. New York: Vintage, 1979.

Lance, James. "What the Stranger Brings: The Social Dynamics of Fieldwork." *History in Africa* 17 (1990): 335–39.

Lee, R.B. *The !Kung San: Men, Women and Work in a Foraging Society.* Cambridge: Cambridge University, 1979.

Legassick, Martin. "The Frontier Tradition in South African Historiography." In *Society and Economy in Pre-Industrial South Africa,* edited by Shula Marks and Anthony Atmore, 44–79. London: Longman, 1980.

———. "The Northern Frontier to 1840: The Rise and Decline of the Griqua People." In *The Shaping of South African Society, 1652–1840,* edited by Richard Elphick and Hermann Giliomee, 358–420. 2nd ed. Johannesburg: Maskew Miller Longman, 1989.

Leibbrandt, H.C.V. *Precis of the Archives of the Cape of Good Hope Reqeuesten (Memorials) 1715–1806,* 5 vols. Cape Town and London: Cape Times Limited, Government Printers (vols. 1–2), 1905. Cape Town: South African Library (vols. 3–5), 1989.

Lewis-Williams, J.D. *Believing and Seeing: Symbolic Meanings in Southern San Rock Painting.* London: Academic Press, 1981.

———. "Introductory Essay: Science and Rock Art." *New Approaches to Southern African Rock Art,* The South African Archaeological Society Goodwin Series 4 (1983): 3–13.

Linebaugh, Peter. *The London Hanged: Crime and Civil Society in the Eighteenth Century.* 2nd ed. London: Verso, 2006.

Linebaugh, Peter and Marcus Rediker. "Hewers of Wood and Drawers of Water." In *The Many Headed Hydra: Sailors, Slaves, Commoners, and the Hidden History of the Revolutionary Atlantic,* 36–70. Boston: Beacon Press, 2000.

Lombard, R.T.J. *Handleiding vir genealogiese navorsing in Suid-Afrika.* Pretoria: Raad vir Geesteswetenskaplike Navorsing, 1990.

Maalouf, Amin. *In the Name of Identity: Violence and the Need to Belong.* New York: Arcade Publishing, 1996.

Mackenzie, Norman H. "South African Travel Literature in the Seventeenth Century." *Archives Year Book for South African History* 2 (1955): 1–112.

Macmillan, W.M. *The Cape Colour Question: A Historical Survey.* Cape Town: A.A. Balkema, 1968.

Malherbe, V.C. "In Onegt Verwekt: Law, Custom and Illegitimacy in Cape Town, 1800–1840." *Journal of Southern African Studies* 31: 1 (2005): 163–85.

———. "Indentured and Unfree Labor in South Africa: Towards an Understanding." *South African Historical Journal* 24 (1991): 3–30.

———. *Krotoa, Called Eva: A Woman Between.* Communications No. 19. Rondebosch: UCT Centre for African Studies, 1990.

———. "The Life and Times of Cupido Kakkerlak." *Journal of African History* 20:3 (1979): 365–78.

Manhire, Tony. *Later Stone Age Settlement Patterns in the Sandveld of the South-Western Cape Province, South Africa.* Cambridge Monographs in African Archaeology. Oxford: BAR, 1987.

Manhire, A.H., J.E. Parkington, and T.S. Robey. "Stone Tools and Sandveld Settlement." In *Southern African Archaeology Today,* edited by D. Avery et al., 111–20. Oxford: BAR, 1984.

Manhire, Tony, John Parkington, and W. J. van Rijssen. "A Distributional Approach to the Interpretation of Rock Art in the South-Western Cape." *New Approaches to Southern African Rock Art,* The South African Archaeological Society Goodwin Series 4 (June 1983): 29–33.

Manhire, Tony, John Parkington, and Royden Yates. "Nets and Fully Recurved Bows: Rock Paintings and Hunting Methods in the Western Cape, South Africa." *World Archaeology* 17: 2 (1985): 161–74.

Marais, J.S. *The Cape Coloured People.* Johannesburg: Witwatersrand University Press, 1957.

Marks, Shula. "Khoisan Resistance to the Dutch in the Seventeenth and Eighteenth Centuries." *Journal of African History* 13:1 (1972): 55–80.

Martin, C.G.C., and K.J. Friedlaender, eds. *History of Surveying and Land Tenure in South Africa.* Cape Town: UCT Department of Surveying, 1984.

Mason, John Edwin. *Social Death and Resurrection: Slavery and Emancipation in South Africa.* Charlottesville: University of Virginia Press, 2003.

———. "Hendrik Albertus and His Ex-Slave Mey: A Drama in Three Acts." *Journal of African History* 31 (1990): 423–45.

Mbembe, Achille. "The Power of the Archives and its Limits." In *Refiguring the Archive,* edited by Carolyn Hamilton, Verne Harris, Jane Taylor, Michele Pickover, Graeme Reid, and Razia Saleh, 19–26. Cape Town: David Philip, 2002.

———. "Necropolitics." *Public Culture* 15: 1 (2003): 11–40.

Meilink-Roelofsz., M.A.P., R. Raben, and H. Spijkerman, eds. *De archieven van de Verenigde Oostindische Compagnie (1602–1795).* The Hague: Sdu Uitgeverij Koninginnegracht, 1992.

McClendon, Thomas V. *Genders and Generations Apart: Labor Tenants and Customary Law In Segregation-Era South Africa.* Portsmouth, N.H. Heinemann, 2002.

Mitchell, Laura J. "Material Culture and Cadastral Data: Documenting the Cedarberg Frontier, South Africa 1725–1795." In *Sources and Methods in African History: Spoken, Written, Unearthed,* edited by Toyin Falola and Christian Jennings, 16–32. Rochester: University of Rochester Press, 2003.

Moore, Donald, and Richard Roberts. "Listening for Silences." *History in Africa* 17 (1990): 319–25.

Morgan, Cecilia. "'A Wigwam to Westminster': Performing Mohawk Identity in Imperial Britain, 1890s–1990s." *Gender and History,* 15:2 (August 2003), 319–41.

Morton, Barry. "Servitude, Slave Trading and Slavery in the Kalahari." In *Slavery in South Africa: Captive Labor on the Dutch Frontier,* edited by Fred Morton and Elizabeth Eldredge, 215–50. Boulder: Westview Press, 1994.

Mostert, Noel. *Frontiers: The Epic of South Africa's Creation and the Tragedy of the Xhosa People.* New York: Knopf, 1992.

Naidoo, Jay. *Tracking Down Historical Myths: Eight South African Cases.* Johannesburg: Ad. Donker, 1989.

Neumark, S.D. *Economic Influences on the South African Frontier, 1652–1836.* Stanford: Stanford University Press, 1957.

Newton-King, Susan. "For the Love of Adam: Two Sodomy Trials at the Cape of Good Hope." *Kronos: Journal of Cape History* 28 (2002): 21–42.

———. *Masters and Servants on the Eastern Cape Frontier, 1760–1803.* Cambridge: Cambridge University Press, 1999.

———. "In Search of Notability: The Antecedents of David van der Merwe of the Koue Bokkeveld." *Collected Seminar Papers* (University of London, Institute for Commonwealth Studies), no. 48, *The Societies of Southern Africa in the Nineteenth and Twentieth Centuries,* vol. 20, 26–50.

Novik, Peter. *That Noble Dream: The 'Objectivity Question' and the American Historical Profession.* Cambridge: Cambridge University Press, 1988.

O'Toole, Rachel Sarah. "Castas y representación en Trujillo colonial." In *Más allá de la dominación y la resistencia: Estudios de historia peruana, siglos XVI–XX,* edited by Paulo Drinot and Leo Garofalo, 48–76. Lima: Instituto de Estudios Peruanos, 2005.

Parkington, John. "Changing Views of Prehistoric Settlement in the Western Cape." In *Papers in the Prehistory of the Western Cape, South Africa,* edited by John Parkington and Martin Hall, 4–23. BAR International Series, Oxford: BAR, 1987.

———. "Late Pleistocene and Holocene Climates as Viewed from Verlore Vlei." *Paleontology Africa* 23 (1980): 71.

———. "Soaqua: Hunter-Fisher-Gatherers of the Olifants River, Western Cape." *South African Archaeological Bulletin* 32 (1977): 150–57.

———. "Time and Place: Some Observations on Spatial and Temporal patterning in the Later Stone Age Sequence in Southern Africa." *South African Archaeological Bulletin* 35 (1980): 73–83.

Parkington, J.E., R.J. Yates, A.H. Manhire, and D.J. Halkett. "The Social Impact of Pastoralism in the South-Western Cape." *Journal of Anthropological Archaeology* 5 (1986): 313–29.

Parkington, John and Martin Hall, eds. *Papers in the Prehistory of the Western Cape, South Africa.* Oxford: BAR, 1987.

Penn, Nigel. *The Forgotten Frontier: Colonist and Khoisan on the Cape's Northern Frontier in the Eighteenth Century.* Cape Town: Double Storey Books and Athens: Ohio University Press, 2005.

———. "The Onder Bokkeveld Ear Atrocity," *Kronos: Journal of Cape History* 31 (November 2005): 62–106.

———. "The Wife, the Farmer, and the Farmer's Slaves: Adultery and Murder on a Frontier Farm in the Early Eighteenth-Century Cape." *Kronos: Journal of Cape History* 28 (2002): 1–20.

———. *Rogues, Rebels and Runaways: Eighteenth-Century Cape Characters.* Cape Town: David Phillip, 1999.

———. "The Frontier in the Western Cape, 1700–1740." In *Papers in the Prehistory of the Western Cape, South Africa,* edited by John Parkington and Martin Hall, 463–93. Oxford: BAR, 1987.

———. "Pastoralists and Pastoralism in the Northern Cape Frontier Zone During the Eighteenth Century." *Prehistoric Pastoralism in South Africa,* South African Archaeological Society Goodwin Series 5 (June 1986): 62–68.

Philips, John Edward, ed. *Writing African History.* Rochester: University of Rochester Press, 2005.

Phillips, Roderick. *Putting Asunder: A History of Divorce in Western Society.* Cambridge: Cambridge University Press, 1988.

Pomeranz, Kenneth L. *The Great Divergence: China, Europe, and the Making of the Modern World Economy.* Princeton: Princeton University Press, 2001.

Prakash, Gyan. "Subaltern Studies as Postcolonial Criticism." *American Historical Review* 99:5 (1994): 1475–90.

Pratt, Mary Louise. *Imperial Eyes: Travel Writing and Transculturation.* London: Routledge, 1992.

Randle, Tracey. "Patterns of Consumption at Auctions: A Case Study of Three Estates." In *Contingent Lives: Social Identity and Material Culture in the VOC World,* edited by Nigel Worden, 53–74. Cape Town: University of Cape Town Press, 2007.

Raben, Remco. "European Periphery at the Heart of the Ocean: The Maldives, 17th–18th Centuries." In *International Conference on Shipping, Factories and Colonization,* edited by J. Everaert, and J. Parmentier, 45–60. Brussels, 24 November 1994. Brussels: Koninklijke Academie voor Overzeese Wetenschappen, 1996.

Richter, Daniel K. *Facing East from Indian Country: A Native History of Early America*. Boston: Harvard University Press, 2003.

Reid, Anthony. "Female Roles in Pre-colonial Southeast Asia." *Modern Asian Studies* 22:3 (1988): 629–45

Ricoeur, Paul. *Time and Narrative*. Translated by Kathleen McLaughlin and David Pellaur. Chicago: University of Chicago Press, 1983.

Roberts, Richard. "Reversible Social Processes, Historical Memory, and the Production of History." *History in Africa* 17 (1990): 341–49.

Roessingh, M.P.H., and W. Visser, comps. *Guide to the Sources of the History of Africa South of the Sahara in the Netherlands*. Translated by J.W. Veenendaal-Barth. Netherlands State Archives Service, New York, London, Paris: K.G. Saur, 1978.

Romero, Patricia. "Some Aspects of Family and Social History Among the French Huguenot Refugees at the Cape." *Historia* 48:2 (November 2003): 31–47.

———. "Encounter at the Cape: French Huguenots, the Khoi, and Other People of Color." *Journal of Colonialism and Colonial History* 5:1 (2004). http://muse.jhu.edu/login?uri=/journals/journal_of_colonialism_and_colonial_history/v005/5.1romero.html

Ross, Robert. "Belonging and Belongings: On the Material Superstructure Of Identity." Paper presented at the Historical Association of South Africa Jubilee Meeting, 26–28 June 2006.

———. *Status and Respectability in the Cape Colony 1750–1870: A Tragedy of Manners*. Cambridge: Cambridge University Press, 1999.

———. "The Kat River Rebellion and Khoikhoi Nationalism: The Fate of Ethnic Identification." *Kronos: Journal of Cape History* 24 (1997): 91–105.

———. "The First Imperial Masters of Colonial South Africa." *Southern African Historical Journal* 25 (1995): 177–83.

———. *Beyond the Pale: Essays on the History of Colonial South Africa*. Johannesburg: Witwatersrand University Press, 1994.

———. "The Rise of the Cape Gentry." *Journal of Southern African Studies* 9:2 (April 1983): 193–217.

———. *Cape of Torments: Slavery and Resistance in South Africa*. London: Routledge and Keegan Paul, 1983.

———. "The First Two Centuries of Colonial Agriculture in the Cape Colony: A Historiographical Review." *Social Dynamics* 9:1 (June 1983): 30–49.

———. *Adam Kok's Griquas: A Study in the Development of Stratification in South Africa*. African Studies Series, edited by John Dunn, J.M. Lonsdale, D.M.G. Newberry, and A.F. Robertson, 21. Cambridge: Cambridge University Press, 1976.

Rupert, Linda M. "Contraband Trade and the Shaping of Colonial Societies." *Itinerario* 30:3 (2006): 35–54.

Sabean, David Warren. *Kinship in Neckarhausen, 1700–1879*. Cambridge: Cambridge University Press, 1998.

Sahlins, Peter. *Boundaries: The Making of France and Spain in the Pyrenees*. Berkeley: University of California Press, 1989.

Sales, Jane M. *Mission Stations and the Coloured Communities of the Eastern Cape, 1800–1852*. Cape Town: A.A. Balkema, 1975.

Saunders, Christopher. *The Making of the South African Past: Major Historians on Race and Class*. Cape Town: David Philip, 1988.

Schama, Simon. *The Embarrassment of Riches: An Interpretation of Dutch Culture in the Golden Age*. London: Fontana Press, 1991.

Schoeman, Karel. *This Life*. Translated by Elsa Silke. Cape Town: Human and Rousseau, 2005.

——. "Die Kort Bataafse era aan die Kaap, 1803–1806—'n oorsig van eietydse bronne." *Quarterly Bulletin of the South African Library* 52:4 (1998): 162–81.

Scholtz, Philippus Lodewikus. "Die historiese ontwikkeling van die Onder-Olifantsrivier, 1660–1902: 'n Geskiedenis van die Distrik Vanryhsdorp." *Archives Yearbook for South African History*, 7–28. Cape Town: Staatsdrukker, 1966.

Scott, James C. *Domination and the Arts of Resistance: Hidden Transcripts*. New Haven: Yale University Press, 1990.

——. *Weapons of the Weak: Everyday Forms of Peasant Resistance*. New Haven: Yale University Press, 1985.

Scott, Joan. "Gender as a Useful Category of Analysis." *American Historical Review* 91:5 (December 1986): 1053–75.

Schrire, Carmel. *Digging Through Darkness: Chronicles of an Archaeologist*. Charlottesville: University Press of Virginia, 1995.

Schutte, Gerrit. "Between Amsterdam and Batavia: Cape Society and the Calvinist Church Under the Dutch East India Company." *Kronos: Journal of Cape History* 25 (1998–99), 17–49.

——. "Company and Colonists at the Cape, 1652–1795." In *The Shaping of South African Society, 1652–1840*, edited by Richard Elphick and Hermann Giliomee, 283–323. 2nd ed. Johannesburg: Maskew Miller Longman, 1989.

Scully, Pamela. "Indigenous Women and Colonial Cultures: An Introduction." *Journal of Colonialism and Colonial History* 6:3 (2005), paragraph 1. http://muse.jhu. edu/journals/journal_of_colonialism_and_colonial_history/toc/cch6.3.html

——. *Liberating the Family? Gender and British Slave Emancipation in the Rural Western Cape, South Africa, 1823–1853*. Portsmouth, N.H.: Heinemann, 1997.

——. "Rape, Race and Colonial Culture: The Sexual Politics of Identity in the Nineteenth-Century Cape Colony, South Africa." *American Historical Review* 100:2 (April 1995): 335–59.

Shell, Robert C.-H. "Immigration: The Forgotten Factor in Cape Colonial Frontier Expansion, 1658–1817." *Safundi* 18 (April 2005). http://www.safundi.com/issues/18/ shell.asp

——. "The Tower of Babel: The Slave Trade and Creolization at the Cape, 1652–1834." In *Slavery in South Africa: Captive Labor on the Dutch Frontier*, edited by Elizabeth Eldridge and Fred Morton, 11–39. Boulder, Colo.: Westview Press, 1994.

——. *Children of Bondage: A Social History of the Slave Society at the Cape of Good Hope, 1652–1838*. Hannover and London: University Press of New England, 1994.

——. "Auctions—their Good and Evil Tendency (Part 1)." *Quarterly Bulletin of the South African Library* 3:4 (June 1985): 147–51.

——. "A Family Matter: The Sale and Transfer of Human Beings at the Cape, 1658–1830." *The International Journal of African Historical Studies* 25:2 (1992): 285–336.

Skotnes, Pippa, ed. *Miscast: Negotiating the Presence of the Bushmen*. Cape Town: UCT Press, 1996.

Sleigh, Dan. *Die Buiteposte: Die VOC Buiteposte onder Kaapse Bestuur, 1652–1795*. Pretoria: Haum, 1993.

Smith, Andrew B. "Competition, Conflict and Clientship: Khoi and San Relationships in the Western Cape." *Prehistoric Pastoralism in South Africa*, South African Archaeological Society Goodwin Series 5 (June 1986): 36–71.

Smith, Andrew, Karim Sadr, John Gribble, and Royden Yates. "Excavations in the South-Western Cape, South Africa and the Archaeological Identity of Prehistoric Hunter-Gatherers Within the Last 2000 Years." *South African Archaeological Bulletin* 46 (1991): 71–91.

Smith, Ken. *The Changing Past: Trends in South African Historical Writing*. Johannesburg: Southern Book Publishers, 1988.

Snyman, Lannice. *Rainbow Cuisine*. Hout Bay: S&S Publishers, 1998.

Southey, Nicholas. "From Periphery to Core: The Treatment of Cape Slavery in South African Historiography." *Historia* 37:2 (November 1992): 13–25.

Spear, Thomas. "Struggles for the Land: The Political and Moral Economies of Land on Mount Meru." In *Custodians of the Land: Ecology and Culture in the History of Tanzania*, edited by Gregory Maddox, James L. Giblin, and Isaria N. Kimambo, 213–40. London: James Currey, 1996.

Spence, Donald. *Narrative Truth and Historical Truth: Meaning and Interpretation in Psychoanalysis*. New York: W.W. Norton, 1982.

Spivak, Gayatri Chatravorty. "Can the Subaltern Speak?" In *Marxism and the Interpretation of Culture*, edited by Cary Nelson and Lawrence Grossberg, 271–313. Urbana: University of Illinois Press, 1988.

Spillhaus, Margaret W. *The First South Africans and the Laws Which Governed them, to Which is Appended the Diary of Adam Tas*. Cape Town: Juta, 1949.

Stearns, Peter N. "Periodization in World History Teaching: Identifying the Big Changes." *The History Teacher* 20:4 (August 1987): 561–80.

Stoler, Ann Laura. *Carnal Knowledge and Imperial Power: Race and the Intimate in Colonial Rule*. Berkeley: University of California Press, 2002.

Strasser, Ulrike. *State of Virginity: Gender, Religion and Politics in an Early Modern Catholic State*. Ann Arbor: University of Michigan Press, 2004.

Swart, Sandra. "A Boer, His Gun and His Wife are Three Things Always Together." *Journal of Southern African Studies* 24:4 (December 1998): 737–51.

Taylor, Jean Gelman. *The Social World of Batavia: Europeans and Eurasians in Dutch Asia*. Madison: University of Wisconsin Press, 1983.

Theal, George McCall. *History of South Africa, 1691–1795*. London: Sonnenschein & Co., 1888.

———. *The Records of the Cape Colony*. London: for the Government of the Cape Colony, 1905.

Townsend, Leslie. "Out of Silence: Writing Interactive Women's Life Histories in Africa." *History in Africa* 17 (1990): 351–58.

Turner, Frederick Jackson. "The Significance of the Frontier in American History." Paper presented at the American Historical Association Meeting, Chicago, 12 July

1893. Reprinted in *The Frontier in American History*, 1–38. New York: Henry Holt and Company, 1920.

Ulrich, Laurel Thatcher. *Good Wives: Image and Reality in the Lives of Women in Northern New England, 1650–1750.* New York: Alfred A. Knopf, 1982.

———. *The Age of Homespun: Objects and Stories in the Creation of an American Myth.* New York: Alfred A. Knopf, 2001.

Vail, Leroy, ed. *The Creation of Tribalism in Southern Africa.* Berkeley: University of California Press, 1991.

van der Boogart, C. and P.C. Emmer. "Colonialism and Migration: An Overview." In *Colonialism and Migration: Indentured Labour Before and After Slavery,* edited by P.C. Emmer. Comparative Studies in Overseas History, vol.7. Dordrecht: M. Nijhoff, 1986.

van der Merwe, C.P. *Van der Merwe Gedenkboek,* 1952.

van der Merwe, P. J. *Die Noordwaarste beweging van die Boere voor die Groot Trek (1770–1842).* Pretoria: Die Staatsbiblioteek, 1988. First published 1937 by W.P. van Stockum & Zoon.

———. *Die Trekboer in die geskiedenis van die Kaapkolonie, 1657–1842.* Cape Town: Nasionale Pers Beperk, 1938.

———. *Trek: Studies oor die mobiliteit van die pioniersbevolking aan die Kaap.* Cape Town: Nasionale Pers Beperk, 1945.

———. *The Migrant Farmer in the History of the Cape Colony, 1658–1842.* Translated by Roger B. Beck. Athens: Ohio University Press, 1995.

van der Spuy, Patricia. "Slave Women and the Family in Nineteenth Century Cape Town." *South African Historical Journal* 27 (1992): 50–74.

———. "'Making Himself Master': Galant's Rebellion Revisted." *South African Historical Journal* 34 (1996), 1–28.

van Duin, Pieter, and Robert Ross. *The Economy of the Cape Colony in the Eighteenth Century.* Intercontinenta 7. Leiden: Centre for the History of European Expansion, 1987.

van Jaarsveld, Floris Albertus. "Veldkornet en sy aandeel in die opbou van die Suid-Afrikaanse Republiek tot 1870." *Archives Year Book for South African History* 13:2 (1950): 187–354.

van Onselen, Charles. *The Seed is Mine: The Life of Kas Maine, a South African Sharecropper, 1894–1985.* New York: Hill and Wang, 1996.

van Rooyen, Gretel and Hester Steyn. *South African Wild Flower Guide 10: Cedarberg, Clanwilliam and Biedouw Valley.* Cape Town: Botanical Society of South Africa, 1999.

van Sittert, Lance. "Seeing the Cedarberg: Alpinism and Inventions of the Agterberg in the White Urban Middle Class Imagination, c. 1890–c. 1950." *Kronos: Journal of Cape History* 31 (November 2005): 152–83.

Vansina, Jan. *Paths in the Rainforest: Toward a History of Political Tradition in Equatorial Africa.* Madison: University of Wisconsin Press, 1990.

———."Historians, are Archaeologists Your Siblings?" *History in Africa* 22 (1995): 369–408.

Viljoen, Russel. *Jan Paerl, a Khoikhoi in Cape Colonial Society, 1761–1851.* Leiden: Brill, 2006.

———. "Indentured Labour and Khoikhoi 'Equality' Before the Law in Cape Colonial Society: South Africa. The Case of Jan Paerl, c. 1796." *Itinerario* 29:3 (2005): 54–72.

———. "'Till Murder Do Us Part': The Story of Griet and Hendrik Eksteen." *South African Historical Journal* 33 (1995): 13–32.

Vinnicombe, Patricia. *People of the Eland: Rock Painting of the Drakensberg Bushmen as a Reflection of Their Life and Thought*. Pietermartizburg: University of Natal Press, 1976.

Walker, Eric. *The Frontier Tradition in South Africa: A Lecture Delivered . . . at Rhodes House on 5 March 1930*. London: Oxford University Press, 1930.

———. *A History of Southern Africa*. 3rd ed. London: Longmans, 1957.

Wallerstein, Immanuel. *World-Systems Analysis: An Introduction*. Durham: Duke University Press, 2004.

Ward, Kerry. "Knocking on Death's Door: Mapping Spectrums of Bondage and Status Through Marking the Dead at the Cape." In *Contingent Lives: Social Identity and Material Culture in the VOC World*, edited by Nigel Worden, 391–413. Cape Town: University of Cape Town Press, 2007.

Watson, R.L. *The Slave Question: Liberty and Property in South Africa*. Hanover: University Press of New England, 1990.

Watt, Jeffrey R. *The Making of Modern Marriage: Matrimonial Control and the Rise of Sentiment in Neuchâtel, 1550–1800*. Ithaca: Cornell University Press, 1992.

Wells, Julia. "Eva's Men: Gender and Power in the Establishment of the Cape of Good Hope, 1652–74." *Journal of African History* 39 (1998): 417–37.

White, Hayden. *Metahistory: The Historical Imagination in Nineteenth-Century Europe*. Baltimore: Johns Hopkins University Press, 1973.

———. *Tropics of Discourse: Essays in Cultural Criticism*. Baltimore: Johns Hopkins University Press, 1985.

White, Richard. *The Middle Ground: Indians, Empires, and Republics in the Great Lakes Region, 1650–1815*. Cambridge: Cambridge University Press, 1991.

Wijsenbeek, Thera. "Identity Lost: Huguenot Refugees in the Republic and its Former Colonies in North America and South Africa, 1650–1750: A Comparison." In *Contingent Lives: Social Identity and Material Culture in the VOC World*, edited by Nigel Worden, 91–110. Cape Town: University of Cape Town Press, 2007.

Williamson, Tom, and Liz Bellamy. *Property and Landscape: A Social History of Land Ownership and the English Countryside*. London: George Philip, 1987.

Wilson, Monica, and Leonard Thompson, eds. *The Oxford History of South Africa*. New York: Oxford University Press, 1971.

Worden, Nigel, ed. *Contingent Lives: Social Identity and Material Culture in the VOC World*. Cape Town: University of Cape Town Press, 2007.

———. "Forging a Reputation: Artisan Honour and the Cape Town Blacksmith Strike of 1752." *Kronos: Journal of Cape History* 28 (2002): 43–65.

———. *Slavery in Dutch South Africa*. Cambridge: Cambridge University Press, 1985.

Worger, William H. *South Africa's City of Diamonds: Mine Workers and Monopoly Capitalism in Kimberley, 1867–1895*. New Haven: Yale University Press, 1987.

Wuras, Rev. C.F. "An Account of the Korana." *Bantu Studies: A Journal Devoted to the Scientific Study of Bantu, Hottentot and Bushman* 3:3 (1929): 287–96.

Yates, Royden, Jo Golson, and Martin Hall. "Trance Performance: The Rock Art of Boontjieskloof and Sevilla." *South African Archaeological Bulletin* 40 (1985): 70–80.

Yates, Royden, Anthony Manhire, and John Parkington. "Rock Painting and History in the South Western Cape." In *Contested Images: Diversity in Southern African Rock Art Research*, edited byThomas Dowson and David Lewis-Williams, 29–60. Johannesburg: Witwatersrand University Press, 1994.

Yates, Royden and Anthony Manhire. "Shamanism and Rock Paintings: Aspects of the Use of Rock Art in the South-Western Cape, South Africa." *South African Archaeological Bulletin* 46 (1991): 3–11.

UNPUBLISHED PRESENTATIONS AND PAPERS

Austin, Gareth. "'Developmental' Divergences and Continuities Between Colonial and Pre-Colonial Regimes: The Case of Asante, Ghana, 1701–1957." Paper presented at the African Studies Association Annual Meeting, New Orleans, LA, 11–14 November 2004.

Groenewald, Gerald. "From Tappers to *Pachters*: The Evolution of the Alcohol *Pacht* system at the Cape, c.1656–1680." Paper presented to the 'Company, Castle and Control' research group meeting, University of Cape Town, 8 September 2004.

———. "Parents, Children and Illegitimacy in Dutch Colonial Cape Town, c. 1652–1795." Unpublished paper, 2006.

Hughes-Warrington, Marnie. "Keynote Address," presented at the World History Association Annual Meeting, Milwaukee, WI, 28 June–1 July 2007.

Mitchell, Laura J. "Sex, Religion, and Other Cultural Exigencies in the Early-Modern Atlantic." Paper presented at the Berkshire Conference on the History of Women, Scripps College, Claremont, CA, 2–5 June 2005.

Newton-King, Susan. "The Pre-Colonial and Colonial Khoikhoi: From Fragile Independence to Permanent Servitude. Part II: Servitude and Resistance." Paper presented to the Africa Seminar, Centre for African Studies, University of Cape Town, 16 May 1984.

Parkington, John. "Western Cape Landscapes." Unpublished paper, 1999.

Ruiters, Michelle. "Re-Imagining and Re-Claiming Identity: Coloured Identities in a Post-Apartheid South Africa." Paper presented at the New England Workshop on Southern Africa, Burlington, VT, 22–25 April 2005,.

Saunders, Christopher. "Historians on South Africa's Pre-Colonial Past: Notes on Early Phases in the Long Search." Paper presented at the Workshop on Pre-Colonial History, University of Cape Town, July 1986.

Upham, Mansell. "In a Kind of Custody: For Eva's Sake, Who Speaks for Krotwa?" Unpublished paper, 1997.

UNPUBLISHED THESES AND DISSERTATIONS

Bugarin, Flordeliz T. "Trade and Interaction on the Eastern Cape Frontier: An Historical Archaeological Study of the Xhosa and the British during the Early 19th Century." PhD diss., University of Florida, 2002.

Campbell, Colin. "Art in Crisis: Contact Period Rock Art in the South-Eastern Mountains of Southern Africa." MSc thesis, Witwatersrand University, 1987.

Clift, Harriet E. "The Assimilation of the Khoikhoi into the Rural Labour Force of Paarl, Drakenstein District." BA Honours thesis, University of Cape Town, 1995.

Dooling, Wayne Leslie. "Agrarian Transformation in the Western Districts of the Cape Colony, 1838–c.1900." PhD diss., St. John's College, Cambridge, 1996.

———."Law and Community in a Slave Society: Stellenbosch District, c. 1760–1820." MA thesis, University of Cape Town, 1991.

Granger, Stephen. "Land Tenure and Environmental Conditions at Wupperthal." MSc thesis, University of Cape Town, 1982.

Guelke, Leonard. "Early European Settlement of South Africa." PhD diss., University of Toronto, 1974.

Host, Elizabeth Anne. "Capitalization and Proletarianization on a Western Cape Farm: Klaver Valley 1812–1898." MA thesis, University of Cape Town, 1992.

Legassick, Martin. "The Griqua, the Sotho-Tswana, and the Missionaries, 1780–1840: The Politics of a Frontier Zone." PhD diss., UCLA, 1970.

Malan, Antonia. "Households of the Cape, 1750 to 1850: Inventories and the Archaeological Record." PhD diss., University of Cape Town, 1993.

Malherbe, Vertrees Candy. "Diversification and Mobility of Khoikhoi Labor in the Eastern Cape Districts of the Cape Colony Prior to the Labor Law of 1 November 1809." MA thesis, University of Cape Town, 1978.

Mason, John. "Fit For Freedom: The Slaves, Slavery and Emancipation in the Cape Colony, South Africa, 1806–1842." PhD diss., Yale University, 1992.

Nell, Dawn D'Arcy. "Land, Land Ownership and Occupancy in the Cape Colony During the Nineteenth Century With Special Reference to the Clanwilliam District." BA Honours thesis, University of Cape Town, 1997.

O'Toole, Rachel Sarah. "Inventing Difference: Africans, Indians, and the Antecedents of 'Race' in Colonial Peru (1580s–1720s)." PhD diss., University of North Carolina, 2001.

Newton-King, Susan. "The Enemy Within: The Struggle for Ascendancy on the Cape Eastern Frontier, 1760–1799." PhD diss., University of London, 1992.

Parkington, John. "Follow the San." PhD diss., Cambridge University, 1977.

Penn, Nigel Garth. "The Northern Cape Frontier Zone, 1700–c.1815." PhD diss., University of Cape Town, 1995.

Raben, Remco. "Batavia and Columbo: The Ethnic and Spatial Order of Two Colonial Cities, 1699–1800." PhD diss., Rijksuniversiteit te Leiden, 1996.

Rayner, Mary. "Wine and Slaves: The Failure of an Export Economy and the Ending of Slavery in the Cape Colony, South Africa, 1806–1834." PhD diss., Duke University, 1986.

Shaw, Susannah. "Building New Netherland: Gender and Family Ties in a Frontier Society (New York)." PhD diss., Cornell University, 2000.

Shell, Robert C.H. "Slavery at the Cape of Good Hope, 1680–1731," vols. I and II. PhD diss., Yale University, 1986.

van der Merwe, Hannalie. "The Social Context of Rock Art During the Contact Period in the North-Western Cape and Seacow River Valley." MA thesis, University of Stellenbosch, 1990.

Viljoen, Russel Stafford. "Khoisan Labor Relations in the Overberg Districts During the Later Half of the Eighteenth Century, c. 1755–1795." MA thesis, University of the Western Cape, 1993.

Worden, Nigel Anthony. "Rural Slavery in the Western Districts of Cape Colony During the Eighteenth Century." PhD diss., Cambridge University, 1982.

ABOUT THE AUTHOR

Laura J. Mitchell teaches African history, world history, and historical theory and method at the University of California in Irvine. She earned a bachelor's degree from UC Berkeley, a master's degree in foreign service from Georgetown University, and a Ph.D. in African history from UCLA. Her work explores the intersections of environmental, social, and labor histories in colonial South Africa. Professor Mitchell is active in the World History Association, FEEGI, and Past Tense. She lives in Irvine with her husband and son, where she enjoys hiking and kayaking.

The author looks forward to corresponding with readers about this book and can be reached by emailing mitchell_at_uci.edu

Lightning Source UK Ltd.
Milton Keynes UK
UKOW04n2054070115

244149UK00002B/22/P